The Complete Communications Handbook

Ed Paulson

Wordware Publishing, Inc.

Library of Congress Cataloging-in-Publication Data

Paulson, Ed.
 The complete communications handbook / written by Ed Paulson.
   p. cm.
 Includes index.
 ISBN 1-55622-238-6 : $21.95
 1. Telecommunication. I. Title.
 TK5101.P32 1991
 384--dc20   92-5984
                        CIP

ISBN1-55622-238-6
10 9 8 7 6 5 4 3 2 1
9203

All inquiries for volume purchases of this book should be addressed to Wordware
Publishing, Inc., at the above address. Telephone inquiries may be made by calling:

(214) 423-0090

Contents

Acknowledgments

This book represents almost 20 years of combined educational and professional experiences. To those customers, co-workers and professors who see a piece of their insight contained in these pages, I give my gratitude. Thank you Mark Judd and Stan Kroder for being last minute information resources, and thank you Lisa Forasiepi for your tireless enthusiasm and proofreading during the final days of manuscript completion.

Without my parents, John and Jean Paulson, the writing of this book would have been virtually impossible. They will always have my love and sincere appreciation for their continuing support.

Introduction

Technology is an integral part of almost aspect of contemporary life. It is almost impossible to watch a few hours of television and not hear about one company's fiber-optic network, or their competitor's special long-distance rates. Our cars talk to us, and people listen to CD music that was recorded in computer language.

Cellular telephones that used to be the exclusive property of the elite are casually used today while people eat lunch. It is almost impossible to do business without a fax machine and almost every business desktop in America is adorned with a computer terminal of some type. In short, communication technology is rapidly changing the way Americans conduct business.

Business managers need to make effective use of technology to remain competitive and the average consumer is continually asked to choose one type of technology over another. Even engineers have a hard time keeping up with the rapid pace of change combined with the special characteristics that make one solution superior to another.

The Complete Communications Handbook is specially written to fill the understanding void that currently exists regarding communication technology and its benefits. Topics ranging from basic telephone operation to optical fiber digital communication are explained in easy-to-understand language that clearly defines industry jargon.

Special sections are included to provided a historical perspective on the evolution of communications technology. The intent is for the reader to understand that the telephone network, data processing industry, and datacommunications technologies are merging into one. Both computer information and telephone conversations are transported in computer language (bits). This development is the result of a natural evolution being driven by consumer demand.

The Complete Communications Handbook is written for the business manager who needs a quick overview of communication technology or for the lay person who simply wants to learn more about this important part of our society. Discussion questions and module quizzes are also included to allow the reader to test his understanding. These questions also make *The Complete Communications Handbook* effective as a telecommunication education program primary or companion textbook.

Thank you for your general interest in telecommunications and your particular interest in *The Complete Communications Handbook*. An earnest attempt has been made to simplify a complicated subject while still providing enough substance to ensure understanding. I look forward to being your technology tour guide, and I hope you enjoy learning about telecommunications as much as I enjoyed explaining it.

Ed Paulson

Austin, Texas

Module One
Communication Fundamentals

All human beings have experience with communication in one form or another and have an intuitive sense of effective and ineffective communication. We communicate most effectively in a structured environment, and many human communication experiences have been incorporated into the methods of technical communication. It is not surprising that this should occur, since human beings defined our technical communication systems. Most of the confusion about telecommunications stems from unfamiliarity with these structures or protocols.

Webster defines communication as "an exchange of information or opinions; the act of transmitting." Telecommunication is defined as "communication at a distance (as by telephone or radio)."

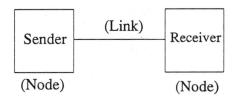

We see that telecommunication facilitates communication over larger distances than possible between human beings unaided by technology. Communication requires a sender and a receiver of information. The connection between these two parties is called a link. If the parties are close to each other, we have personal communications. If they are farther apart, then other methods of communication are needed and this is the purpose of telecommunications.

American Indians once communicated by sending information in coded smoke signals.

The next chapter is a historical perspective on the impact of the telephone on society. It shows that the ability to communicate largely determines the ability of a society to progress. Relationships can be established over larger geographic areas instead of being limited to a restricted area.

Without effective communication there is the possibility for misunderstanding instead of understanding. In an age of increasing globalization, the need for effective communication becomes increasingly more important.

As seen with humans, there is a specific sequence of events that must be followed before telecommunication can occur. 1) The parties need to be defined. (Who is it that we want to call?) 2) The receiver needs to be located. (We look up their telephone number.) 3) The receiver needs to be notified that communication is to occur. (The telephone rings on their end.) 4) A communication link needs to be established that allows the required communication to occur. (The receiver answers the telephone and establishes a connection.) 5) The parties need to communicate in a common language. (If one speaks English and the other German, little communication will occur.) 6) The parties need to understand what they are communicating about. (The overall context or purpose of the call is established.) 7) Both need to understand when the communication is finished. (We say "Goodbye.") 8) The communication link needs to be broken when communication is completed. (The telephone connection ends when both parties hang up.)

If any portion of the sequence does not occur properly, there will be minimal communication or transmission of information from the sender to the receiver.

A similar process can be outlined for sending a letter. The concept of an envelope with from/to addresses and contents is fundamental to the *packet switching* technology (sending information in electronic envelopes). This is rapidly becoming the communication mode of choice.

In essence, human communication follows an unwritten but fairly defined procedure, and this procedure or *protocol* has been incorporated into technological communication. There is a connection (link) "setup" procedure, then the transmission or exchange of information over that link, a confirmation of information reception (error checking), and finally a "tear down" procedure after communication is completed (breaking the link).

The transmission of information from one party to another is the ultimate goal of communication, but a link must be established before that information can be transmitted. The link consists of the network connection between the two parties and the equipment at each end sending and receiving. Establishing that link requires interaction between the sender and receiver, their respective equipment, and the telecommunication network.

For example, if a toaster is plugged into the telephone network, its presence is not recognized. Point: The equipment connected to the network endpoint must be a form that the network recognizes.

Replace the toaster with a telephone set and assume that the caller (sender) dials an improper telephone number or several insufficient digits. The network will inform the caller that the number is invalid and instruct him to try again. Point: The established procedure for communicating instructions to the network must be followed, or the network cannot understand the request and make the desired connection.

The receiver also must have equipment that is compatible with the network, or receiving the telephone call is not possible (see the toaster example above).

Also notice that as the call connection process progresses, the caller gets audible feedback about the network status via dial tone, busy, ringing, and other tones.

When the receiver answers the telephone, if she does not say "hello" so that the caller can introduce himself, the caller may wait on the line and eventually hang up even though the connection is made and the called party has been reached. Point: The telecommunication equivalent of a *handshake* is necessary to ensure both parties are aware of the connection. In fact, computers introduce themselves to each other using procedures called handshakes in which the communication ability of each terminal device is communicated to the other.

If the caller only speaks German and the receiver understands only Spanish, then there also will be a communication breakdown even though the connection through the network was properly established. Point: Both parties in a communication link need to talk the same language or structure to ensure the information transmitted is received intact.

Once the network connection is established, the greetings completed, and the common language defined, it is still critical that both parties transmit/receive information in a compatible form. For example, assume that the caller reads data from a form that relays personal information in a last name, first name, address, telephone number sequence. Also assume that the receiver fills in a form that sequences the information as first name, last name, telephone number, then address. If the information received over the link is directly copied onto the receiver's form in the order received, the last name, first name will be reversed with the address and phone number. The intention of the communication will be lost and only meaningless numbers and letters will be recorded on the receiver's form. Point: During the communication session, the *application* performed on either side of the link must be compatible.

Transmitted Data Order

Lastname: *Paulson*   **Firstname:** *Ed*
Address: *7777 West 57th Street, Austin, Texas*
Phone: *(512) 555-7777*

Firstname: *Paulson*   **Lastname:** *Ed*
Phone: *7777 West 57th Street, Austin, Texas*
Address: *(512) 555-7777*

Incorrect Received Order

Human beings are adaptable and consequently take for granted much of what occurs in a communication process. If variations in the data transfer occur, such as reversing the first name/last name order, we can recognize the change and insert the names in the proper location on our form. Computer and telephone networks are not very adaptable. So, automated communication (or telecommunication) requires highly standardized procedures and processes to occur effectively.

Much of the information contained in this book is an outline of the accepted standards and procedures used in contemporary communication systems. The intent of the standards is to ensure the completion of all parts of the communication process without a problem.

There is much jargon and history included in the way communication systems of today operate. In the midst of any confusion that may arise, please refer to the communication procedures outlined in this module. They form the intuitive foundation upon which telecommunication standards are based.

In particular, the later discussions about layered protocols such as Integrated Services Digital Network (ISDN) and Systems Network Architecture (SNA) are based upon models that closely replicate the connection/communication procedures outlined in this module. The International Standards Organization (ISO) has developed the seven-layer Open System Interconnection (OSI) model that draws from the communication procedures discussed in this chapter, but adds the necessary additional levels of standardization needed to deal with communication procedures that we as humans rarely have to address.

For example, a human being traveling from Chicago to New York would travel in a straight line between the two. It seems completely unreasonable to travel to Miami before going to New York. Life is not so simple in the world of telecommunications. Much of today's information may indeed travel to Miami, Atlanta, or even San Francisco while getting from Chicago to New York. The transmission occurs so quickly that the time lost traveling to Atlanta is negligible and may turn out more efficient in the grand scheme of things. This is perhaps a source of major confusion in telecommunications and a point that will be demystified by the end of this book.

Finally, remember that the acceptance of these communication standards allows the existence of the advanced level of telecommunications we enjoy today. As globalization increases, the need for more comprehensive standards dealing with multicultural/lingual situations will increase. Those future standards probably will stem from standards that are already in place. A basic understanding of American business managers of communication procedures will pay large dividends for years to come.

In our discussions, telecommunications will be used to mean both voice and data communication. As we will see later, the two modes of information transmission look identical once inside the telecommunications network (binary one and zero bits of information) since voice is typically transmitted in digital form. The network is simply a high speed pathway for moving ones and zeros. It is the equipment used and the procedure followed at each end of the link that determines the outcome of the transmission.

Module Two
Telephone Development and Network Evolution

It is difficult for us today to imagine a world without a telephone. The telephone was invented in 1876 just a few years after the end of the Civil War. Horse and buggy was the accepted means of transportation. The letter was the dominant method of communication and instant communication was provided by the telegraph, which was only 30 years into its commercialization.

The United States as we know it was still relatively unfounded, and large distances were a critical impediment to the migration of civilized society to the central and western parts of the North American continent.

It is difficult to understand the current regulatory and technological environment in the United States without understanding the historical evolution of the American telephone system. This chapter looks at the invention of the telephone, the relationship between Bell and Watson, and the evolution of the Bell Telephone System from the standpoint of an evolving start-up.

Today we talk about start-up companies, but there have been few start-up companies on the scale of the telephone and its ensuing network as originally conceived by Bell, Watson, and two relatively unknown men named Hubbard and Vail.

The telephone in the United States alone has spawned an industry with hundreds of billions of dollars worth of annual revenues. Globally, there are trillions of dollars worth of capital equipment and U.S. dollar equivalence spent annually in communication services. Many of the foundations laid by the initial founders of the telephone system are currently assumed as guidelines for the operation of the current American telephone system.

Bell, Watson, and the Invention of the Telephone

Alexander Graham Bell was born in Scotland to Melville Bell, who was a respected *elocutionist* (speech teacher). As an elocutionist, Bell's father developed methods of teaching people with speech impediments the most effective ways to work with their impediment so that they could verbally communicate. The character of Professor Henry Higgins in Bernard Shaw's famous work *Pygmalion* was modeled after Melville Bell.

Alexander Graham Bell followed in his father's footsteps and became an elocutionist before coming to United States with his father. His father originally immigrated to Canada and later moved to Boston. In 1872, at the age of twenty-five, Alexander Graham Bell founded the School of Vocal Physiology in Boston. The charter for the school was "to correct stammering and other defects of utterance and to provide practical instruction in visible speech."

Bell's original inclination was with speech and the inability of speech. Some assert that from this passion came his desire to provide a method for people to speak over great distances.

While teaching in Boston, Bell came in contact with a gentleman named Gardiner Hubbard, a Boston attorney whose daughter was hearing impaired from the age of five. Hubbard's daughter, Mabel, had a difficult time with other speech teachers so Hubbard took her to Bell for instruction. Bell's instruction techniques proved to be successful, and Hubbard became a believer in Bell and his techniques. Simultaneously, Bell and Mabel fell in love and eventually married.

This entire encounter was fortuitous in that Hubbard was instrumental in the funding and counselling of Bell as the telephone became a reality. The telephone may have been invented without Hubbard's assistance, but it would never have become commercially successful within the same timeframe. Also, the Bell system that we know would almost certainly not exist with its current structure.

Bell met Thomas Watson in 1874. Watson was one of the most respected mechanical designers and machinists of the time and had a renowned ability to take other people's concepts and convert them into a physically operating product. He was fascinated with the existential aspects of life, electromechanics, and not afraid to take a chance. Watson was to become an integral part of the Bell system legacy. When Bell Telephone Company was first founded in July of 1877, it was Hubbard, in conjunction with Watson, who cofounded the Bell Telephone Company.

In 1874 Bell was working on a product called the harmonic telegraph. A harmonic telegraph had the ability to send several telegraph signals of different frequencies over the same piece of wire. The concepts involved with the harmonic telegraph were paramount in Bell's mind at the time. He had no concept, however, that transmitting speech would be a viable option.

In Bell's early days he read, in German, a paper by the German scientist Helmholtz in which he understood that Helmholtz had sent tuned sounds via the telegraph. It turns out that Bell's German was not very good and that he had misread the German paper. That is not at all what it said. His mistake may have been lucky in that he thought the harmonic telegraph had been done before, which gave him the confidence to keep pursuing it. It was not until later that he learned of his mistake in reading the paper and realized that he had been working on something completely new for the times. "I thought Helmholtz had done it and that my failure was due only to my ignorance of electricity. It was a very valuable blunder. It gave me confidence. If I had been able to read German, I might never have begun my experiments in electricity."

The Invention of the First Telephone

The harmonic telegraph required accurate tuning of the mechanical devices connected on either side of the wire. One day Watson broke a wire while tuning his device, and Bell heard the sound of the breaking wire on his side of the wire. He realized that he had heard more than just the tone. He had heard the actual plucking sound of the wire and not just the individual tone as he would have expected. That started Watson on a design attempt that would allow sounds, and not just tones, to be sent over wire.

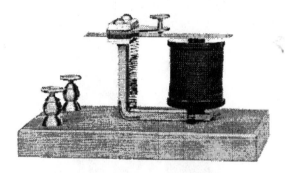

Harmonic Telegraph

They had been wrestling with sending sound over wire but could not quite comprehend the possibility of sending a randomly changing electrical signal as is generated by sound over a piece of wire. The logic at the time was that only tones or singular electrical signals could be sent. This accidental breaking of the wire started them down a path that would eventually lead to the telephone.

The original telephone was essentially an electromagnet attached to a large paper diaphragm. As sound pressure waves came into contact with the diaphragm, the diaphragm would move in proportion with the pressure of the sound wave. When the diaphragm moved, it would move components within the electromagnet, which caused a varying signal to be transmitted over the wire.

At the other end of the connection, another electromagnet would sense the varying electrical signal and move another paper diaphragm back and forth, which created another sound pressure wave (acoustic) that could be heard by someone on the receiving side.

The concept was simple and seemed to work on very short distances, but the sounds needed to be very large to generate a large enough electrical signal to eventually be converted back into sound. Nevertheless, the patent was filed on February 14, 1876. The patent was granted on March 3, 1876, and officially issued on the March 7, 1876.

It turns out that at the time of the patenting, no fully intelligible sentence had been translated via the telephone line. In fact, all that had been translated were some sounds, and that was enough to warrant the issuance of a patent. The next development step was to devise a way of magnifying those sounds and their electrical signal so that they could become more intelligible.

Watson initially developed the idea for using a sulfuric acid solution on either side of the connection. The intent was to use the sulfuric acid solution as a medium that would sense the variations in the transmitted electric signal. As the electrical signal variation was sensed, a larger physical fluctuation could be created and the paper diaphragm could be moved over larger distances causing larger sounds to be created.

It was this sulfuric acid testing procedure that gave rise to the commonly referred to first sentence heard over the telephone line. Bell was in one room with the sulfuric acid solution based device and Watson was in another. When Watson listened to his end of the connection he heard Bell say, "Mr. Watson, come here. I want you." He felt a sense of urgency in Bell's voice and ran into the room to learn that Bell had spilled sulfuric acid all over himself.

Bell was not hurt by the acid and the two men clearly realized that the device had worked. The initial product had been put together in a way that worked. More sophisticated prototypes would be developed and the empire of the phone was about to begin.

The Commercialization of the Telephone

Philadelphia was holding the World Exposition in June of 1876. The exposition was attended by England's Lord Kelvin, who was famous for his contributions in mathematics and physics. Also attending was Don Pedro, the emperor of Brazil and a strong supporter of scientific development.

Hubbard arranged for Bell to have a booth at the exposition. He also arranged for members of the exposition's technology selection committee to visit Bell's booth and see his new device. Seeing an apparatus that could actually transmit speech over wire made the committee members ecstatic, and they immediately proclaimed it as one of the most astounding inventions they had ever seen.

Kelvin offered to take the product back to England so that patents could be filed in England. In his haste, Bell gave Kelvin a unit that was not packed very well and by the time Kelvin arrived in England, the product did not function properly and the patent was never issued. This turned out to be a lucky occurrence because if the patent had been issued in England, there may have been legal complications in the United States and other countries. A second design of the product was later patented in the United States and eventually patented in England under the new design.

Bell wanted Watson's full time and attention on the telephone, and he offered Watson one-tenth interest in the Bell patent if he would give up his full-time job and devote his attention to the development of the telephone. Watson had misgivings about the long-term financial viability of the telephone, but he finally signed a contract for half of his time at a wage equal to that of his current job, plus 10 percent of the patent's worth. Watson needed to make a living while they speculated on the telephone eventually becoming a financially viable operation. If Watson had not made this kind of commitment, there is a good chance that the telephone would not be the way we know it.

In late 1876 Watson and Bell strung cabling around their neighborhood in Boston and transmitted the first telephone conversation over a two-mile distance using standard telegraph wire. This marked the advent of the first "long-distance" telephone call. In 1877 the first commercial telephone, called a box telephone, was developed. In May of 1877 six telephones were in use. In November of 1877 three thousand telephones were in use. By 1880, 133,000 telephones were in use. People had finally realized and appreciated the value of the telephone, and from this point on, there was no going back.

Even though the telephone was widely accepted in late 1877, early 1877 found Alexander Graham Bell with no income to support his family. To address this problem he sold admission to telephone demonstrations and used the admission revenues to feed his family.

Bell's financial problems had already become serious in 1876. He had actually attempted to sell his patent to Western Union, the major telegraph company, for $100,000. They refused his offer in the belief that the telephone was a short-lived product and that the telegraph would remain the dominant mode of future communication. They changed their mind in 1877 and tried to purchase the rights. This time it was Bell's turn to refuse.

In 1878 Western Union retaliated by coming out with their own telephone set that consisted of a carbon transmitter very similar to those used as telephone transmitting devices up until the late 1970s. Western Union contracted the design of this carbon transmitter to Thomas Edison. Watson took the concept of Edison's design and embellished it to make the telephone offered by the Bell group technologically superior to any competitor's product.

Around the same timeframe, Watson came into contact with Theodore M. Vail, the superintendent of the Post Offices Railway Mail Service. Vail was making excellent money at his current job but was very impressed with the prospects of Bell and Watson's telephone company. Vail was a professional manager and Watson and Bell were scientists being guided in business by Hubbard. The Bell company needed a general manager. The job was offered to Vail, who accepted it.

Vail was an influential person in molding the telephone company into what it is today. His vision was very simple. He wanted to advance the telephone network through speed, quality, and efficiency. These three chartered objectives were carried throughout the Bell system until its breakup in 1984.

At the same time, Emile Burliner was brought on board to work with Watson on technological developments, such as a loose carbon microphone that would compete with the one designed by Thomas Edison. They succeeded with this process.

In 1878 Bell filed a suit against Western Union for infringement on his design of the telephone set and won the suit. When Western Union was officially instructed to stop selling its telephones in violation of the patent, it sold its telephone facilities to the Bell system. National Bell, founded in 1879, and Western Union's operations were combined and became American Bell in 1880.

The National Bell Company was founded in 1879 under Vail's tutelage. The purpose of the National Bell Company was to license Bell's telephone technology to other companies that might be interested in providing telephone service. This a classic start-up situation where people with a great idea have limited financing. The Western Union Company had tried to move in on the telephone market, and only through the legal patent protection had Bell and his people been able to defend their right to the product. But the protection provided by the original Bell patent would run out in the early 1890s, so it was in their best interest to expand the system as quickly as possible.

National Bell needed to provide telephone technology to the nation as quickly as possible so that the industry would standardize on the Bell design. The best way to do this was to license the technology to investor groups who would then provide telephone service to their own subscribers. This allowed the telephone system to grow and provided the National Bell Company with critical financial support. This approach has been taken in many start-up situations where the founders are typically undercapitalized.

In 1879 the New England Telephone Company was created to sell licenses to operators in the New England area. That same year New England Telephone Company was superseded by National Bell Telephone Company, which was developed to provide licenses throughout the country. At the same time Metropolitan Telephone and Telegraph was created to provide service to the New York area.

As the licenses were sold, hundreds of small companies sprung up around the country using Bell in their name, since they had been legally licensed. The parent company to the system was to remain American Bell.

In 1877 the first operator-manned switchboard was created. When a caller wanted connection to another telephone, he rang the switchboard via a hand crank. When the operator answered, the caller gave the operator the name of the party she wanted to speak to and the operator then provided the connection to the second party using a *patch cord device*. The terminology for the pair of wires that transmit the telephone signal, "tip and ring," are a carryover from the operator's plug, in that one wire was connected to the tip of the plug and the other was connected to a ring on the shank of the plug. The original switchboard was created to allow doctors in the Hartford, Connecticut, area to communicate with the drug stores in the area.

Switchboard

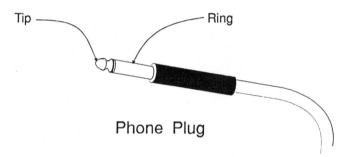

Early Telephone Switchboard

At this period of time, the operators knew by name who owned each telephone and consequently did not need a numbering system to provide the proper connections. In 1880 a doctor in Lowell, Massachusetts, petitioned the telephone company to install a telephone numbering system so that the system would not be shut down if an operator got sick. The complaint was that whoever replaced that operator might not know the phone extensions of the individual parties by name, and telephone service could be interrupted. It took a few years, but in 1895 a numbering system was introduced that allowed subscribers to call the operator and request the number of the party to whom they wished connection.

American Telephone and Telegraph was created in 1885 as the long-distance arm of the telephone company. AT&T's charter, as defined by Vail, was to connect every city, town, or place in the state of New York with each and every other city, town, or place in New York, the United States, Canada and Mexico, and also the rest of the known world as might become desirable. In essence, AT&T was started as a long-distance company whose charter was to connect New York with every place else (typical start-up mentality). Obviously, Vail had a global vision for AT&T which really knew few boundaries.

In 1887 Vail left the AT&T network because the system had substantially become a financially vs. operationally run company. Vail's emphasis was providing quality and quick telephone service to his subscribers. The financiers of National Bell Telephone were more interested in providing their optimum investors with optimum dividends. Vail felt this was a conflict of integrity for him and decided to leave his position. Vail was eventually brought back in 1907 as the system started falling into disarray.

The first automated switching system was patented in 1891 and first installed in 1892. The inventor of the product was a Missouri undertaker named Almon Strowger. Necessity is the mother of invention, and such was the case with Mr. Strowger. He began to believe that the operator in town was transferring more requests for undertaker service to his competition than to him. After some research, he discovered that the operator in question was actually the wife of the other undertaker in town. Strowger set out to correct the situation by developing a device that allowed the calling party to automatically select the telephone number as opposed to the manual selection performed by an operator, who was obviously biased in this case.

His switching device is called a Strowger step-by-step switching system and it saw substantial use within the Bell system which adopted it for use in 1918, nearly 20 years after its invention. In fact, as of 1978, over 23,000,000 American subscribers were still served by telephone switches based upon the Strowger design.

In 1896 the first telephone was designed to work in conjunction with the Strowger switching system. It was a dial telephone which was limited to 99 numbers. The switching equipment and telephone set were both created by Automated Electric Company which is still active as a telecommunication equipment designer.

The 1893 telephone subscriber paid roughly $100 per year for a residence telephone, and $150 per year for a business telephone.

In 1893 and 1894 the original telephone patents would expire and the free market economy would start to step in and drive the telephone industry. As expected, when the original patents ran out, everybody who could put together a telephone system jumped into the marketplace. Many people became dependent upon a particular telephone company, but quite often that company went out of business due to lack of funding and intense competition.

This situation prompted the development of the United States Independent Telephone Association (U.S.I.T.A.) which is still in existence today as the U.S. Telephone Association. A major goal of USITA was to provide stability of service across the many telephone companies. Many smaller local organizations, such as the Texas Telephone Association, exist to address local telephone company issues.

The system was expanding rapidly and eventually outgrew the legal constraints placed upon American Bell by the Massachusetts incorporation laws regarding capitalization limits. In 1899 AT&T became the parent organization for the Bell System, including American Bell, and was incorporated in New York because it had more flexible capitalization laws.

The years between 1893, when the patent expired, and 1907, when Vail again took the reins, were full of disruption and turmoil. Many financial arrangements had to occur to allow the Bell companies to work together and still provide improved service while substantial industry growth occurred.

In 1909, with Vail back at the helm, AT&T bought Western Union in the interest of wrapping telephone and telegraph service under one organization. Vail's idea of the telephone network was that every person in the United States should have access to a telephone, and that they should all communicate with each other. From 1907 until his departure a number of years later, Vail brought his vision of one system with universal service to the operation of the telephone company.

His concept of things was that if you work in conjunction with the public, the public will reward you. Consequently, he did not create an antagonistic environment between the telephone company and the public and saw the telephone company as a service organization to the public.

His personality was probably more critical than anything to setting the precedent for how we currently view the expected quality level of the telephone system in the United States. Some sources contend that the acquisition of Western Union was, in Vail's mind, a way of wrapping voice communications and telegraphy under one organization to provide a higher level of service to the people.

On the other hand, the federal government viewed the consolidation of the two as a violation of the Sherman Act. In 1913 the federal government used the antitrust laws as a basis for instructing AT&T to divest itself of Western Union. This was the beginning of an ongoing litigious relationship between the Bell system, the federal government, and others.

Indeed, in 1918, during the first world war, President Wilson nationalized the telephone telegraph operations and put them under the auspices of the post office. Vail worked cooperatively with Albert Burleson, who was then postmaster general. He convinced Burleson that the telephone company could work more effectively in support of the U.S. government's efforts if left on its own. In July of 1919 the government gave AT&T back control over the telephone company.

Vail died in 1920. At that point the Bell telephone company was fairly well established and its evolution is marked primarily by litigation between the federal government and AT&T establishing the guidelines under which it would be allowed to operate as a service organization to the general public.

Even though Vail may have had the best of intentions regarding the role of the Bell system in serving the general public, AT&T's methods in promoting this goal have often been questionable. Much of the antagonism that exists between the Bell system and the independent telephone suppliers exists because of AT&T attempting to provide service to subscribers to the exclusion of any other potential suppliers. A later section is dedicated to the evolution of the current regulatory environment.

Summary

Event Time Frame Summary

Date	Event
1874	Bell is working on the harmonic telegraph
1876	Patent for the first telephone
1876	First long-distance telephone conversation
1877	First commercial telephone developed
1877	First operator-manual switchboard
1878	Bell files an infringement suit against Western Union
1880	Telephone numbering system developed
1885	AT&T created as the long-distance arm of the company
1891	First automated switching system
1893-1894	Original telephone patents expire
1899	American Bell changed to American Telephone & Telegraph

The business and technology of the telecommunications market is becoming more complex instead of less. There are more contenders for the individual dollars of the telecommunication subscriber, and the confusion to the subscriber is increasing. The complexity of technology is increasing, and the diversity of commercial offerings is also increasing.

These are relatively new responsibilities that have been thrust upon the consumer. Up until recently, AT&T was the one dominant telephone company. Subscribers could easily procure equipment, long-distance and local service from the same source. Many subscribers wish that the simplicity of the days of AT&T dominance would return.

In many ways, the legacy of AT&T's market dominance is still in place. The telecommunications industry has always been controlled by a single major entity, and the industry consequently developed around an established set of standards. The way a telephone talks to the network was standardized by AT&T and is used almost exclusively today as a means of accessing the public network. The level of transmission quality we expect from the telephone network is also a tribute to Vail and Watson's commitment to excellence and quality.

Many parts of the world do not even have telephone service, yet Americans believe that a telephone, with its ever-present dial tone, is almost a God-given right and actually get angry when it is not readily available or if it is taken away. This expectation is also the result of many years of quality and service provided by a single carrier.

There is a strong case to be made for making the telephone marketplace less of a monopoly and more competitive. Technological advancements will migrate into the residence and workplace at the maximum speed that the market will allow. But the strong history of standardization and virtually uninterrupted service provided by the Bell system will be an ever-present benchmark against which each new public offering will be compared.

It is not suggested that AT&T is a preferred supplier over any of the other major vendors of telecommunications equipment. The AT&T of today resembles the previous company in name only, and in many ways it has suffered from deregulation and divestiture. What is suggested instead is that the level of service provided by a uniform national entity that was virtually transparent to the end user is the legacy of the Bell system to which Americans owe a debt of gratitude.

We live in an exciting stage of development for the telecommunications industry. Companies that effectively manage the transitions occurring in the marketplace will far exceed the progress of their competitors. Telecommunications is here to stay, and the history of the Bell system will provide the springboard for future growth.

We in the United States enjoy a uniform telephone system that provides a high degree of service reliability. The original patent and the original idea for the telephone should be credited to Alexander Graham Bell and Thomas Watson, but the structure of the organization and the service that we expect as subscribers can heavily be credited to Vail and his vision of the telephone company as a service organization whose job is to provide high quality, quick, and efficient telephone service to all subscribers in the United States. The obvious benefits of the telephone to the general public allowed the telephone to proliferate through American society the way it did. The competitive pressures of the open market kept the system in a constant state of improvement and will drive that improvement into the future.

Technology is changing quickly and the organizations that provide it must be willing to adapt and adjust to the circumstances. Any person who plans on using telecommunication equipment to further his or her own personal or business goals must stay in touch with what is happening on both a technological and a regulatory basis.

Module Three
Information Transmission and Electrical Signal Characteristics

The previous module describes the development process followed by Bell and Watson to design a device that converted sound pressure waves into electrical signals. The telephone network takes advantage of some characteristics of human speech to optimize network performance while not compromising sound quality. In addition, much of communication technology is based upon taking full advantage of the characteristics of a particular information signal. A conceptual yet complete understanding of electrical signal analysis is important to understanding the later topics.

If you are nontechnical, please do not get scared away from this section. The presentation is extremely nontechnical and easily understood by nearly everyone, and the benefits derived by a basic understanding of these concepts will far outweigh any momentary confusion that may occur.

Signal Frequency

The most fundamental of electrical signals is a *sine wave*. Notice that a sine wave has a particular shape that repeats itself after it has gone through one *cycle*. The number of times that a sine wave repeats itself in one second is called its *frequency*, which is measured in the number of *cycles per second* or in *hertz*, abbreviated *Hz*. The shape of an electrical signal is called its *waveform*.

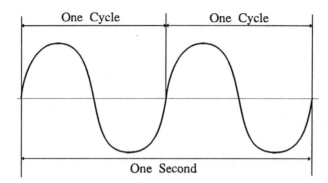

A Two Cycle Per Second Sine Wave (2 Hz)

We regularly hear the term hertz in our daily lives, but we rarely take notice of it. Look at the label on any piece of electrical equipment and notice that it lists *60 Hz* as one of its parameters. This is the frequency of the electrical signal provided to this equipment by the power company in the United States. In many other countries around the world, the frequency standard for power is 50 Hz, which means that their power is delivered with a signal that repeats itself 50 times per second.

Take a look at any FM/AM radio and notice that the frequency of the FM band is measured in Mhz (megahertz or millions of hertz) and the frequency of the AM band is measured in KHz (kilohertz or thousands of hertz). These terms are not uncommon but simply ones not used in everyday discussion.

Signal Amplitude

Another major descriptor of a sine wave is its peak amplitude, usually referred to simply as the amplitude. The amplitude of a sine wave is the distance from the neutral axis (zero point) of the wave and its peak point. The stronger a signal, the larger its amplitude. The weaker a signal, the smaller its amplitude.

Notice that a sine wave has both a positive and a negative peak amplitude that are equal in absolute value but opposite in sign, since one is positive and the other is negative. In general, both the positive and negative portions of the wave must be transmitted to maintain signal quality. The distance from the positive peak to the negative peak of the waveform is referred to as the *peak-to-peak amplitude*. This equal positive/negative characteristic of a sine wave is sometimes referred to as *symmetry*.

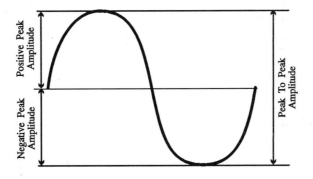

Sine Wave Amplitude Measurements

Signal Phase

The phase of a waveform relates to the timing of the signal based upon the timing of some other referenced waveform. For example, assume that a sine wave begins its positive movement at a time that we will arbitrarily call time-zero. Also assume that a second waveform begins its positive movement precisely at the time when the first waveform is reaching its maximum or peak amplitude.

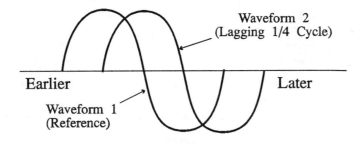

Phasing Relationship Between Waves

If we assume that the first wave is the reference wave, then we can say that the second wave is behind in time (or *lagging*) the first wave by one quarter of a cycle. Remember that a full cycle has occurred when the wave begins to repeat itself. In other words, the second wave is out of phase, or time, with the first wave by one quarter of a cycle and is referred to as lagging the reference wave by 90 degrees.

The Degrees of a Sine Wave

The degree reference is derived from the relationship between a sine wave and a circle. Imagine a circle with a radius of one unit that has a pen at the zero-degree point of the circle (marked A). Also imagine that a piece of paper lies underneath the pen and that the paper moves to the left at the same time that the pen moves around the circle in a counterclockwise direction.

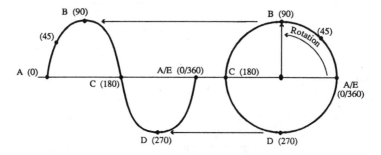

The Degrees of a Sine Wave

We see that the pen starts at zero degrees on the circle, which corresponds with the neutral (zero) axis of the waveform. Imagine that the pen moves around the circle then stops at the 90-degree point or top of the circle (point B). Notice that the pen would have drawn the first one-quarter cycle of the sine wave we have referenced throughout this section. We say that the waveform has moved through 90 degrees or a one-quarter cycle.

As the pen continues its rotation around the circle, notice that it moves through the 180 degree (point C), 270 degree (point D), and 360/0 degree (point E) points and draws a full sine wave just as we drew earlier.

This relationship between a sine wave and a circle gives rise to the accepted practice of referring to a location on a sine wave as its degree location. The positive and negative peaks are the 90 and 270 degree locations respectively, while the starting and half-way zero crossing points are referred to as the 0/360 and 180 degree locations respectively.

When dealing with modems, which will be discussed in a later module, reference is also made to the 45 degree locations, or the half-way points between zero and 90 degrees, and so forth, around the full circle.

Coming back to our previous example, we now see that the second wave lags behind the first wave by one quarter of a cycle or 90 degrees. The timing of the second wave is behind the first by 90 degrees, so it is *out of phase* with the first wave by 90 degrees.

If the second wave started its positive movement after the first wave had completed one-half of its cycle and was moving in a negative direction, then the second wave would be one-half cycle or 180 degrees out of phase from the first.

The concept of phasing is a little abstract, but it is fundamental to understanding many aspects of telecommunications. This is especially true when dealing with modems.

Electrical Signal Analysis

A French mathematician named Fourier showed that virtually any signal or waveform can be broken into a combination of sine waves of different frequency, amplitude, and phase. His findings form the basis for the current transition from analog to digital technology as the transmission standard.

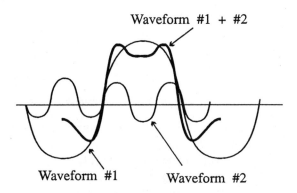

Waveform #1 + #2

Waveform #1

Waveform #2

Sinsoidal Signal Components

It can be shown that if a continuous waveform of a known minimum and maximum frequency is sampled at discrete points often enough, that the discrete samples can be reassembled so that the original waveform is recreated without loss of information.

The proper sampling rate was determined by Harry Nyquist in 1933. Mr. Nyquist determined that sampling a waveform at a rate equal to at least twice the maximum sine wave frequency contained in the waveform would ensure that the samples contained all important signal information. Consequently, if the sampling process could be reversed, the original analog waveform could be reproduced without loss of information. Sampling at twice the maximum signal frequency is referred to as the *Nyquist sampling rate.*

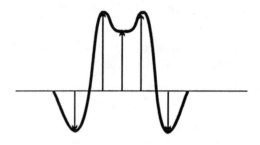

Sampled Continuous Signal

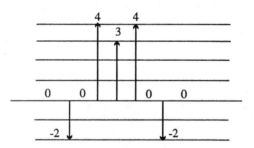

Discrete Digital Samples with Same Information

The primary benefits associated with discrete sampling versus continuous waveforms is that computers "think" in discrete *binary* terms. Consequently, they can effectively process information in any discrete form that is translated into binary computer code. The fundamental building blocks of binary code are the discrete states of one and zero. All computer applications, no matter how they may ultimately look to us, are the result of a large number of binary (one/zero) operations performed very quickly by the computer.

Once a discrete waveform sample is taken, it can be converted into a stream of ones and zeros, referred to as computer bits, which can be stored, processed, or transmitted by any computerized network.

Fourier's mathematical discovery regarding signal sine wave composition broke signals into frequency parts. The ability to sample a continuous wave at discrete levels and not lose information, combined with the ability of computers to quickly process discrete information levels provides the background against which the communications industry is moving into a completely digital world.

The Concepts of Digital Storage of Signal Information

As discussed previously, any waveform with a maximum sine wave frequency component can be sampled at the Nyquist sampling rate of twice that maximum frequency without any loss of information content. We also noted that this particular sample could be stored in binary (one and zero bits) form so that computers could work with the information.

The number of bits used to store the sample is an important component in determining the ability to recreate the waveform that was initially sampled. In addition, modems use many of the techniques discussed in this section for increasing the amount of information they transmit over the telephone link of fixed transmission capacity. A brief conceptual discussion of *digital encoding* is in order at this point. Once again, please do not get scared off simply because the topic sounds technical. The discussion will be conceptual in nature and calculators are not required.

Assume that we have only a single bit of computer information. This single bit can only be in one of two states. It can be either one or zero. Period. This is true for any computer bit of information, no matter what it is used to represent.

Picture a straight vertical line and assume that a one bit means that a treasure is buried at the top end of the line, and a zero means that the treasure is located at the bottom end of the line. Notice that it is only possible to represent two possible locations with this single bit designation but that the zero/one state of the bit carries very clearly defined information.

Now assume that we have two bits with which to represent locations. Each bit can be either a one or a zero which gives rise to four possible states (00,01,10,11). To illustrate this situation, imagine a room with four corners. Let the upper left corner, the upper right corner, the lower right corner, and lower left corner correspond to the 00, 01, 10, and 11 states of the two bits, respectively.

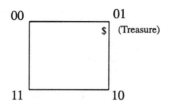

Two Bit Encoding Combinations

If you were told that "01" represented the location of the buried treasure, you would know just where to go to become a rich person (and have the opportunity to pay a large portion of your find in taxes). Notice that there were only four locations possible with a two bit representation, but that there is absolutely no confusion about the meaning of a "01" designation in the context of this example.

As a final example along these lines, assume that we have three bits with which to represent locations. As before, each bit can be in either a zero or one state which gives rise to eight possible one/zero bit combinations (000,001,010,011,100,101,110,111). Picture an octagon (eight-sided object) and begin labeling the corner locations with each successive bit combination starting with "000" in the "10 o'clock" corner location.

Once again, if you were told that the treasure was buried at the "100" location, you would quickly become rich by digging at the "5 o'clock" corner location.

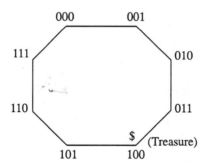

Three Bit Encoding Combinations

Of interest to us in this example is that a specific combination of one and zero bits can have very specific meanings. In addition, the greater the number of bits involved, the larger the number meanings possible. To be specific, the number of states is determined by raising the number two to the power of the total number of bits (i.e., three bits provide two to the third power or 2x2x2=8 possible meanings). These different meanings are referred to in computer jargon as the total possible states of the three bit combinations.

This discussion has particular meaning when we move on to digitizing an analog voice signal using the Nyquist sampling criteria. Just as more bits allowed us to define more buried treasure locations, more bits allow greater precision when recording the magnitude of the analog wave at the time it is sampled.

If only one bit is used, then we can only record whether the wave is on or off at the time of sampling. If two bits are used, then four possible magnitude levels are possible. If three bits are used, then eight magnitude levels are possible, and so forth. This process of correlating possible bit combinations with different levels or states is called *digital encoding*.

The U.S. industry accepted standard used for encoding voice information uses seven bits to define the state of the analog wave when sampled and an eighth bit to define whether the wave was in a positive or negative state. This allows for encoding of two to the seventh power or 2x2x2x2x2x2x2= 128 different waveform levels on the positive side of the waveform and 128 different levels on the negative side of the waveform. In addition, a specific method of weighting the waveform signals is used to optimize the quality of the encoded information.

Converting the analog waveform to digital information is called *modulation* and the specialized weighting procedure is called *companding*. The standard used for digitizing voice signals in the U.S. is Pulse Code Modulation (PCM) using a mu-law compander. The device that performs this analog-to-digital (A/D) conversion is a CODEC (short for coder/decoder). It takes one codec to convert the analog wave into digital form. It takes another to reverse the process and turn digital bit streams into analog electrical signals that the telephone receiver can ultimately convert back into sound.

Once again, the specifics of the techniques are not covered here. The intent of this section is to demystify some commonly used industry terminology. The reader should now understand that the 64 kilobit PCM using a mu-law companding technique used by industry is nothing more than a standardized procedure for converting analog voice into a 64,000 bit per second digital form.

We will see in the next section that voice information signals contain information with a maximum frequency of 4,000 hertz. If this signal is sampled at a Nyquist rate of twice 4,000 hertz, then a total of 8,000 samples must be taken per second. Based upon the previous discussion of PCM encoding, a total of 8 bits are used for each sample taken.

Performing some simple multiplication shows that 8,000 samples x 8 bits per sample= 64,000 bits (64 kilobits) of information per second are needed to properly sample an analog voice signal and not lose information. This is indeed the American industry sampling rate and the basic multiplier used when calculating voice bandwidth requirements on digital telecommunication links.

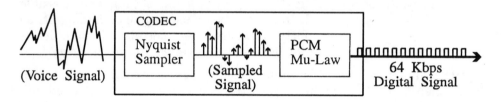

Voice Signal Digitizing Sequence

Module Four
Communication Link Types and Their Physical Configuration

Communication Link Bandwidth

The objective of any communication link is to provide a connection for the transmission of information between a transmitter and a receiver. Since most information in the telecommunications arena is electrical, it is assumed that telecommunication signals are composed of a series of sine waves of different frequencies, amplitudes, and phases.

Most signals have specific frequency characteristics that allow for processing of the signal such that the transmission process can be optimized. Most signals contain combinations of sine waves with lower and upper frequency limits and various frequency components in between these limits. This range of frequencies from the upper to lower limits is called the *bandwidth* of the signal.

The term bandwidth is also used in conjunction with the upper and lower frequency transmission capabilities of a particular link type. In effect, the transmission link will only transmit signal frequencies within that bandwidth range. All frequencies outside of the specified bandwidth of the link will be essentially blocked from transmission.

The human voice is composed of sine waves within the frequency range of 100-10,000 hertz, but the bulk of the voice information required to transmit intelligible speech is between 200-4,000 hertz.

It is in the best interest of the network designers to limit the frequencies transmitted to the smallest possible bandwidth since it is more expensive to transmit information requiring a larger bandwidth. Consequently, the telephone network limits its conduction frequencies to a voice channel bandwidth extending from 0-4,000 hertz.

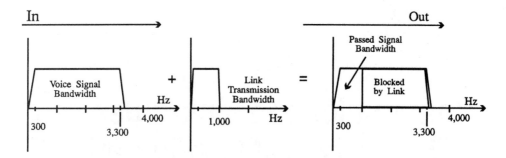

Effect of Link on Signals

Within that voice channel a bandwidth extending from 300-3,000 hertz is reserved for transmission of the actual voice signal (the voice sounds we hear when we talk on the telephone). The bandwidth left over between the voice channel bandwidth of 4,000 hertz and the bandwidth reserved for voice transmission is used by the telephone network for various communication control functions.

This extra bandwidth is also used to separate telephone conversations from each other by providing a guard band between conversations that are transmitted over a common media using the frequency division multiplexing.

Media Transmission Characteristics

As mentioned previously, any signal contains information that can be broken into sine waves of different frequencies. The range of those frequencies from the lowest to the highest is the bandwidth of the signal.

If the range of frequencies containing the bulk of the information is transmitted without change, then the received signal will closely resemble the information transmitted. If the characteristics of the sine waves (i.e., amplitude, phase) within that range of frequencies are modified as they are transmitted, then the received signal will be a distorted representation of what was originally transmitted. If the modification is severe, the received information may not resemble the transmitted information and the entire purpose of the communication is lost.

As a signal is transmitted over a communication link, the electrical characteristics of the link affect the signal and introduce some level of distortion. This distortion comes from the finite bandwidth of the transmission link. A water analogy is often useful for explaining the actions of electrical products.

Just as a water pipe can only pass a certain amount of water in any given period of time, a communication link of a specified bandwidth can only transmit a certain amount of signal information.

With a water pipe we refer to the size of the pipe by its diameter. A pipe of a larger diameter, and consequently larger cross-sectional area, can pass more water in a second than a smaller pipe with smaller cross-sectional area. Imagine that a three-inch-diameter pipe carries water that feeds into a one-inch-diameter pipe. It is obvious that the amount of water coming out of the one-inch pipe will be determined by the one-inch pipe since its water carrying capabilities limit the amount of water flow.

If the objective is to pump 10 gallons per second through the three-inch pipe, but the one-inch pipe can only carry 1 gallon per second, then the combination of the two pipes can allow 1 gallon per minute of water flow.

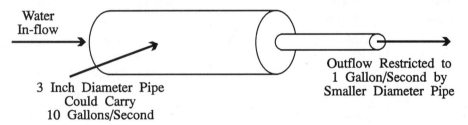

Communication links are similar to water pipes in that they have different bandwidth carrying capabilities. A link with a larger bandwidth has the ability to transmit larger amounts of information than a link with a smaller bandwidth.

This concept of bandwidth becomes critically important when matching the bandwidth carrying capability of the link with the bandwidth of the information to be transmitted over that link. Just as a smaller water pipe restricts that flow of water through it, a communication link of smaller bandwidth will restrict the transmission of signal information to that which is within its transmission bandwidth. It will block the passage of those frequencies outside of its transmission ability.

It may help to think of a links transmission capacity as a pipe of a specific diameter. The water pipe has the ability to pass water through it up to a certain capacity. Flow rates below that capacity will pass without obstruction, where flow rates above that capacity will be restricted to the capacity of the pipe. Objects at either end of the pipe that are dependent upon higher flow rates will see their performance hampered by the lower water flow rate allowed by the smaller diameter pipe.

Communication transmission links are like pipes of different diameters with the bandwidth of the link correlating to the diameter (and cross-sectional area) of the pipe. A transmission line with a higher bandwidth capacity corresponds to a pipe with a larger cross-sectional area. A transmission line with a lower bandwidth capacity corresponds to a pipe with a smaller cross-sectional area.

Think of electrical signals of a specific bandwidth as transmissions that require a specific amount of cross-sectional area to be effectively transmitted.

If the cross-sectional area requirement of the signal (sine wave information content bandwidth) is larger than the cross-sectional area (bandwidth capacity) of the communication link, then the information to be transmitted will be distorted during transmission just as water flow would be restricted by a smaller pipe.

If the cross-sectional area requirement of the signal (sine wave information content bandwidth) is smaller than the cross-sectional area (transmission bandwidth capacity) of the communication link, then the information will be transmitted without distortion.

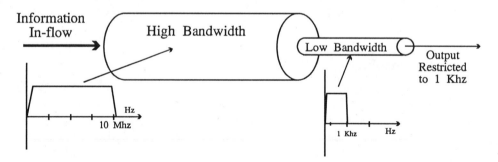

The physical characteristics of the communication link (material type, diameter, layout of conductors) determine its transmission bandwidth. So far in this discussion of networks, the term communications link has been used frequently but without describing what it is. The generic term for physical links is *transmission media*. Transmission media types over which information is communicated fall into four categories: 1) Twisted-pair (copper wire), 2) Coaxial Cable, 3) Optical Fiber Cable, and 4) Wireless Media.

In general, standard telephone network unshielded twisted pair wire has the lowest bandwidth of conventional communication links. Coaxial cable, similar to that connected to a television set but of many different physical types, is the next highest. Microwave and satellite, which transmit radio waves using air as the link, are the next highest. Optical fiber cable is the fastest and most reliable medium available today.

Fiber-optic cables are becoming increasingly popular because of their ability to carry enormous amounts of information (thousands of times that of standard twisted pair wire), simply because of their large bandwidth capacity.

The length of the link inversely affects the maximum frequency that can be effectively transmitted. The longer the link, the lower the maximum frequency. The shorter the link, the higher the frequency. For this reason, different media types will have wide ranges of frequencies that they can transmit. Notice that these limits are for different link lengths.

Transmission Characteristics of Select Media

Medium	Total Data Rate	Repeater Spacing	Cost
Twisted Pair	4 Mbps	1 - 10 km	low
Coaxial Cable	140 - 500 Mbps	1 - 10 km	Moderate
Satellite	2 Mbps	Geosynch Orbit	High
Optical Fiber	2 Giga bps	10 - 100 km	Moderate to High

To refer back to the pipe analogy, a pipe with a one-inch cross-sectional area has a diameter of approximately one inch. A pipe big enough to carry one thousand times the water flow (as is so with fiber optics when compared to twisted pair wire) would have a diameter of around 36 inches, or three feet.

Copper Wire
Equivalent Pipe
(1 inch Diameter)

Optical Fiber
Equivalent
Pipe Diameter

3
feet

Twisted Pair

Twisted Pair is a copper wire medium that is the primary carrier for voice communications. It is widely available, well understood by telephone networking technicians, and is currently the least expensive medium. Pairs of wires are twisted together under tight control (hence the name) to form a cable. Twisting minimizes the interference created between adjacent pairs when large numbers of pairs are bundled together. Wire sizing is determined in accordance with the *American Wire Gauge (AWG)* standard. The larger the AWG rating, the smaller the wire diameter. Typical telephone wiring ranges from 18 to 24 AWG.

A major beneficial aspect to twisted pair is that every home or business worker location in the U.S. has some form of twisted pair running to it. It has been in such widespread use that it is sometimes referred to as the *ubiquitous wiring scheme* (present in all places). Many vendors have developed high speed data and voice transmission equipment that takes advantage of the universal nature of twisted pair. In fact, the 10BASET local area network standard defines methods of passing LAN data over twisted pair wiring and was developed specifically to capitalize on the wealth of installed twisted pair cable.

Some older bundles of telephone wiring were not twisted and are sometimes referred to as *straight cable*. It is generally a good idea to remove straight cable and replace it with modern twisted pair wiring to eliminate intermittent failure of transmission links.

Twisted pair bundles generally come in 2,4,8,25,50, and 100 pair bundles. Notice that a 4 pair cable has eight wires.

When used for sending data communications signals, however, this medium poses some problems. First, the electrical characteristics of twisted pair wiring preclude the transmission of very high speed data over distances longer than a few hundred feet. To overcome these electrical limitations, the data signal power is increased, which poses problems with the second deficiency area associated with twisted pair wiring.

Secondly, wire emits and absorbs a large amount of electrical interference, resulting in high error rates that pose problems where data security is important.

Special twisted pair wiring with a signal shield is used for data transmission needs. The shield reduces the amount of electromagnetic interference received by the wiring and also reduces the amount of electromagnetic interference caused by the twisted pair wiring itself. The shielding does affect the transmission characteristics of the line and reduces the number of feet over which a signal can be effectively transmitted. This is generally not a problem for most business applications, but it is a cautionary note worthy of attention.

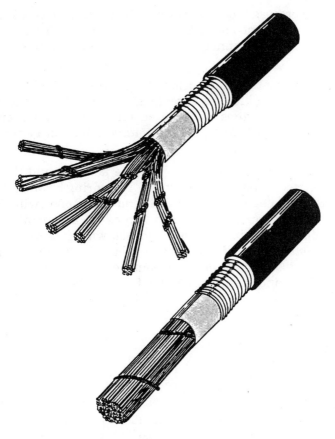

Twisted Pair

An attractive aspect of twisted pair wiring is its ease of installation. The telephone company has used twisted pair wiring for decades, and a great deal of experience has been obtained regarding its installation and maintenance. Most businesses use a star topology twisted pair wiring scheme to route cable throughout their organization.

Twisted pair wiring is generally run to a *punch down block* that consists of metal tabs into which the twisted pair wiring is inserted through the use of a *punch down tool*. When the wire is pressed onto the tabs, the wire insulation is pierced and the wire makes electrical contact with the tabs.

The tabs are then connected in various ways to route the electrical connections to the desired locations.

The punch down process is easily accomplished and relatively inexpensive. Connecting from one punch down block to another is called a *cross connect* and is generally used to connect an incoming telephone line to a specific worker location.

The lines between the telephone company and the customer terminate on a punch down block which represents the point where the telephone network responsibility stops and the customer premises responsibility begins. This point is referred to as the *demarcation point* or simply as the "demarc."

In general, the wiring between the telephone network and the customer terminates at a specific point in a building. The wiring between the worker location where the telephone is installed and telephone switching equipment follows a star topology and terminates at a central point. This centralized point of distribution for premises wiring is called the *main distribution frame (MDF)*. It is usually more convenient to run cable bundles between floors of a building to points called *intermediate distribution frames (IDF)* and then make the final cable run to the worker telephone station.

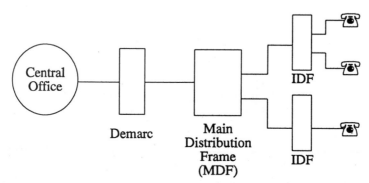

Both main and intermediate distribution frames are located in *wiring closets*, which are named such for obvious reasons.

Many organizations have implemented a specially designed wiring *patch panel* that allows for twisted pair wiring to be cross connected without the need for punch down blocks or tools. Patch panels are a series of standard modular telephone outlets and special cables with compatible plugs. When connections are desired from one line to another, a patch cord is plugged into the appropriate outlets and the connection is complete. These systems cost a little more to install but generally pay for themselves within a few years of installation.

Coaxial Cable

Coaxial cable overcomes many of the transmission problems associated with twisted wire pairs. It supports high-speed, high-capacity data transmission, exhibits high immunity to electrical interference, and maintains a low incidence of errors. In coaxial cable, a central *carrier wire* is covered by an insulating material and surrounded by a fine copper wire mesh or extruded aluminum sleeve and a protective outer shield.

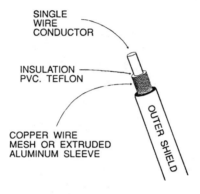

SINGLE
WIRE
CONDUCTOR

INSULATION
PVC. TEFLON

COPPER WIRE
MESH OR EXTRUDED
ALUMINUM SLEEVE

OUTER SHIELD

Coaxial Cable

Coaxial cable is used by the public telephone companies for carrying long-distance calls between telephone company switching offices. It is used extensively by the cable television industry because "coax" has the capacity for carrying many television channels at the same time over a single cable. Coaxial cable is moderate in cost and readily available.

Some problems associated with coaxial cable are the size of the wire itself and the skill level needed to make error free cable terminations. In addition, patch panels are the only effective way to work with coaxial cable wiring plans, and consequently the cost of a coaxial-based installation is substantially higher than a twisted pair network

Many terminal devices, such as the IBM 3270-based terminals, use coaxial cable for transmission of data between a special controller and the worker's terminal. The amount of cable involved in routing the communication capability throughout an organization has caused some companies to remove elevator shafts simply to have enough room to run 3270 terminal coaxial cable. These organizations drove the efforts to find other methods of transmitting the same information but over twisted pair. The *balun* is the result of these efforts.

A balun is a passive device that does not amplify or modify the information content of the high-speed, coaxial-based signal. Instead it converts the signal into a form that can be transmitted over both twisted pair and coax. One media is referred to as *balanced* and the other is called unbalanced, based upon how the electrical signals are routed. This device converts *balanced* to *unbalanced* signals. Thus the term balun.

Twisted Pair

The balun allows companies to use the already installed twisted pair wiring to route information that would typically be coax based. The cost savings derived in not using coaxial cable easily pay the incremental cost of the balun.

Fiber-Optic Cable

Fiber-optic cable allows for data transmission with light as the "signal" carrier. Optical fibers are thin strands of glass or plastic that act like pipes, preventing light from escaping the fiber except at the ends. In addition, optical fiber medium is nonconductive (does not conduct electricity) and therefore cannot be affected by electrical noise in the area.

Fiber-Optic Cable

The signal transmitted over a fiber-optic link is also nonelectrical. The signal is light which is composed of photons which do not create any noticeable electrical field as they traverse the optical fiber path. The net effect is that optical fiber systems are highly noise resistant and also do not emit any significant electrical noise that could interfere with surrounding equipment. This lack of radiation transmission characteristic makes fiber communication attractive in many government applications where information security is critical. Without a transmitted electromagnetic field, the signal is difficult to tap into and therefore very secure.

Speed of transmission is a principle asset associated with optical fiber communication. The information is transmitted at the speed of light (186,000 miles per second) which means that a trip around the world only takes around 1/8th of a second. In addition, the bandwidth of optical fiber is in the billions of bits per second range versus the millions of bits per second found on coax or twisted pair media.

Networks that use fiber-optic communications translate electrical messages into light pulses using a *modulator* and transmit those pulses over the fiber to a receiver where they are detected and converted back into their original electrical form by *photoelectric diodes*. The light signal can be either analog (a continuous wave) or digital (a series of light pulses). Analog light signals vary by light intensity, while on/off light pulses represent the 0/1 bits used in conventional digital signaling.

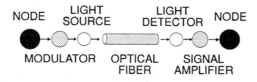

Fiber-Optic Transmission System

It is easy to see why the future of data communications is so strongly tied to optical fiber technology. Fiber-optic cables have substantially more bandwidth than coaxial cable, transmit information faster, and exhibit error rates that are almost negligible. There truly is a remarkable difference in sound quality between a long-distance call routed over a conventional analog network and one digitally transmitted over a fiber-optic link. Fiber-optic transmission is "quiet" since it is unaffected by electrical interference or electromagnetic effects.

Optical fibers have traditionally been difficult to work with. Installation was typically tedious and subject to error because of the extreme precision required when splicing fibers at junctions. The splice must be aligned just right for the cable to work.

Recent advancements in technology have overcome this problem and the cost of fiber installation is decreasing rapidly as more communication companies begin to standardize on fiber. Optical fiber splices are now relatively simple to accomplish and the test instruments that qualify the quality of the splice are becoming easier to operate and less expensive.

Optical fiber comes in three basic flavors: *multimode, multimode graded index*, and *single mode*. The number of *modes* refers to the number of paths available to the light as it passes through the fiber link.

Optical fiber construction consists of three parts. The inside contains a center *core* that actually conducts the light and a *cladding* that surrounds the core and reflects the light back into the core. The outside of the optical fiber is a *jacket* that protects the cladding and core from damage. Notice that the core actually conducts the light beam which is guided down the path by the cladding. The jacket is simply a protector.

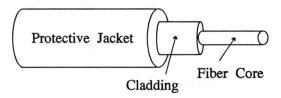

Optical Fiber Cable

If the core is very narrow, then there is not enough room for the light beam to bounce from one side of the core to the other. Since there is only one path for the light to follow (down the center of the core) this is referred to as "single mode" optical fiber. Since all light beams travel the same path, little signal degradation is encountered with single mode fiber and the transmission distances can be largely compared to multimode.

Single mode fiber is the most expensive optical fiber to purchase and is also the most difficult to work with since the alignment tolerances are so tight due to the small core size.

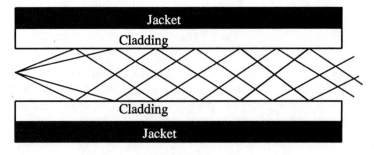

Multimode Optical Fiber

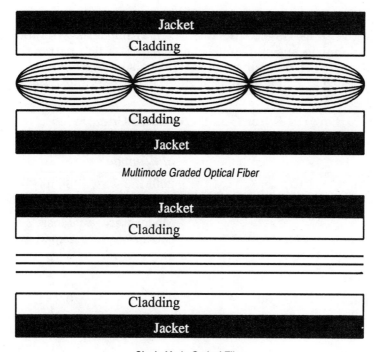

Multimode Graded Optical Fiber

Single Mode Optical Fiber

If the core is very wide relative to some characteristics of the light beam, then the beam will bounce back and forth as it moves down the optical fiber line. There may actually be many different paths for the light to follow, which gives this type of optical fiber the name "multimode."

The major problem with multimode fiber is that the light source follows different paths as it progresses through the fiber line. Different portions of the light source arrive at the end of the journey at different times since some of the light rays travel a farther distance than others due to the extensive bouncing experienced during the trip. The effect of the different distances is to erode the characteristics of the initial signal transmitted and the signal received may look very different from the one initially transmitted.

Consequently, the transmission distance cannot be as far as with single mode because the signal must be recaptured and regenerated in its original form. There is also a larger amount of signal power loss with multimode than with single mode. Multimode is the least expensive of the optical fiber options.

Graded index multimode cable has a core designed to allow multiple modes but controls the travel path for the light beam so that the light arrives at

relatively the same time. Graded index multimode is a compromise between single mode and multimode in that it is much better than multimode, but not as good as single mode. It is also less expensive and easier
to work with than single mode but more expensive and tougher to work
with than multimode.

Optical Fiber Characteristics Comparison

	Multimode	*Graded Multimode*	*Single Mode*
Bandwidth	Up to 200Mhz/km	200Mhz - 3Ghz/km	3Ghz - 50Ghz/km
Cost	Least expensive	Moderately expensive	Most expensive
Core Diameter (micrometer)	50 - 125	50 - 125	2 - 8
attenuation (db/km)	10 - 50	7 - 15	0.2 - 2

The telephone companies want to eventually run fiber to the curb of every
house and building in America. The standard twisted copper pair wiring
that is already in place has limited bandwidth and consequently limited
information carrying capability. The installation of an optical fiber to a
household opens up virtually unlimited possibilities regarding voice, video,
data, and graphical information transmission. This one optical fiber could
replace the coaxial television cable and the telephone lines and provide
substantially more services.

The RBOCs (Regular Bell Operating Company) have been working on the
Justice Department to allow them to provide information services to the
public. The RBOCs claim that access to that marketplace would provide
the financial justification needed to pursue the multibillion dollar investment necessary to install fiber to the curb.

In October 1991 the Justice Department allowed the RBOCs access to the
information services marketplace. The transition has begun to occur and
the ultimate outcome of the migration process will almost definitely
include a ubiquitous optical fiber network.

Wireless Media

Wireless media, such as *radio* and *microwave*, are slowly gaining acceptance for the transmission of voice and data information.

The era of wireless transmission was ushered in by Marconi's first intercontinental radio transmission between England and France in 1898. Microwave technology came along 50 years later. Not until the early 1950s was it possible to reliably transmit microwave signals. But with this technology came an easier and more cost-effective means of long-distance communication. It was no longer necessary to string thousands of miles of wire to carry information between two distinct points.

Both radio and microwave use the air as the communication link. Of the two, microwave signals have a higher information-carrying capacity than the typical radio link. Microwave transmission, however, has a few limitations. First, microwaves are stopped by things such as hills, buildings, and other solid objects. This is referred to as *line of sight* transmission in that an unobstructed view must exist between the sending and receiving stations of a microwave connection. Microwave transmitters are usually situated on high ground away from obstructions and other sources of ground clutter to minimize transmission interference.

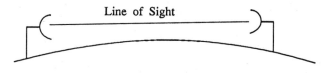

Microwave Communication Link

Microwaves follow straight paths, but the Earth is curved. Microwave relay stations must therefore dot the landscape at regular intervals to intercept and retransmit the signals before they speed off into outer space. A rule of thumb for two 100-meter-high antennas is that they must be placed no farther than 82 km from each other.

Satellite Communications

Some communication networks use microwave to transmit information to orbiting satellites which then relay the signals back to earth. Virtually every point on the globe can be reached by satellite communications.

Communication satellites are placed into stationary orbit around the earth, which means that the location of the satellite is always the same and can be easily found at any given time. To achieve this high level of positional stability, the satellite is placed in orbit 22,300 miles above the earth. At this point, the satellite does not fall towards the earth and also does not try to fly away. The satellite circles at a rate that keeps the satellite at the same point above the earth at all times as it rotates. This synchronized rotation is called a *geosynchronous orbit*.

Notice that signals are sent to the satellite and also broadcasted back to earth from the satellite. If the satellites were too close together, signals meant for one satellite might be intercepted by another. To limit this possibility, the satellite locations in space are limited to one every 3 or 4 degrees of a circle, dependent upon the frequency band of the microwave communication links. This proximity restriction places an upper limit on the number of satellites that can be put into geosynchronous orbit.

An earth-based *ground station* points its microwave antenna at the satellite location and transmits information to the satellite over an *uplink*. The satellite then boosts the signal and transmits the information back to the earth over a *downlink* but in a broadcast mode. This means that satellite communication is private on the uplink but unprotected on the downlink. This characteristic is either an advantage or a deficiency depending upon the communication application.

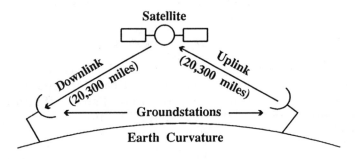

Satellite Communication Link

For television broadcasts, the ability to cover more of the earth from a given satellite is desirable. For this application, the broadcast characteristic of satellite communication is ideal. On the other hand, sensitive government or company communication is available to anyone listening to the proper satellite microwave channel; this is undesirable. Encryption devices are used to *scramble* (shift the form and/order of information) the transmitted information is such a way that the receiver can understand the information but any unauthorized person listening in will receive garbage.

Notice that a complete satellite communication path requires an uplink and a downlink, each of which is 22,300 miles long. Thus the signal must travel 44,600 miles in each direction of transmission. Microwave signals travel at the speed of light (186,000 miles per second), which means that the signal takes around ¼ of a second to make the journey. This delay characteristic makes satellite communication unsuitable for many interactive applications. Most of us have seen the effect of this delay on television shows between foreign countries where the two parties get off in their timing.

Frequency Division and Time Division Multiplexing

Imagine looking at the cross section of a large water pipe. Also imagine that this cross section is divided into a number of equal circular areas. Depending upon the size of the pipe, there are a specific number of these smaller circular areas that can be fit into the pipe.

Think of each one of these smaller circular areas as individual voice paths of 4,000 hertz each. Through a process called *modulation* these individual voice paths can be placed into the different circular locations of the pipe's cross-sectional area until the pipe is full.

Modulation is a common technique used in the communication industry for combining different signals over the same transmission media. Pulse Code Modulation (PCM) is a common method of representing an analog voice signal as a stream of digital ones and zeros.

Two other modulation techniques we see every day are the FM (frequency modulation) and AM (amplitude modulation) bands on our radios. In essence, many radio signals are being transmitted over a single communication link (air). The transmission bandwidth of air is much higher than that required by one radio signal (the pipe is much bigger than that required for one signal), so frequency and amplitude modulation techniques are used to "fill" the area of the pipe.

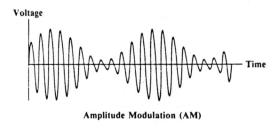

Amplitude Modulation (AM)

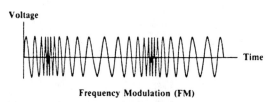

Frequency Modulation (FM)

Types of Modulation

Frequency modulation techniques *shift* (also referred to translate or move) the basic signal information into a section of the transmission frequency bandwidth not already in use by another signal. This is the equivalent of moving the water flow to a particular portion of the pipe.

When many different signals are shifted into various different frequency locations via this modulation process, we have combined or *multiplexed* these many signals onto a single transmission link. A single physical communication link now has the ability to serve as a communication link for many different signals. The frequency bandwidth of the link has been divided into subpaths for multiplexed signal transmission. This is the essence of *frequency division multiplexing*.

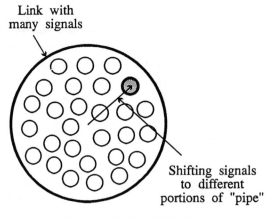

Frequency Division Multiplexing

Frequency division multiplexing is used in the transmission of analog signals since the process divides aggregate frequency carrying capacity into many smaller frequency components.

When digital (one and zero *bits* of information) signals are transmitted over a communications link, a technique known as *time division multiplexing (TDM)* is used whereby individual bits of information are interspersed within a one-second time period. Multiple digital signals are still transmitted over a single physical link, but the timing of the individual digital signals is shifted instead of the frequency. In essence, the time capacity of the link is divided and the digital bit signals are multiplexed (inserted) into their respective time slots.

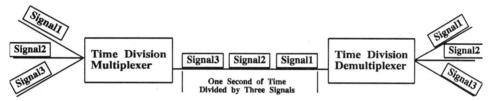

Using the terminology of the frequency division multiplexing example, the second of time is like the overall frequency bandwidth of the conductor (size of the pipe) and the individual bit streams from each signal are like the smaller frequency components (individual water flows). With frequency division multiplexing, the frequency of the information signals was shifted to the proper frequency location within the overall link bandwidth. With time division multiplexing, the bit stream of the individual information signals is shifted in time within the one-second time interval.

The overall capacity is still used, but with frequency division multiplexing the divided capacity is frequency bandwidth, and with time division multiplexing the divided capacity is one second of time.

Module Five
Network Physical Configurations or Topology Types

Networks are connected in combinations of several well-accepted physical configurations or *topologies*: star, bus, ring, multidrop, hierarchical, and mesh. These connections are chosen based upon many criteria but primarily to minimize monthly tariff charges to the telephone companies, to optimize performance, and to minimize maintenance complexity.

Star Topologies

A star topology is probably the most common. The standard telephone network is a fine example of a communication network configured in a star shape. Think of the central office as the center of the star and each communication link between the central office and the customer premises as a point of the star. Star topologies have a common center point and many "ray" end points.

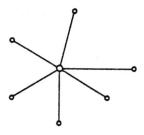

Star Network

Notice that a telephone network star topology uses more wire than if a single wire were run from the central office that connected each house, but determining who desired access to the network at a particular time would then become a problem. Remember that the central office looks for "loop current" to determine when a caller desires access to the network.

In essence, the loop current is the network access protocol defined for a star topology central office switch. If two subscribers on the same single loop lifted their receivers at the same time, the central office would not know which subscriber to serve, since both would draw loop current and there is no physical method of separating one caller from another.

Running a separate line for each house uses more wire but precludes the possibility of more than one person using a particular central office line at one time. This one-to-one correspondence between lines and subscribers was needed in the early days of telecommunications, but technology has improved to the point that multiple subscribers can now use the same physical link and reserve their own portion of frequency or time within which to transmit. These technological improvements gave rise to the bus and ring topologies.

Bus Topologies

A *bus topology* LAN has all user nodes and servers connected into one single physical transmission link over which all devices communicate. The single transmission path is called the *bus* and has a definite beginning and end point. Notice the problems that arise with this scenario when two devices simultaneously desire access to the communication link. The electrical signal has no way of knowing who has access or even which node is transmitting or receiving.

A bus is analogous to a meeting in which every person tries to talk at the same time. There is a lot of chatter, but little communication. Defining a protocol by which speakers gain communication control allows the meeting to proceed in an orderly fashion. In a similar way, bus topology LANs define a method by which nodes gain access to the communication bus. There are many different access protocols, but they all are referred to as *media access control* (MAC) methodologies and apply to different LAN topologies.

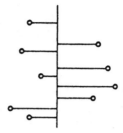

Bus Network

It is important that the topology and the media access method not be confused. Media access protocols are needed when a common path is shared by many devices. In the case of the central office, the switching equipment is the common path and loop current is the media access control. In the case of LANs, a carefully defined digital protocol is used to determine who may use the path at a particular time.

The most common bus topology LAN is *Ethernet* which is also referred to as the IEEE 802.3 standard, even though there are some minor differences between the two. *Token bus* (IEEE 802.4) is another bus topology LAN, but it is not widely used except in some specific manufacturing networks.

Ring Topologies

Ring topologies are also a shared pathway for communication, but the path does not have definite beginning or end points and looks like a ring. In a typical ring topology LAN, each node receives the information transmitted on the line and either processes the information if appropriate or passes it to the next node. Notice that under these conditions, if one node fails, the entire ring may be broken.

This issue is addressed by having redundant paths, one going clockwise and the other counterclockwise. If the link between two nodes is broken for a particular reason, then the information is routed in the other direction using the second path. For this type of ring to fail, both paths must be broken, which is unlikely.

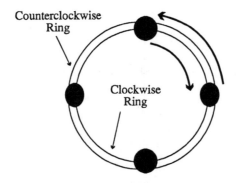

Dual Ring Network

Since the information is passed to each node, then for a brief moment each node has control of the network. This control procedure is formalized as the *token passing* protocol. A "token" is passed over the LAN from one station to another in a specific order. When a node has control of the token, it also has the right to transmit over the LAN. It only controls the token for a brief period of time and then must pass it on to another node. This token passing methodology controls the single path/multiple user issue discussed in the bus topology section. The node with the token can "speak" while the others listen.

The most popular token passing scheme is the IEEE 802.5 token passing ring (*token ring*) spearheaded by IBM. This scheme allows for data transmission at 4 and 16 megabits per second and generally uses shielded twisted pair wiring as the transmission medium.

Notice that the token passing scheme is simply a method of determining which node may access the network. It is used in either a ring or bus topology. The method of accessing the network is different from the topology of the LAN.

Point-to-Point and Multidrop Circuits

IBM networks make extensive use of multidrop circuits and any discussion of networking techniques would be incomplete without a short introduction to point-to-point and multidrop operation concepts.

Point-to-point connections are exactly what they sound like — network connections between two specific points at either end of a link. Point-to-point is easy to understand and is widely used in telecommunications.

Point-to-Point Connection

Examples of point-to-point connections are telephone calls, modem connections, and DTE-to-computer connections. Notice that this connection type describes a physical connection and may not accurately define the logical connections or channels conveyed by the link. There may actually be multiple communication channels transmitted within a single point-to-point link. Fixed point-to-point connections are used when data rates are sufficiently high to warrant a dedicated line connection between two points.

Multidrop circuits usually are divided into several different segments with intermediary nodes along each leg of the overall length. Assume that there are physical connections (links) between point A and B, then B and C, then finally C and D. If point A wishes to contact point D, then the request for contact must pass through B and C before reaching D. Once the connection is established between A and D, there is a single channel but multiple physical drop points along the communication path. Node A could just as easily contact Node B or Node C using the same technique just applied to the Node D connection.

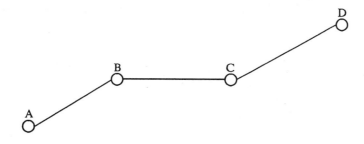

Multidrop

Multidrop circuits are generally used to decrease recurring monthly network charges by the telephone company. Instead of requiring separate lines connecting A to B, A to C, and A to D, multidrop allows for the installation of a single physical connection to handle all required communication. Notice that with the reduced number of physical links being shared by several nodes, some type of access scheme is required. Multidrop is a typical polling or token passing application.

Using multidrop allows a decrease in networking cost due to reduced tariffed links, but an increase occurs in network complexity and end-point equipment cost.

Hierarchical Topologies

A network with a *hierarchical topology* resembles an inverted tree in that the root (central) node of the network is at the top of the network. Under the root node are branches that each span out into other branches. The source point for each series of branches can act as a local processing center for the branches that stem from it. For example, a central computer may contain information that is only needed on a national level. From it may stem three regional computers, each of which has several district computers, each with its own terminal users.

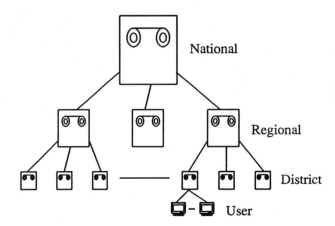

Each terminal user will generally only retrieve data from its district computer unless regional information is needed, in which case the district computer will query the regional computer for the information. Should national information be required, then an information query is routed to the national computer. Notice that most data communication traffic is between the district computer and its terminal users, and minimal information is routed to the regional and national computers. There is a hierarchy for information access which gives rise to the hierarchical topology designation.

Mesh Topologies

Mesh Topology Network

The initial telephone networks started out as *mesh topologies* in that every telephone was interconnected with every other telephone. This meant that if ten telephones were in use, then each telephone would have ten wires connected to it (one for each telephone). When the number of telephones is small, then the mesh topology is not a major problem, but when the number of telephones increases slightly, then the complexity of the wiring plant increases substantially. To minimize the complexity of the network, the telephone network quickly moved to a star topology with a human operator as the central switching device.

Mesh topologies are still used in connecting several switching centers into a uniform network because a mesh provides redundant paths for communication.

Assume that the network consists of four central switches, each with their group of subscribers. To route a call from a switch-one subscriber to a switch-four subscriber, the call can route directly from switch one to switch four over pathway A or route through switch two or three on the way to switch four over pathway B.

This may not seem important unless the pathway A link between switch one and four is cut by a construction crew. Without the additional paths for routing information, switch one to switch four calls would be impossible. This higher level of network *redundancy* is critical to a high level of network reliability. The level of network complexity increases, but the reliability increase is probably worth the expense.

Telephone Network Wiring Discussion

The receive and transmit sides of the conversation are separate within the telephone network and within the telephone. Each telephone set transmitter and receiver has its own pair of wires. But between the telephone company and the telephone set only one pair of wires is used.

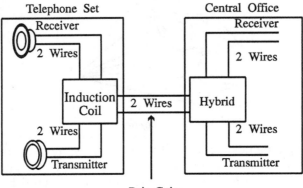

Pair Gain

This reduction in the number of wires used is something seen often in telecommunications. Many of the improvements seen within the network were developed to increase the efficiency of the network while also decreasing the installation and maintenance costs of the network.

A major cost for the telephone company is the installation of cable between its facilities and the subscriber's premise. Most residences have a two-pair (or four-wire) cable installed to the street. Only one pair is needed for a standard telephone connection, due to the hybrid arrangement described earlier. This means that a telephone company can provide service to twice the number of subscribers from a given number of wire pairs using a hybrid arrangement than without the hybrid.

For example, a cable containing 100 pairs of wire that is installed between the telephone company and a particular neighborhood can connect 100 telephones using a hybrid (one-pair) configuration but could only connect 50 telephones using a nonhybrid (two-pair) configuration. The telephone company has essentially gained 50 connections over the same size of cable using hybrid equipment at each end of the subscriber loop.

This process of installing equipment to increase the number of connections or conversations that can be conducted over installed facilities is common practice for the telephone company and is sometimes referred to as *pair gain* in that the network has gained the equivalent number of pairs of wires. In the previous example, installing the hybrid causes a pair gain of two or a doubling of the carrying capacity of the installed 100 pair cable.

The extra pair allows for easy installation of a second telephone line to any outlet within the building since two pairs are installed to every telephone jack. Without the extra pair, an entirely new cable would be required to each location. This new cable installation process would be much more expensive than simply connecting the second pair of wires already installed with the first telephone.

We see here another concept that is critical to understanding the management of telephone networks: dealing with future telephone moves, adding additional telephones, or changing the level of service provided to a telephone user, which is often referred to as *moves, adds, and changes (MACs)*.

On average, a business office telephone user moves his location every nine months or 1.3 times per year. If it is difficult or costly to move this person and their associated telephone equipment, then the expense of MACs can quickly overshadow the cost of the equipment and service.

Combined Topologies

Many contemporary premise equipment suppliers have integrated the best parts of each topology into a single device and increased performance while decreasing maintenance cost.

The most common example is using a bus topology for connections internal to the main device and a star topology to connect between the central device and the desktop equipment. This scenario makes perfect sense when the universal presence of twisted pair is considered.

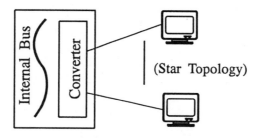

Hybrid Topology Equipment

If the central box is installed near a main or intermediate distribution frame, then the installed twisted pair wiring can be used to distribute the desired capability to each of the desktops without installing additional wiring. Problems arise when one considers that the device's internal operations expect an ethernet or token passing configuration, which is not compatible with the star topology distribution to the desk. The device design must make the proper conversions to ensure that both the desktop link and ethernet bus work in a complimentary fashion.

These types of *mixed topology* devices are popular with users because they are easier to maintain, since they use inexpensive twisted pair, and also more secure, since the mission-critical centralized equipment is contained within a controlled area. They are sometime referred to as having an internal token bus topology with an external star topology.

Mixed topologies are becoming more popular in many areas. For example, IBM's token ring network uses a star distribution network between the central distribution node and the desktop but retains an internally "logical" token ring standard. The internally logical designation ensures software logical compatibility.

This combination provides the best of both worlds for users in the token ring environment. They get easy distribution of communication capability to the user desktop because of the twisted pair star network, but they retain compatibility with the predictability of token ring for their overall network operation.

Module Six
Telephone Network Operation

The Basic Functions of a Telephone Set

A telephone set is a relatively complex instrument that performs a conceptually simple function. It takes sound waves, such as those created by a speaking person, and converts those sound waves into electrical signals that are transmitted over telephone wires. Looking at the telephone from a block diagram approach aids in understanding how it works.

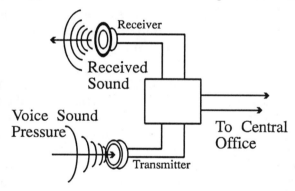

When we speak, our vocal cords create sound pressure waves that are transmitted through the air. These waves strike objects and move objects in proportion with the intensity of the sound pressure.

The transmitter of the telephone set contains a sensing device (previously a loose carbon microphone but more frequently today an electrical microphone is used) that converts these pressure wave variations into electrical signal variations that are transferred to another part of the telephone set. The transmitter of a carbon microphone has a metal diaphragm that senses the pressure of the sound waves and then moves the carbon granules in such a way as to vary the magnitude of electrical source. These variations in electrical signal represent an *analog*, or an electrical copy, of the variations in sound pressure waves. This electrical waveform is referred to as an analog wave and has been the primary electrical form of telephone conversation transmission since the telephone's first invention.

The telephone set contains two wires that connect to the handset's transmitter and two wires that connect to the receiver. This is a total of four wires, but only two wires are used to transmit the telephone conversation to the telephone company's central office. This four-wire to two-wire conversion inside of the telephone set is accomplished through the use of a device called an *induction coil* and reconverted back onto four-wire form in the central office through the use of a *hybrid transformer*.

The only real difference between the induction coil and the hybrid is that the induction coil is designed to allow a certain amount of signal generated from the transmitter to be heard on the receiver. This is to provide the caller with feedback as to loudness of their own speaking voice. This feedback is called the *sidetone*. Many inexpensive electronic telephones have dropped the sidetone as a cost saving measure only to receive complaints from the users that they did not like the phone and wanted a new one.

The electrical operation of a hybrid or induction coil is beyond the scope of this book. It is mentioned only to eliminate any confusion that may arise due to the four-wire/two-wire transformation.

The transmitted electrical signal is passed through the network and eventually arrives at the receiver side of the receiving party's telephone set where a process that converts the received electrical signal back into sound pressure waves occurs. In essence, an electromagnet contained within the receiver converts the electrical signal into a magnetic force that attracts a diaphragm in proportion with the magnitude of the electrical signal. The larger the signal, the larger the diaphragm's movement and the larger the sound pressure waves. These pressure waves are sensed by the ear, and sound is heard. The larger the sound pressure waves, the louder the sound.

The network technology used in moving the sound information from one end of the telephone network to the other has changed substantially since the initial invention, but the fundamental design of the mechanism has remained substantially the same.

Signalling Between the Telephone Set and the Network

We now have a method for converting the sound pressure waves created by speech into electrical signals and reversing the process. Once two telephones are connected by a transmission link, the required electrical signals carrying the necessary voice information can be transmitted and a conversation can occur.

The topic of this section is the accepted procedure for instructing the telephone network about which telephone, out of the millions installed around the world, is desired for connection at this particular time. As mentioned earlier, we are not only concerned about the information transmitted but also the *call setup* instructions required to establish the desired network link between transmitter and receiver.

Pulse and Tone Signalling

Call setup information can only be sent within the bandwidth restrictions established for voice communications. This means that any signalling between the telephone set and the telephone network must happen within the frequency confines of the 4,000 Hz bandwidth restrictions mentioned in the previous section.

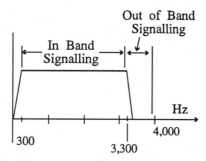

Signalling information sent as tones or pulses within the standard voice bandwidth are called *in band signals*, where those sent at frequencies outside of the standard frequency range are called *out of band signals*.

The network is also an electrical device and as such operates using electrical voltage and current. Referring back to a water analogy, electrical voltage is like pressure on a water hose and electrical current is like the flow of water through the hose. If there is no pressure then no water will flow. Similarly, if there is no voltage then no current will flow.

In addition, for water to flow from one point to another there must be a continuous path over which the water can flow. Similarly, electrical circuits need a closed, or continuous, path over which current can flow. When an electrical switch is opened, the path is broken and no current can flow. Electrical power stops. When the electrical switch is closed, current can now flow over the continuous path and electrical power is available.

It is this presence of electrical current that provides the initial signalling to the telephone network that a caller wants to place a telephone call. When the telephone receiver is resting in the cradle of the telephone set, the button is depressed which opens the path for current flow from the telephone network and no current is allowed to flow. This button on the telephone set is referred to as the *switchhook*. When the receiver is resting in the cradle, it is referred to as in the *on-hook* position.

The term switchhook is a carryover from the days when the telephone transmitter and receiver were separate pieces. The receiver was literally hung over a hook upon completion of the call. This hook also served as an on/off switch for the telephone connection. Thus the name switchhook was adopted and has carried over into modern telecommunications.

When the telephone set receiver is lifted, the switchhook button is released and the path for current from the telephone network is completed. This is called the *off-hook* position for the receiver. Electrical current now flows under the pressure of a 48-volt *battery* located in the central office. This current flow is referred to as *loop current* since it flows in a loop from the telephone company's central office to the customer's premise then back to the central office. This loop of wire that extends from the central office to the customer premise and back to the central office is referred to as the *local loop*.

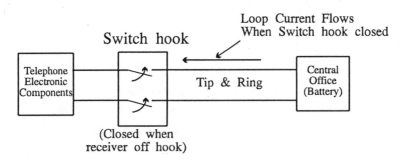

When the telephone network sees the flow of loop current to the telephone set, it sends a tone over the line to the telephone set receiver which we hear and refer to as *dial tone*. This is a notification from the network that it is ready to receive your calling instructions. Dial tone is actually a combination of 350 Hz and 440 Hz sine waves. Notice that these frequencies are both within the 4,000 Hz voice bandwidth.

The prevalent dialing mechanism in use until recent years was the *rotary dial* telephone. It is sometimes referred to as a *pulse dial* telephone since the customer's telephone actually sends a number of electrical pulses down the telephone line that equal the number dialed. For example, if the number three is dialed, the electrical connection between the telephone and the central office would open and close three times to indicate the dialing of a three on the part of the caller. Similarly, if a seven is dialed, then the connection would open and close, or pulse, seven times.

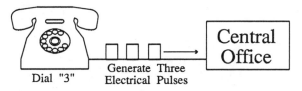

Dial "3"   Generate Three
                  Electrical Pulses   Central Office

If one listens carefully to a rotary dial connection while it is dialing, he will hear the sounds of the path being opened and closed.

To keep the network from interpreting the opening/closing of the dial pulse as being a depressed switchhook, very specific timing restrictions are placed on pulses and valid switchhook flashes. A rotary dial telephone generates up to 10 pulses per second, with each pulse only around 1/20th of a second in duration and around a 1/20th of a second time delay between pulses. The network also expects around a 7/10th of a second delay between the different digits dialed. This provides the network with a way of knowing when one digit is completed dialing and the next is beginning. Otherwise, the digits would blend together and the network could not know which telephone number the caller is requesting.

A valid *flashing* of the switchhook (opening and closing the switchhook) must see the switchhook connection open for a specified period of time. This action is also referred to as a *hookflash*.

The specific timing of the pulse telephone is not as critical to our discussion as are the timing principles they outline. Notice how several factors all come together to provide accurate information to the network regarding the specific number dialed, the number of digits dialed, whether the breaking of the loop current is pulse dialing or hookflash, and when service is no longer needed (on-hook). This type of timing specification is seen repeatedly in telecommunications and is the important principle to be learned from this section.

As anyone who has ever dialed a long-distance number on a rotary dial phone can attest, it is a time-consuming process and can be annoying if the number is misdialed and the process needs to be repeated.

Another process that uses tones instead of pulses is now the dominant method of dialing telephone numbers in the U.S. This process uses a keypad with 12 buttons as the input device. Each row and column of the keypad corresponds to a certain tone and actually creates a sine wave of a specific frequency. Each button lies at the intersection of two tones. When a button is depressed, the two tones are generated by the telephone set and sent over the local loop connection to the central office, which has the ability to read the different tones and understand which button was pressed.

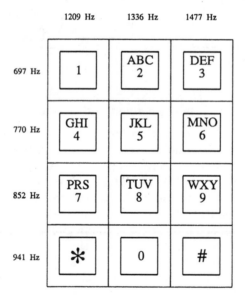

Dial 8 = 852 Hz + 1336 Hz

DTMF Dialing Pad

For example, pressing the number "eight" simultaneously generates both an 852 Hz and a 1336 Hz tone. These tones are sent over the local loop and received by the central office switching equipment. When the central office recognizes the 852/1336 Hz tone combination it knows that an "eight" was dialed by the caller. Along the same lines, dialing a "four" generates a

770/1209 Hz combination which is interpreted by the central office equipment as a "four." Notice that the "*" and "#" keys also have dual tones associated with them, which allows them to be used for additional signalling functions.

Since multiple frequencies are available and pressing a key generates a specific dual tone combination, this type of dialing is referred to as *dual-tone-multifrequency (DTMF)* dialing. It is faster than pulse dialing and allows for the dialing of additional keys such as * and #, which provides an additional level of network control. The Bell system tradename for DTMF dialing is *Touchtone*.

On average, the normal person can dial a number 10-15 times faster using a DTMF dialing system than using a rotary dial phone.

A closer look at the telephone dialing discussion shows that a central office system designed to only look for dialing pulses would completely ignore the tones generated by a DTMF telephone. Even though the plugs may look the same, the methods of signalling between the two telephone types are very different and must be installed in conjunction with the dialing information expectations of the telephone network. As was mentioned earlier with regard to the ineffectiveness of hooking a toaster onto a telephone line, the same can be said of connecting a DTMF telephone to a line designed only to sense dial pulses.

Many residential subscribers stay with their pulse telephones simply because they do not make a large number of calls and there is usually an additional charge for lines that provide DTMF service. As more people migrate to DTMF telephones, the pulse dial lines may become obsolete and the additional charge may be levied against those lines. Notice that this situation will change only after the approved tariffs are also changed and that more than technology and customer preference dictate whether this change will occur.

The Telephone Network Numbering Scheme

Most Americans are familiar with the standard telephone numbering structure in that a local number is dialed using a seven-digit sequence and long-distance numbers are dialed using a 1-Area Code-telephone number type of sequence.

We are also aware that 800 numbers are toll free and that 900 numbers are becoming a major abuse problem in contemporary communications since they are billed by the minute and directly to the person's telephone bill.

There is actually a definite structure to how telephone numbers are distributed, and this section will explain them on a cursory basis.

The most general form of a telephone number is an up to three-digit country code, and up to three-digit area/city code, a three-digit exchange code and a four-digit subscriber code. There are certain restrictions placed upon what numbers can be in specific locations. For example, the first number in the area/city code may not be a "0" to avoid confusion with a party dialing a "0" to reach the operator. The center digit of the area/city code may only be a zero or a one to avoid confusion with exchange codes.

A quick look at any listing of American area codes shows that they all indeed have a zero or one as the center digit. i.e., 214 for Dallas, 312 for Chicago, and 202 for Washington, D.C. Industry practice shows that although zero is a valid number for use in the last position of the area code, it is not used as such.

This numbering scheme has worked well for the United States in the past, but there are potential problems looming on the horizon. Only nine numbers are allowed in the first location, two in the second location, and only nine are used in the third. This provides 9x2x9=162 possible area codes and only 160 are available in practice. A new "903" area code was recently introduced in northeastern Texas, a "210" area code will go on-line in central Texas in 1992, a "310" area code was added in Los Angeles in 1991, along with a "510" area code for the San Francisco area.

The restriction on the center digit of the area code limits the total number of area code numbering options, and this restriction will remain in place until all telephone companies standardize on the need for dialing a one before any long-distance number. This eliminates possible confusion with exchange codes and allows for up to 800 different area codes. In late 1991 there were only five unassigned North American area codes.

The *Consultative Committee on International Telegraphy and Telephony (CCITT)* is an international standards group that defines, among other things, a numbering scheme that ensures that all telephones around the world have a unique number. CCITT divides the world into nine basic areas, then provides a means for defining each country, city/area code, exchange, and individual subscriber in each of these areas. The general form of this definition was shown in the beginning of this section.

Toll Calling and Long Distance

The geographic areas of the U.S. are now divided into separate areas called *Local Access and Transport Areas (LATA)*. These LATAs define the region over which a local telephone carrier may provide local and long-distance telephone service. LATAs are also sometimes called *Regional Calling Areas*. The state of Texas is divided into 16 LATAs.

If a call is placed from one subscriber to another within the same LATA, then the local carrier may provide the end-to-end connection for that call. This is referred to as an *intra-LATA* call. The distance may indeed be hundreds of miles, but as long as the call is intra-LATA it may be handled by the same regional carrier without the assistance of a long-distance interexchange carrier.

If a called party's extension lies within another of these geographical LATA areas, then the call must be transferred on an *inter-LATA* basis through the use of an *interexchange carrier (IXC)*. Even though the call may be placed to a business just across the street, if it lies within another LATA, the call must pass through an interexchange carrier to be completed.

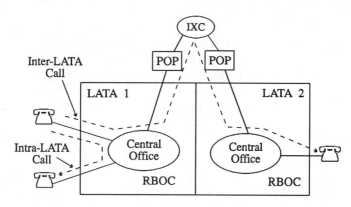

LATA Related Calling

This situation becomes more interesting when one considers that a call from one point to another within an RBOC's territory has to travel through an IXC even though both the caller and the receiver are within that RBOC's territory. This situation is caused simply by the existence of LATAs.

A call can still be placed within a LATA and be considered a toll call. LATAs are divided into toll and nontoll or local areas. Local calls are treated according to the specific arrangements you have established with the common carrier that services your area. Many have special plans set up to address specific geographic circumstances, such as the Chicago land area which has a 312 area code for the city proper and a 708 area code for the suburban area. Plans have been established that allow all calls placed within a specific geographic region to be treated as local calls, but at a monthly premium.

The two general types of plans are *flat rate service* where unlimited local calls can be made for a fixed monthly total, and *measured rate service* where calls are billed based upon their duration, distance, and volume.

When a call must use the services of an interexchange carrier (IXC) then the call is transferred to a *point-of-presence (POP)* for that particular carrier. The POP is the point in the network where all long-distance or IXC companies receive calls that must pass between LATAs.

We see that all calls within a LATA or intra-LATA calls are handled by the local carrier. These calls can be either local or toll calls based upon the geography and specific arrangements between the carrier and the subscriber. Any calls that pass between LATAs, or inter-LATA calls, are passed to an interexchange carrier (IXC) through its particular point-of-presence (POP). The advent of the POP allows for the implementation of equal access for long-distance carriers.

Every long-distance carrier has a particular code associated with its services. This code informs the local carrier about which IXC is to be used for routing of a particular call. The general form used by the central office for routing of calls is 10 (access code) -XXX (specific carriers code) - N0/1X (standard area code) -NXX-XXXX (standard telephone number).

This numbering scheme looks similar to that discussed in the previous section except for the addition of the carrier code. The carrier code is different for each carrier. For example, AT&T uses the carrier code 288 (ATT on the telephone buttons). MCI and Sprint also have their own, along with the other IXCs. Thus, to dial a long-distance call using the AT&T network a caller would dial 10-288-312-555-1212.

This process is shortened substantially when a telephone subscriber chooses a primary IXC over which to route all calls. This choice does not preclude the use of the other carriers, but it indicates a preference for one carrier over another. This is the basis for the deluge of Sprint, AT&T, and MCI commercials continually seen on television. The IXCs are actively seeking to become that carrier of choice because all long-distance calls made by that subscriber will be routed over that particular carrier's network and billed back to the subscriber at that carrier's rates. The other carriers are still available, but additional numbers must be dialed and most consumers will not go to the trouble.

Equal access means that each long-distance carrier is provided equal access to the telephone network and is provided a POP. *One plus dialing* (1+) defines the ability of the local carrier to allow a subscriber to select the IXC over which all inter-LATA (long-distance) calls will be routed. The two terms are often used interchangeably, but have different meanings.

International calls may be direct dialed by dialing the *international access code*, 011, before dialing the country code and the other necessary numbers that must follow.

Wide Area Telecommunication Service (WATS)

Many businesses subscribe to a volume discount calling service called *wide area telecommunication service (WATS)*. This service was pioneered by AT&T, but they did not legally protect the name and WATS type of products are offered by most major long-distance companies.

WATS customers typically have the need to provide higher volumes of telephone traffic to specific geographic regions, either domestic or international. The realization of this higher volume allows them to take advantage of volume discounting provided by WATS plans.

WATS is defined by the direction of the calls (either inbound or outbound calls), the geographic locations (within the same state, interstate, or international) and the coverage area which is divided into bands of coverage. It is important to understand that each WATS call requires a dedicated line. If the WATS calling volume is expected to be large, then multiple WATS lines should be installed. Refer to the section covering traffic analysis for items to consider when determining the number of WATS lines needed to address a specific situation.

Most 800 numbers are a form of WATS service which is an *"inbound"* WATS service from the perspective of the business providing the 800 number. No calls are made in an *"outbound"* direction from the business's offices using these 800 WATS lines.

800 numbers are typically used to entice customers to call regarding a company's products or services. Many times the orders are taken directly over the telephone. This used to be considered a special service and is now rapidly becoming a mandatory requirement for many retail businesses, particularly in the mail-order sector.

Another use for 800 numbers is to allow field salespeople a toll free line to the company. This reduces the need for calling cards, which are typically more expensive, and also reduces the possibility of calling card abuse on the part of the salesperson. Many companies find that providing 800 service for its field sales personnel reduces costs and increases communication.

Outbound WATS is typically used when a large number of calls are made to a specific geographic region. Using outbound WATS reduces the long-distance charges without any loss of service. Calls to non-WATS coverage areas are routed over the standard IXC long-distance routes. Most modern telephone systems, whether PBX or key, have the ability to route calls over the least expensive path based upon criteria placed into the system at the time of installation.

Intrastate WATS comes in both inbound and outbound flavors and is designed to handle both inbound or outbound calls that originate and terminate within the same state.

Interstate WATS has several bands of coverage that vary depending upon the geographic location used as the hub of the network. Each band is a concentric ring centered on the state of the hub office. Each successive band covers approximately 20 percent of the total telephones in the United States but based upon the hub office as the center. Consequently, WATS coverage bands determined for the state of Illinois will not be the same as those determined for Idaho. Each set of bands has a different coverage area based upon the center of the bands.

WATS service is typically billed as a fixed charge for the WATS lines provided and also a variable charge depending upon the amount of calling traffic. A higher call volume typically translates into lower charges on a per minute of use basis. Each IXC will provide a different program based upon their particular technology. A determination of the number of lines and the total monthly call volume should be made, then the IXCs can be asked to provide estimated costs to the consumer for providing the expected level of service.

Cellular Telephone

A few years ago the only people with cellular telephones were those wealthy folks driving their BMWs on the Los Angeles freeways. The cost of the telephone set itself was very high (around $2,000) and the cost of the cellular service was generally too high to easily justify daily use.

It is not uncommon today to see people in a restaurant talking over their pocket-sized cellular telephone unit in small towns around the country. The cost of the unit has come down along with its size. The telephones are now priced under $500 and truly are the size of a pocket calculator.

This technology has the possibility of becoming the local loop provider in the 21st century. As the cellular prices continue to decrease and the RBOCs continue to get deeper into information services and further away from the regulated subscriber loop, we may see a shift in the industry towards cellular being the principle connection to the network.

In light of cellular's increasing importance and popularity, a brief discussion of cellular telephone operation is provided.

Cellular telephone companies divide geographic areas into smaller *cells* that each contain a *cell site* with an antenna. Each of these antennas has the ability to communicate with a subscriber's cellular telephone unit over a radio frequency channel. The FCC has allocated 833 separate channels for use by all cellular carriers within a specific geographic area. Each of these channels has the ability to carry a standard voice grade telephone conversation.

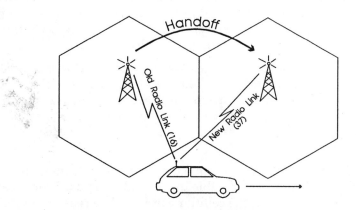

Cellular Telephone Call Handoff

When a caller desires cellular service, their cellular unit requests service, over the radio link, from a local cell radio tower. That tower scans the radio channels it has available and allocates one of the channels to that particular caller and provides dial tone. That radio channel is kept live and reserved for that caller until he either terminates the call or moves to another cell site. This is a fascinating aspect of cellular telephone systems.

The power level of the conversation is continually monitored by the cellular tower. As the power level begins to reach a certain threshold level, the cell site that has control of the call requests that the neighboring cell sites monitor their sensed power levels for the particular telephone in question. The request is routed to the other sites over a packet switched network that is internal to the cellular carrier's facility.

The queried sites provide feedback to the controlling site, who then decides which site is the most likely site to handle the caller's projected movement. A central control processor is then brought into the sequence to handle the ultimate handoff of the call to a neighboring site. That site is requested to reserve a radio channel (not necessarily the same channel frequency currently being used) for use by the caller once he enters into that cell's territory. The mobile unit is then instructed to make the transition from the radio frequency it currently is using to the new frequency chosen by the new cell site.

At the moment of handoff, both the old and new channels are held open and a bridged connection exists between the old cell site, the new cell site, and the cellular unit. Once the new connection is established the old radio channel connection is dropped, which frees that radio channel for use by another customer in that cell.

A tremendous amount of coordination must occur for the handoff to work properly, and this type of technology would not have been possible just a few years ago. The processing power was just not there to handle the intense background operational data communication.

Cellular telephones come in a few basic flavors: *mobile*, *transportable*, and *portable*. The mobile units are installed in automobiles and not designed for use outside of the car. Transportable are units that have their own battery power supply but tend to be bulky and relatively heavy. Portable units are small trim units that are easily carried in a briefcase or even in a purse or suitcoat breast pocket.

It is easy to see that the more accessible the telephone, the more likely one is to use it. Consequently, the portable units tend to be used the most and are the units of preference by the cellular carriers. The reason: they bill for the number of *airtime* minutes the telephone is used. The billing rate varies from around 20 cents per minute for off-peak hours up to over 50 cents per minute for peak time.

The economics of cellular appear to dictate the methods of use. Seventy percent of cellular calls are from the mobile user to a *land based number* (a standard business of residential telephone), 25 percent of calls are from a land based location to the mobile user, and the other 5 percent is between mobile users. This scenario makes sense when viewed from an economic perspective.

Airtime minutes are billed by the cellular carrier whether the call is inbound or outbound from the mobile unit. Consequently, most cellular users only provide their cellular number to those critical persons who really need to have it. This minimizes the likelihood of the cellular user paying large fees for receiving less important calls.

Most cellular subscribers use voice mail in conjunction with a beeper to notify them if they have received a call. The user then retrieves the message, usually at no airtime charge, and determines whether to use valuable airtime minutes to return the call. This scenario requires paying for a beeper and voice mail, but it is cheaper than paying for unwanted airtime minutes. (Note: Some carriers charge airtime minutes while the message is being left, which affects the overall benefits derived from this operational scenario.)

The cellular carriers are slowly installing more cell towers and decreasing the amount of radiation power from each site and decreasing the size of the cell. The networking extreme of this progression is called *micro-cellular* technology. This allows the carriers to more evenly cover a geographic area, provide service to more customers, and not exceed their respective number of allocated radio channels.

As the number of towers increases, so does overall call carrying capacity. Eventually, cellular may become cost effective to the point of replacing the home telephone line completely. Telephone users may only have one telephone number issued to them that they carry with them all the time — even when traveling outside their normal geographic area.

The cellular carriers provide a unique service called *roaming*. This service allows a Dallas-based cellular customer to notify the Chicago cellular carrier of his presence in Chicago. The Chicago carrier notifies the Dallas carrier that all calls to the subscriber's Dallas number are to be automatically routed to Chicago.

A call made to the Dallas number instantaneously rings the subscriber's cellular telephone in Chicago and the caller is not aware of the transfer. This type of service truly makes time and distance irrelevant in today's business world. Telephone-based business can now be transacted on a national scale that is independent of the cellular carrier's location.

NCR and AT&T recently merged and have introduced a notebook computer that contains an integral cellular telephone for data transmission. Anything that can be transmitted over a standard telephone line can also be transmitted over a cellular connection. FAX machines are now marketed with cellular connections included. NCR predicts that cellular computing is the wave of the 1990s, and they may be right.

By 1996 Motorola intends to have their Iridium global cellular system up and running. This is a network of 23 satellites that will circle the earth in a low orbit (not geosynchronous) and provide cellular service on a global basis. This means that an Iridium customer in Chicago who is somewhere in Africa can be contacted by a Chicago customer simply by dialing the Chicago number, and the Iridium system will ring his phone in Africa.

This project still has many stumbling blocks in the way of completion. A major one is the level of cooperation required by the countries around the world in allowing the service into their respective geographic regions. Should a call placed from Nigeria be billed at American rates or Nigerian rates? Who controls the airwaves in Nigeria? What is the sociological impact of providing telephone service to remote areas that barely have electricity? Iridium raises these questions and many more, but Motorola contends that the system will work on schedule. Only time will tell.

There are many fascinating and complex aspects to the cellular industry. As the industry continues to mature and the level of service and transmission quality continues to improve, one thing is certain; cellular is here to stay.

The FAX Explosion

Recent technology advancements have moved facsimile (FAX) machines into mainstream business to the point that it is possible to instantly order equipment or lunch, request a song, or even get a date by FAX. It is a useful business tool and many businesses find that they are increasingly faced with the need for a FAX machine.

A FAX machine allows a copy of a document to be immediately transmitted anywhere there is a telephone. The alternative to FAX are the overnight carriers such as Federal Express who can move a document across the country overnight and cost between $8-13.

Sending a FAX usually involves long-distance toll charges. The telephone time required for FAX transmission is dependent upon the number of pages sent, the resolution (or clarity) required, and the speed of transmission. The longer the transmission time, the higher the long-distance toll charges.

The standard speed of transmission in use today is Group 3. The original Group 1 standard is obsolete and older Group 2 is primarily used for international communication. Most new machines have Group 3 capability with Group 2 provided as an option. The machine should automatically select the right transmission/reception speed based upon the other machine's group type.

FAX paper types vary from thermal paper to bond paper. Thermal paper machines are common and less expensive, but the thermal image fades over a period of time. Bond paper FAXs are similar to laserjet printers and have a higher quality output along with higher equipment costs. Make sure the machine uses standard paper that is available from multiple sources.

After sending a FAX, the receiving machine sends a verification to the sending machine regarding the number of pages received. The sending machine then generates a confirmation report that shows the date, time, telephone number, and number of pages sent.

Many legal, purchasing, and sales organizations use the confirmation reports as verification to their clients or vendors that information was sent. Some machines keep a record of all FAXs sent or received and can generate a summary report for checking against telephone or client records. This may be a valuable feature if your business requires a degree of accountability.

Two other items that should be high on a list of features are a paper cutter and an automatic document feeder.

Thermal paper comes in continuous rolls of paper. The FAX machine will copy the received information onto the paper until the entire document is received. Without a paper cutter, the receiving side may end up with a very long single sheet of paper that must be cut by hand at the page breaks. A FAX machine equipped with a paper cutter automatically cuts the thermal paper at the end of each received page. This may sound like a trivial feature, but hand-cutting a continuous roll 20-page FAX is right up there with being audited by the IRS.

An automatic document feeder is handy because it allows the machine to send a FAX without a person individually feeding the pages of the original document. For only a few pages this may not be critical, but for documents of five pages or more sent on a regular basis a document feeder is recommended.

To send black and white pictures by FAX the machine must support gray scale imaging. It takes longer to send the photograph, but the quality is much better. The more scales provided (16 scales is typical), the more accurately the photograph will be reproduced on the receiving end.

Other FAX machine features make machine operation more convenient. Delayed transmission (sending the FAX at a later predefined time) and auto redial (the machine automatically calls back if the line is busy) are useful for unattended operation of the machine and allow for transmission in the evening when long-distance toll charges are typically lower.

Speed dial lists are helpful if there are many different FAX machines that you need to contact on a regular basis. Some expensive machines can automatically send the same FAX to several different locations simply by programming in the transmit time and the speed dial numbers to use.

Almost all machines allow you to use them as both FAX machines and low volume backup copiers.

In summary, if you anticipate sending/receiving a few text-only FAXs per month of only a few pages in length, then a basic machine should be adequate. If sending many multiple page documents across time zones is anticipated, then consider a machine with more convenience features.

There are trade-offs between price, service, and application flexibility. Take a few minutes to estimate the number, length, and type of FAXs you expect to send and receive, the level of technical competency and turnover of personnel, and where the FAXs will be sent. This information will help you make an informed and satisfactory FAX machine purchase decision that is within your budget and yet meets your needs.

Module Seven
Evolution of Data Communications

The data industry evolved in a completely different manner from the telecommunications industry. Where the telecommunications companies had a dominant industry force that determined standards for the industry as a whole, the data processing industry evolved as a group of individual companies with specific areas of expertise.

The people and companies who needed this specific expertise typically fell within the same market segment, and the companies who provided equipment and services to that segment did what they could to ensure that other companies (competitors) could not penetrate these customer accounts and take away the customers.

As a result, every manufacturer of data processing equipment developed their own method of solving their target customer's problems including customized software, hardware, and communication protocols.

This customization provided the end users with systems that performed well for their designed applications but also locked the customer into buying equipment exclusively from the major supplier, since that company was the only one that provided equipment compatible with that which was initially purchased.

In this way, the vendors acquired customers for life and the customers were essentially at the mercy of the vendor.

This situation has changed dramatically over the last few years with the customers demanding systems that are nonproprietary and consequently available from multiple sources. The customer protects his investment by ensuring multiple sources for equipment and also finds bargains due to competitive bidding between the vendors.

The First Modern Day Computer

Computational devices have been around for centuries, but computing as we know it today really began with the introduction of the electronic computer in the 1940s.

John Mauchly, a professor at Ursinus College in Pennsylvania, developed the Electronic Numerical Integrator and Calculator (ENIAC) computer with the assistance of J. Presper Eckert. The basis for the system was modeled after work done by John Atanasoff, another professor with Iowa State University, and his Atanosoff-Berry computer (ABC).

The ENIAC had over 17,000 vacuum tubes and mechanical gears that made a huge racket when operated. The system was programmed from Hollerith punch cards.

Around the same time, John von Neumann took an interest in ENIAC and developed some specialized applications for its processing power including the development of the atomic bomb. Von Neumann's contribution was in the development of the contemporary computer inter-component design, or internal communication *architecture*, which calls for a central processing area, memory and peripheral devices, and sequential step by step operation. He called the central processing capability the *mainframe*, and the term is still used today but generally in reference to a large, centralized computer.

During World War II development centered on using the computer for military applications such as aiming and firing of armaments. Bell Telephone Company was active in this area and acquired more computer related patents than any other contemporary company.

The success of the computer during the war did not carry over into a peacetime world. The expected postwar market for computers in the U.S. was assumed to be around 20, and the United Kingdom was expected to use no more than 18. Tom Watson, president of IBM, met with Mauchly and Eckert after the war and offered them jobs designing electronic calculators (not computers), since Watson did not believe there was a market for computers. The two men refused and went on to found the Electronic Control Corporation and the Binary Automatic Computer (BINAC), which caught the attention of Northrop and the Census Bureau.

Mauchly and Eckert delivered the Universal Automatic Computer (UNIVAC) to the Census Bureau in 1951 for $1 million and received roughly $80,000 each for their development efforts when their company was bought by the Rand Corporation. The first commercial unit was purchased soon afterwards by General Electric.

AT&T was also investigating the use of computers as switching devices within their telephone network. AT&T was to develop substantial expertise in this area for AT&T internal use in making the telephone network more efficient.

IBM was still selling calculating devices in the early 1950s when Rand merged with the Sperry company to become Sperry-Rand. General Douglas MacArthur was chairman. Sperry-Rand appeared to rest on its successes during this phase, and little dynamic development occurred.

IBM, on the other hand, had begun development of the 701 scientific computer which was introduced in 1953. It leased for $15,000 per month, and soon after introduction IBM was shipping one 701 System per day. Quickly after that IBM introduced the 702 general purpose computer. In 1955 IBM replaced the 701 with the 704, and the 702 with the 705.

In 1959 IBM introduced a *solid state* (transistorized) computer called the 1401 and ushered in the age of the second generation computer. This introduction cut deeply into Sperry-Rands Univac II sales and placed IBM as the premier American computer vendor.

During this same period companies like Burroughs, Honeywell, NCR, and RCA marketed their own versions of computers with varying degrees of success.

Where was AT&T during this period? It was in the wings developing the telephone network and avoiding actions that could bring down the wrath of the government. The Kingsbury Commitment between AT&T and the federal government of 1913 kept AT&T out of any industries that it could potentially dominate and create an antitrust situation.

This situation was interesting since it was Bell Laboratories that developed the transistor in 1947, and the transistor was the base technology that allowed for the development of the solid state computer. Shockley, the inventor of the transistor, left Bell Labs and became a founder of the semiconductor industry in California's silicon valley.

In 1956 AT&T settled another antitrust suit with a *consent decree* which forbade it from manufacturing any equipment which was not for the exclusive use of the Bell system, with the exception of the federal government and AT&T internal use. AT&T was now allowed to manufacture computers for internal use only and could not market commercial products in competition with IBM. This situation provided IBM with a large playing field and few comparably sized competitors.

Digital Equipment Corporation (DEC) entered the market in 1960 with its Programmed Data Processor (PDP) line of computers which were smaller than the IBM mainframes and were called *minicomputers*. The product could be purchased by customers and was priced reasonably compared to the IBM systems currently available. The products were marketed to a highly technical group that had been ignored by IBM and the others. DEC did very well and is today a major player in the computer industry.

In 1964 IBM introduced the 360 series of computers which included microchips (integrated circuits) as a key component. The product was extremely successful, and IBM's fortunes have increased ever since.

The microcomputer was introduced to the processing world in 1975 as the Altair, which was based upon the Intel 8080 processor. This Altair should not be confused with Motorola's new Altair Networking System. Other companies started into the industry during the same period including Commodore with their PET computer and Radio Shack with their TRS-80 computer. The Apple I computer appeared on the scene in 1976 and IBM finally "blessed" the microcomputer industry with its Personal Computer in 1981.

When introduced, IBM expected to sell around 250,000 PC units over the product's lifetime. Over 600,000 were sold in 1983 and 1991 estimates have over 85 million PCs in use around the world with annual hardware, software, and service sales revenues in excess of $100 billion. Happily for IBM and many others, their market projections were off.

The advent of the PC brought processing power to the level of smaller companies and individuals. Supply and demand worked its wonders, and the use of terminal equipment increased dramatically as the price decreased.

1991 has shown a major shakeout happening in the computer industry. IBM has seen its earnings drop dramatically from 1990 and actually showed its first losing quarter. It layed off 20,000 people in 1991 and plans to do the same in 1992. In addition, IBM is going to start manufacturing its products for resale by other companies under their private label. IBM is becoming an *original equipment manufacturer (OEM)*, which is a radical shift from its typical *not invented here (NIH)* proprietary original philosophy.

WANG Laboratories, once a major minicomputer manufacturer, hovers on the edge of extinction and has essentially become a marketing arm of IBM. UNIVAC, the result of a merger between Sperry and Burroughs, still holds strong position in the federal government markets but has shown cautious signs of financial weakness.

On the other hand, many smaller computer companies such as Apple and Dell have shown great strength and explosive growth. The new age seems to belong to the microcomputer. The more processing becomes decentralized, the more the industry needs methods of networking that equipment together.

Much of this book is dedicated to methods of transmitting digital information. Special emphasis is placed on communication between microcomputers over local area networks (LANs) with an occasional emphasis on micro to mainframe communication. Even though the LAN is quickly sculpting out a large niche for itself, there is still a great deal of existing mainframe equipment installed around the world. Any network design must deal with this fact and responsibly address this venerable giant of an installed base.

Computer Evolution Time Table

Date	Event
1940s	First electronic computer introduced.
1947	Bell Laboratories develops the transistor.
1951	First Univac delivered to Census Bureau.
1953	IBM develops 701 scientific computer.
1956	AT&T not allowed by law to manufacture computers for the commercial market.
1959	IBM becomes the premier American computer vendor with the introduction of the solid state computer.
1960	Digital Equipment Corporation (DEC) enters the market with minicomputers.
1964	IBM introduces the 360 series of minicomputers.
1970s	Distributed processing emerges.
1975	Microcomputers introduced based on Intel's 8088 processor.
1976	Apple I introduced.
1980s	Personal Computers and Local Area Networks moving into businesses.
1981	IBM Personal Computer introduced.
1991	IBM lays off 20,000 people.
1991	IBM shows first losing quarter.

The Migration from Stand-Alone to Networked Systems

The early computer systems were essentially centralized processing machines that processed information for the on-site users of the equipment. Many of the early systems had only one terminal connected to them, and that was for the exclusive use of the system operator. The need for networking was minimal in that the operator terminal was located directly adjacent to the computer and only one terminal was active.

As recently as 1976, computer programs were entered into the computer using a set of cards with punched holes, called Hollerith cards. The method of encoding information on the punch card was developed by Hollerith in the 1880s.

Computers from this era performed their work in *batch mode*. In batch mode, each computer user submitted programs to a computer operator who gave the computer a batch of these programs at a time (hence the name) to perform. The user had no direct interaction with the program while it was running. When the computer completed a program, the operator returned the results, usually in the form of a printed listing, to the user.

The Batch Environment

On-line terminals were installed in the 1960s. Access to these computer terminals was restricted and usually available through some type of *time sharing option* (TSO) that allowed users to instruct the computer regarding their specific program operation. This gave users greater control and quicker results but programs were still executed in batch mode (a block of data at a time).

As the number of people requiring computer services increased, the methods of accessing the computer were improved. Instead of having only one terminal that was exclusively for operator access, there were many terminals installed for use by any of the people desiring computer access. These people were not allowed to tamper with the performance of the computer but were simply allowed to run their programs from terminals instead of by feeding punch cards into a card reading machine.

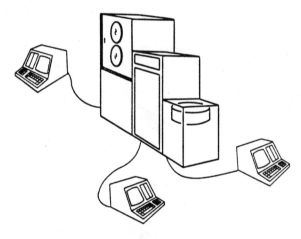

Time Sharing

To ensure security in this environment, each user was given his own password that he needed to enter before being allowed access to the system. Once again the need for networking was minimal in that the terminals were still located in close proximity to the computer.

As the number of people with programming expertise grew, so did the need for terminal access. It was natural to expect that terminal device locations would also become more diverse and that is exactly what happened. Instead of the devices being located in close proximity to the computer, they were actually located in a number of different physical locations around the building or office complex.

During the 1970s the increasing demands for local computing power led to the development of *distributed processing*. In a distributed processing system, smaller computers in remote locations may still be connected to a central *host computer*. The outlying computers reduce the load on the host by performing many of the tasks previously done by the host. By connecting the outlying computers to each other in a network and distributing tasks among them, the host computer often could be replaced.

Collectively, the network provided more processing power than could possibly be built into a single central computer. The need to connect computer to computer further increased the requirement for advanced data communications technology.

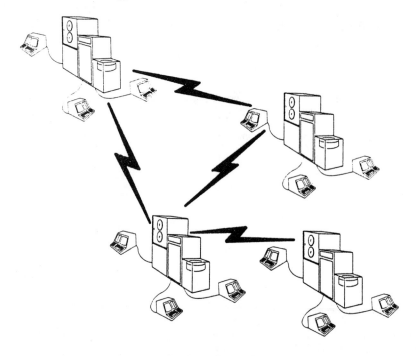

Distributed Processing

Methods of connecting, or networking, these remote systems were developed. The users in distributed processing systems remained close to their main processor because the processor was installed on their site.

Techniques were also designed to network terminals into efficient communication systems which could communicate back to a central processing site. Instead of a distributed processing system, the processing was still centralized and only the user locations were distributed. The IBM 3270 communication network is still in use today and is designed to group terminal users into distributed clusters. These clusters revolved around a cluster controller which, in turn, communicates terminal information back to the central mainframe computer.

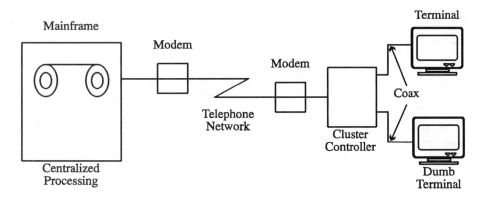

Typical 3270 Cluster Controller Network

The introduction of the PC in 1981 changed processing forever. Dramatic processing power would quickly become available for a reasonable cost, and microcomputers would begin springing up around the world. The terminal equipment was no longer being provided by the same vendor who made the mainframe. Indeed, many of the microcomputer users wanted to take control of their own data processing operations and worked diligently to avoid dealing with the mainframe.

The problems with this approach was that much of the corporate information base resided on the mainframe, so some way needed to be developed to allow a PC to access the mainframe database. Terminal emulation software presented the answer.

Data Terminal Devices and Terminal Emulation

Mainframes and minicomputers dominated the computer industry in 1981 when the PC was introduced. Users accessed these centralized processing devices by using data terminal devices. These devices would either sit on the user's desk, or be placed in a centralized area where people in a group could "log on" to the computer when needed.

Each manufacturer had its own special mode of communication between the terminal and the mini or mainframe. IBM used a single coax cable-based system that connected expensive terminal devices to a 3270 communication *cluster controller* which then connected to the mainframe in various ways. Wang Laboratories used a dual coaxial cable network to connect directly into their minicomputer.

DEC used its "VT" family of asynchronous communication terminal devices for direct access to its VAX minicomputer line and used its own control language to direct data operations in the terminal device. Hewlett-Packard used its own version of RS-232 compatible terminal devices but spoke its own control language over the RS-232 link.

Consequently, a user could have two systems that both used RS-232 as the communication link but could not interchange the terminal devices because the data would not be displayed properly. In this way, the vendors locked their customers into using their products or risk installing equipment that was incompatible with that already existing. In essence, each vendor had a type of monopoly on its customers. The PC changed all that.

The microcomputer has the ability to look like, or emulate, other terminal devices by running special terminal emulation software. In this way, the same microcomputer could look like a DEC VT terminal and a few moments later look like an HP compatible terminal. The same RS-232 port could be used for both.

This capability was also extended into the coaxial communication arena so that a customer could buy a PC, use it for the standard PC productivity functions, and still retain communication capability with the mini or mainframe computer information. The vendor lock on terminal devices had been broken.

As more microcomputers were installed, the need to organize the processing power and information storage developed. The local area network was a natural development from the rapid acceptance of the microcomputer.

LAN'scaping America

Local area networks are a logical outgrowth of data communications technology. They offer great potential for changing the way we work and, eventually, the way we live. By making information resources easily accessible, LANs will alter our work styles, stimulate productivity, and increase our individual choice. LANs also expand the possibilities for global resource sharing by offering standards of information exchange between different kinds of equipment from different manufacturers and between other local and remote communications networks. For now, local area networks are pretty much confined to the work place. But, someday, LANs will be as common as the telephone.

In the 1980s distributed network systems were moving into the office, the factory, and other "local" environments. The primary benefits these local networks offer a business organization are rapid communications and resource sharing.

Within any organization, keeping track of information is a vital and time-consuming task. It is a generally accepted rule of thumb in business that 80 percent of the information used within an organization is generated by the organization; only 20 percent comes from outside. Moreover, 80 percent of the information generated internally is used within the organization and only 20 percent is sent outside.

The advantages of local networks are the economies and efficiencies made possible by accessing and sharing valuable distributed resources — equipment, computing power, databases, and specialized software — for efficiently handling this mountain of data. Information handling time (required for typing, filing, and reporting) is reduced, thus freeing users for more productive pursuits.

Summary

Just as the rapid acceptance of the telephone drove the development of a uniform telephone switching network, the rapid deployment of data terminal devices drove the development of data communication networks.

Then the processing was centralized, the problem to solve was efficient methods of connecting remote terminal locations with a centralized processing location. As distributed processing developed, the issue became methods of tying the distributed processors together so that they performed in conjunction with each other.

The introduction of the microcomputer placed substantial processing power on the desk of the user and forced the development of the local area network. Now the processing and information sharing resources of the networked devices could be linked together, and economies were realized.

The evolution of our current communication systems is a natural progression that developed as a partnership between the end user and the technology developers. Portable computers, such as the notebooks, are taking processing to another level of geographic challenge. Cellular technology appears to be the networking solution, and the vendors are already developing products to address that need.

The immense aggregate processing power present in today's networks is beyond anything imagined in 1950 when the first solid state computer was introduced. We are now roughly 40 years into the lifetime of the electronic computer and only 10 years into the lifetime of the PC. The pace of computer integration into daily life can only be expected to increase, and the need for networking will increase along with it.

Module Eight
RS-232 Data Communications and Modems

A study of telecommunications and data communications would not be complete without an investigation into the operations of the Electrical Industry Association (EIA) RS-232-C interface standard which has also been adopted by the CCITT international standards body as the V.24 standard.

In the early 1980s nearly half of all data communications was accomplished using an RS-232 interface. Nearly all modems use RS-232-C as the communication interface between the modem and the personal computer, and nearly all data processing equipment has an RS-232-C compatible interface port. Its importance to telecommunications and data communications cannot be minimized but its longevity may be in question with the adoption of other digital communication standards such as ISDN and FDDI.

This section looks at the RS-232-C standard. It discusses how compatible devices operate and the basics of RS-232-C operation, asynchronous and synchronous communications, and differences between serial and parallel communication. A brief discussion of modems is also included.

RS-232-C Interface Voltage Levels

As discussed earlier, digital information is simply a sequence of ones and zeroes. The only criterion for determination of whether something is a one or a zero is an easily discernible change of state. Voltage is an easy and natural criterion to monitor in electrical circuits and is the basis for the RS232 Standard.

The standard assumes that anything with a positive 3 volts or greater value is considered a zero, "on," or "space," and anything with a minus 3 volts or less is considered a "one," "off," or a mark. Any voltage level between plus and minus 3 volts is considered undefined. Let's take a closer look at the standard.

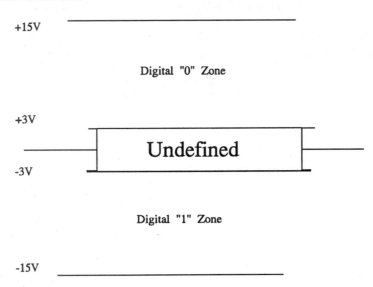

An arbitrary +3 volt/–3 volt value for zero and one digital representations has been established, respectively. We also know that any voltages between +3 volts and –3 volts are undefined. These relative voltage levels were chosen with a specific purpose in mind.

Most noise that may appear on the data lines will typically be in the low voltage range and consequently should be filtered out in the +3 volt/–3 volt range. Consequently, the RS-232-C interface has the ability to accurately discriminate between zeroes and ones since if a voltage level is seen as outside of the +3/–3 volt guard band, then it can be assumed as a valid zero or one.

Data Terminal Equipment (DTE), Data Circuit-Terminating Equipment (DCE), and Null Modems

The physical connection between two RS-232-C pieces of equipment is provided by a cable referred to as an RS-232-C cable. Each end of the cable has a 25-pin connector referred to as a *DB-25 connector*. One end is of a female configuration and the other end is a male configuration (anyone over the age of 16 should be able to figure out which is which). Each of the pins in the connector performs a different function as defined by the RS-232-C interface standard.

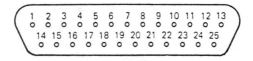

DB-25 Connector

On one end of the cable is a piece of *DCE*, or *data circuit-terminating equipment*, and on the other end is a piece of DTE, or *data terminal equipment*. Data circuit-terminating equipment typically communicates between the telephone network and whatever is connected on the other side. DTE is essentially an input/output device.

The purpose of the RS-232-C standard is to allow DTE and DCE devices to communicate with each other in an effective manner that allows for the transfer of information in a readily understandable manner. In practice, its use ultimately allows the transmission of ones and zeroes from one DTE to another DTE over the telephone network using DCE on either end of the network to perform the proper transformations. A typical DCE device is a modem.

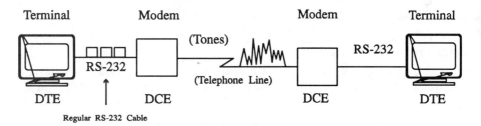

Modem stands for Modulator/Demodulator. Its function is to take the ones and zeroes generated by the DTE and convert them into tones or other forms of information that can be sent down the telephone line within the 4 kilohertz bandwidth provided by the telephone company.

Most RS-232-C connections essentially use pins 2, 3, 4, 5, 6, 7, 8, and 20. The pins have the same names and the same functions for both DTE and DCE, except for pins 2 and 3, which reverse roles and reverse names depending on whether they are for DTE or DCE equipment.

```
        (Terminal or Computer)                    (Modem)
                  DTE                               DCE

       Transmit   2  ─────────────────►   2    Receive
        Receive   3  ◄─────────────────   3    Transmit
 Request to Send  4  ─────────────────►   4    Request to Send
   Clear to Send  5  ◄─────────────────   5    Clear to Send
  Data Set Ready  6  ◄─────────────────   6    Data Set Ready
         Ground   7  ─────────────────    7    Ground
 Carrier Detect   8  ◄─────────────────   8    Carrier Detect
Data Terminal Ready 20 ◄────────────────  20   Data Terminal Ready
```

When using a standard RS-232-C connection between DTE and DCE the DTE pin 2 is a transmit line upon which data is transmitted, and pin 2 on the DCE is the receive line. This makes sense since if one device is to transmit, the other must receive. To ease cable confusion, pins 2 and 3 are reversed so that a direct pin 2-to-pin 2 cable connection allows for transmission by the DTE and receiving by the DCE.

The reverse is also true. When information is received from the network by the DCE (i.e., modem) that needs to be transmitted to the DTE, it is transmitted from the DCE on pin 3 and received by the DTE on its pin 3. In summary, pins 2 and 3 (transmit and receive) are opposite for DTE and DCE. This reversing of transmit/receive for DTE and DCE allows for the usage of what is called a straight-through cable.

If two DCE or DTE components are connected together, such as from one modem to another, a special *null modem* cable or connector is required. This cable or device switches lines 2 and 3 in such a way that transmitting from one DTE on pin 2 is connected to pin 3 on the receiving DTE, and vice versa.

In summary, the wiring in a null modem crosses to allow similar devices (DTE to DTE, DCE to DCE) to transmit and receive on the proper pins. For all other standard DCE to DTE communications the standard RS-232-C cable is generally used.

RS-232-C Interface Protocols

Let's take a look at the steps that are involved in setting up a standard RS-232-C connection.

1. Pin 20 is activated, which tells DCE that the data terminal equipment is ready to transmit information.
2. The DCE responds on pin 6 back to the DTE saying that the DCE is ready to receive information.
3. The DCE performs its functions, dials through the network to contact another modem, and notifies the DTE that it has detected a *carrier* signal, which is the indication from one modem to another that the connection is made and that communication can occur.
4. The DTE requests of the DCE the opportunity to transmit information.
5. The DCE responds back to the DTE saying that it is ready to receive or that the DTE is cleared to send information.
6. Information is transmitted from the DTE to the DCE.
7. The DTE receives data information from the DCE.

Notice that the DTE and DCE go through a clearly defined, specific sequence of steps before they can communicate with each other. This sequence, referred to as a *protocol*, must be gone through in the proper order or the communication can be marred.

Many RS-232-C communication devices do not use most of the 25 pins provided. Many RS-232-C compatible terminals only use transmit, receive, power, and ground. Most modem devices, smart terminals, and printer devices that are connected using RS-232-C interfaces use the sequence defined here.

Many businesses use a four-wire cabling system which allows them to transmit up to four pins worth of information. This information is usually transmit, receive, power, and ground. There are also devices that will receive all RS-232-C interface pin signals and then encode them onto the wires in such a way that they can be decoded on the receiving side and actually present a full RS-232-C interface. Notice that the number of wires has been reduced using this communication scheme, but extra equipment was added to perform the added functionality of encoding and decoding the RS-232-C signals. The information is still being communicated, but in a different way.

Serial Versus Parallel Data Transmission

Notice that only pins 2 and 3 transmitted or received information. Consequently, if information is transmitted from DTE to DCE, all bits have to leave DTE on pin 2 and follow a single path until they arrive at DCE on pin 3. This means that a sequence of one hundred bits sent from DTE to DCE will follow each other in a serial fashion down the wire between pin 2 of DTE and pin 3 of DCE. This transmission of data in a serial fashion is referred to as *serial data communications*.

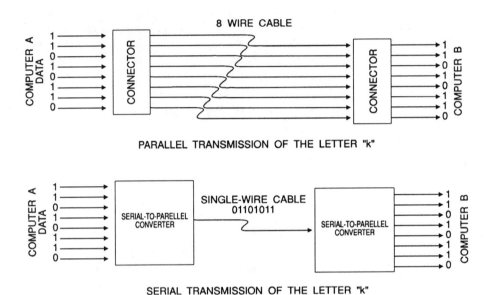

PARALLEL TRANSMISSION OF THE LETTER "k"

SERIAL TRANSMISSION OF THE LETTER "k"

Parallel-to-Serial Conversion

There is another basic form of data transmission called *parallel communications* whereby multiple paths for information transmission is available. Notice that on a parallel path there may be 7 or 8 paths or wires over which data bits may travel from sender to receiver. That means that at any given point in time 8 bits are being simultaneously transmitted versus one bit per time unit as seen with serial transmission.

Most personal computer printer devices use parallel communications since the cable runs are short, and 8 data bits can be transferred at once, which substantially speeds up the transmission process. RS-232-C is a serial information transmission standard.

Asynchronous Versus Synchronous Communication

It is difficult to discuss data transmission concepts without covering asynchronous and synchronous communication.

Asynchronous communication is often used when the amount of delay experienced on the transmission line is erratic and unpredictable. To accommodate this unpredictability, special bits are inserted before and after each character transmitted.

Synchronous transmission is generally used in conjunction with transmission lines of predictable timing nature which allows for the transmission of fewer special timing oriented bits. Each transmission method has its benefits under the proper circumstances.

Synchronous communication means that all data transmission and receipt within a network is performed between devices working in a synchronized manner. The devices at each end of a transmission path have internal clocks that allow them to precisely know when to transmit or look for the presence of a data bit. If the clocks within the respective devices get "out-of-synch" with each other, then the particular time that a specific bit was transmitted will not be surveyed properly by the receiving end and the communication can be lost. Therefore, it is critical that devices connected to a synchronous communication network have clocks that are kept in close time with each other.

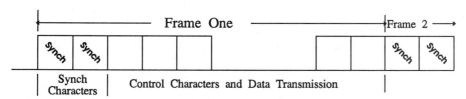

Typical Synchronous Data Transmission Framing

Remember that a computer device determines whether a data bit is a one or a zero based upon the electrical levels present on the line at the time of sampling. If the line is sampled at a time that is off from the proper time of sampling, the electrical levels sampled may actually be for a different stream of data and inaccurate one/zero bit status determinations made.

To ensure proper timing for device clocks, a special set of timing or synchronizing pulses are typically transmitted over the transmission line. These pulses may be contained within the actual data and have a specialized form that is recognized by the receiving side as the synchronizing or clock pulses. When the receiving side receives this particular bit stream, it automatically recalibrates its own clock to match that of the sender. Consequently, a high level of synchronization is achieved.

As the name implies, asynchronous transmission of information from one point to another is done in a nonsynchronous manner. The universal clock timing arrangement defined for synchronous communication is not used for asynchronous communication. Instead, receiver timing is started and stopped each time a character is received.

Start Bit	←—— 5 to 8 data bits depending upon code ——→								Parity	Stop Bit
1									Even Odd None	1 bit 1.5 bit 2 bit

Conceptual Model of Asynchronous Transmission

This is accomplished by adding a start and stop bit to each piece of data transmitted down the line. The start bit sequence, when received by the receiver, tells the receiver to begin looking for information at a given point in time and continue to look for data bits until it receives a stop bit sequence. Notice that there is a start bit and a stop bit sequence for each character transmitted using asynchronous communications.

This procedure allows for information to be transmitted from one point to another over links that are not timing consistent. The timing at the receive side is determined by when the information is received and not determined by the precise time that the information was transmitted. Consequently, asynchronous communication is much more network delay tolerant than synchronous communications.

The benefit of synchronous over asynchronous is seen clearly when the efficiency of the communication link is evaluated. Assume that we want to transmit 100 characters of 7 bits each from a sender to a receiver. The 7-bit designation for a character is in accordance with the *American Standard Code for Information Interchange (ASCII)* accepted method of representing alpha/numeric characters (a,b,c,d,1,2,3,4,etc.) with a 7-bit combination. At a minimum, we must transmit 100 x 7=700 bits to accomplish the transfer.

But life is not that simple when data communications is involved. Asynchronous communication requires a start bit before and stop bit after each character transmitted and sometimes a parity bit. This means that each character requires the transmission of 7 bits for the character and 2 bits for start/stop for a minimum total of 9 bits per character. Thus, transmitting 100 characters over an asynchronous link requires the transmission of 100 x 9 = 900 bits.

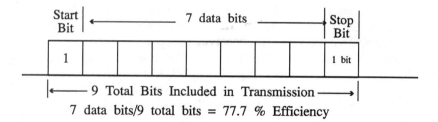

7 data bits/9 total bits = 77.7 % Efficiency

Out of those 900 bits only 700 (100 characters X 7 bits/character = 700 bits) are for actual information use, and the other 200 are used to facilitate the link or are used as communication link *overhead*. A common way to evaluate this situation is to look at the efficiency of the transmission, or how many bits of actual data were received out of all the bits sent. In this case, 700 out of 900 bits were for information which yields a 7/9 or 77.7 percent *transmission efficiency*. If parity were included, the efficiency would be even worse.

Synchronous communication does not include start and stop bits for each character. Instead, a synchronous link will treat the entire 700 character related bits as a *block* of information that is transmitted at one time. Within that block of data bits, a set of synchronizing characters (usually between 1 and 4 character equivalents) are included to maintain sender/receiver timing clock integrity as mentioned before.

The synchronous information may start and end with specific timing characters and may contain a specified number of characters in the middle of the block. The total number of characters located from the beginning to the end is referred to as a *frame*, and since the information is transferred as a whole block instead of as individual characters, this mode of transmission is often referred to as *block mode* communication.

A quick efficiency calculation shows that we still have 700 bits of data character related information being transmitted, but we have only 28 bits (4 characters X 7 bits/character = 28 bits) sent as communication link overhead instead of the 200 sent with the asynchronous example. Sending the 100 characters over the synchronous link requires a total of 728 bits and yields an efficiency of 700/728 or 96 percent. This is 19 percent higher than the equivalent transmission using asynchronous communications.

Most asynchronous communications allow for one start bit, 7 or 8 data bits for character representation, a parity bit (which we will discuss next), and a stop field which can be set at one, one and one-half, or two bits in length to signify to the DCE or DTE that the character information being received has ended.

An important concept to understand when working with RS-232-C is that both DTE and DCE need to be configured to understand the number of data bits, the type of parity, and the number of stop bits being used. If the DTE is operating with one set of parameters (i.e., 8 data bits, no parity bit, 1 stop bit) and the DCE is operating with another (i.e., 7 data bits, odd parity, and 2 stop bits), the two parameters are going to conflict and the bits of character information will not be intelligible on the receiving side of the link.

This situation is worthy of a detailed look. Even though the voltage levels transmitted are those defined in the RS-232-C standard, and even though both devices are RS-232-C compatible devices, communication is still impossible since they are configured to transmit and receive in different modes, like one speaking in Spanish and the other in Japanese. Consequently, it is important when working with RS-232-C devices to ensure that the number of data bits, the parity, and the number of stop bits have been configured the same on each end of the communication link.

Transmission Error Detection and Correction

Humans beings adapt well to noise, static, or incorrectly received information but computers cannot do this very well. A computer will process whatever information it receives in a diligent and flawless manner. Consequently, if incorrect information is received, the computer will perform its defined processes with that incorrect information. This particular characteristic of computers has given rise to the GIGO effect: Garbage In-Garbage Out.

The more links and connections that are contained in a communication network, the more possibility there is for unwanted electrical signals to be injected into the transmitted data. This unwanted electrical interference is referred to as noise and can cause serious problems if the noise signal becomes large when compared to the information signal. In particular, noise can affect the voltage levels sensed by receivers and occasionally cause bits transmitted as ones to appear a zeroes to the receiver, and vice versa. Changing a computer bit from one state to another can completely alter the information received.

For example, assume that the sender transmits the message "Meet me at the car," and the "c" in "car" gets changed to a "b" due to the effect of noise on the transmission line. The receiver will get the message "Meet me at the bar" and the two parties will probably not find each other. The more complex the operations being performed generally means that a single bit change can dramatically impact the outcome of a computer operation or a database record.

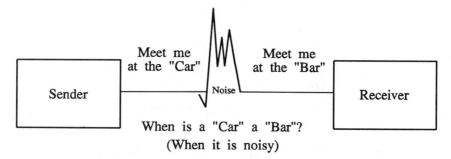

Since the analog telephone network was initially designed for adaptable human beings, it was not designed with a high degree of noise resistance. The telephone network is considered relatively "dirty" from a data communications perspective, which means that it has a significant amount of stray noise on the line. When computers began using the telephone lines for communication, a method of correcting for this noise was needed.

There are many different types of PC communications software on the market, such as Crosstalk, XYcom, Procomm, and the current terminal product contained in Microsoft Windows 3.0. These packages all contain options for transmitting files in a binary or ASCII mode and with different types of error detection/correction.

One method already introduced is the concept of *parity* checking, which checks to see if there is equivalence (parity) between the number of bits sent and the bit used to represent the proper status. This method is used extensively in asynchronous communication. Within each asynchronous character frame is a bit location reserved for parity information. The options provided are *even*, *odd*, or *no* parity.

No parity is the easiest to explain and means that the sender did not include any parity information and the receiver should not expect or look for any. Even parity means that including the parity bit, there are an even number of ones included in the character frame transmitted.

For example, the seven-bit ASCII code for the letter "C" is "1000011." To transmit this letter with even parity would require that another "1" be added to the bit stream giving a total of four "1" bits, which is an even number. Consequently, the even parity bit stream for transmission is "10000111" with the last bit representing the parity bit.

Odd parity is implemented in a very similar way except that the parity bit is set at zero or one to make the number of "1" bits an odd number.

Transmitting the previous letter "F" using odd parity would involve the transmission of a "10000110" bit stream which has an odd number of "1" bits.

<pre>
          Parity Bit
              ↓
    1000011   "C" With No Parity
    10000111   "C" With Even Parity
    10000110   "C" With Odd Parity

    10000110   Bad Transmission
                         With Even Parity
</pre>

The real significance of the parity bit is realized on the receiving side. When both sides are set up for the same level of parity checking (i.e., even or odd), then the receiver can make valid determinations as to the validity of the information received.

Assume both are set for even parity, and the receiver reads "10000111." It checks the number of "1" bits and sees that it is indeed an even number, which indicates that the bit stream received is indeed the same as that transmitted. Dropping the last "1" the receiver can now refer to the ASCII coding table and determine that the bit stream represents the letter "F" and perform its appropriate functions with that information.

Still set for even parity, assume that the receiver reads "10000101." It again checks the number of ones and sees that there is an odd number of ones. This conflicts with the even parity protocol established in the beginning and implies that the bit stream just received has had an alteration in one of the bits. The received data has been corrupted in some way, and the receiver requests of the sender a retransmission of the same character. Notice that the first seven digits, "1000010," correspond to the letter "B" in the ASCII code. Had this mistake not been detected by the parity checking scheme, the receiver would have gone to the bar instead of the car.

Although these methods of error detection and correction take up computer resources and decrease the efficiency of the communication link, it is a small sacrifice to make to ensure that the information is transmitted and received correctly. It should also now be clear that a consistent error correction method is required on both ends of the communication link to ensure that valid information is read by the receiver.

A final note regarding parity checking involves the possibility that two bits may change at the same time (i.e., a one become a zero and a zero become a one). In this situation the parity would still appear correct but the character received would be inaccurate. Many different types of error detection and checking schemes have been developed to address this particular situation and others that relate to the transmission of long data blocks and links involving long transmission times.

A term that we may encounter is *cyclic redundancy checking (CRC)*. This is a mathematical procedure that the sender undergoes to create a particular bit combination that reflects the one/zero status of the data block to be transmitted. This procedure is a more complex evaluation of data block integrity than that provided by parity checking, but the net result is the same. The receiver has a method of determining whether the data received matches that sent and can ask for retransmission of the data if it does not check properly.

Techniques that evaluate received data for errors and request retransmission to correct data deficiencies are called *backward error correction (BEC)* techniques since feedback is required from the receiver for error correction to take place.

Another useful technique provides the receiver with a method of correcting the received data without requesting retransmission by the sender. It is called *forward error correction (FEC)* and comes in several flavors, such as Hamming, Hagelbarger, and Bose-Chaudhuri. Each is a different technique for performing the same forward error correction procedure, but at the cost of many additional bits being transmitted for a given block of information. As seen earlier, when additional bits are transmitted a corresponding decrease in transmission efficiency is also seen. This type of trade-off decision is common in telecommunications and is generally made on a company strategy basis instead of purely technological.

Remember that these techniques are needed because of the electrical noise present on analog telecommunication circuits. As the networks become increasingly digital and eventually fiber-optic based, the *bit-error-rate* (number of bit errors per million of bits transmitted) of telecommunication links will improve dramatically and the critical need for extensive error checking will decrease in proportion. The introduction of high quality end-to-end digital networks such as integrated services digital network (ISDN) may eventually obsolete the need for error checking and correction. This situation is still years in the future and the use of error correction in telecommunications is a must for ensuring data integrity.

Error correction is the main function of most communications software packages and their various data communication protocols such as XModem and Kermit. They serve a valuable function in today's communication arena and have become relatively easy to use in conjunction with the modern software packages.

This section has prepared you with a foundation for clearly understanding the intent, if not the specifics, of error detection and correction on communication links. The form of the error detection may change, but the reason for using it and the trade-off with regard to transmission efficiency should now be clear.

A modem is designed to convert digital information into analog signals that can be transmitted over analog telephone lines. We have already seen that telephone lines are "dirty" by data communication standards and are prone to inducing noise and resultant bit errors. Error detection and correction is critical in these types of environments.

Modem Fundamentals

Modems are designed to convert digital (one/zero) information, generally received from DTE, into representative tones that are transmitted over telephone lines. Once these tones are received by another modem, they are transformed back into digital (one/zero) form and generally passed on to the DTE at the receiving end.

We see then that modems allow for the transmission of digital information from a sender location to a receiver location with the analog telephone network as a long-distance link between them. The error correction mentioned in the previous section ensures that data transmitted over the noisy telephone network is received intact and that the sender DTE bit stream arrives at the receiver DTE in the precise order of transmission. The RS-232-C protocol defined earlier in this section outlines a method of communication between the modem (DCE) and the terminal or computer (DTE).

The introduction of the modem into the communication link also introduces another communication protocol. Different modem types will encode the DTE digital bit stream in different ways. Consequently, even though two modems are connected to the same physical telephone line there is no guarantee that they will be able to communicate with each other unless they both are transmitting and receiving tone encoded information using the same protocol.

There are several different modem transmission techniques in use today. The primary modulation techniques rely upon *amplitude modulation (AM)*, *frequency shift keying (FSK)*, and *phase shift keying (PSK)*. These techniques provide a method for creating analog waves with attributes that are modulated, or changed, by the incoming digital bit stream.

The term modem is actually a contraction of MOdulator/DEModulator (MODEM). To understand the basic operation of a modem, we need to briefly review sine waves and basic modulation techniques.

Sine waves have three basic descriptive characteristics: amplitude, frequency, and phase. The peak amplitude of the sine wave is defined as the distance from the neutral zero point of the wave and the wave's peak.

The frequency of the sine wave is a measure of how often it repeats itself in one second and is measured in the number of hertz of the sine wave. For example, a power outlet in the United States has a 60-hertz, or 60-cycle-per-second, sine wave presented to it. Consequently, that wave repeats itself 60 times in one second. The phase of a sine wave refers to the timing of a particular wave as taken in reference to a second base time. Phase is a critical concept and is used extensively with respect to phase shifting.

When a frequency shift key based modem sees a digital one or zero come down, the RS-232 line converts that one or zero into a tone of a frequency based upon whether the modem is in send or receive mode and whether the bit is a one or a zero.

Let's look at two modems communicating over a telephone line using the Bell type 103 standard. The modem initiating the call is referred to as the originate modem (sender) and the modem on the receive end is called the answer modem. Even though they both have the ability to transmit and receive, the originate/answer designation will be established for each modem connection depending upon who calls and who receives.

Once the originate/answer status is established, two frequencies are set aside for each modem's use when it wants to transmit a one or a zero down the line. The answer side automatically adopts two frequencies for its one/zero tones (2225Hz and 2025Hz, respectively). The originate side also selects two tones for its one/zero transmission use (1270Hz and 1070Hz respectively).

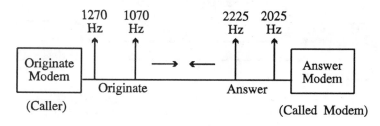

FSK Modem Arrangement
(Bell 103 Type)

Since different tones are used for one/zero communications in both originate and answer modes, information can be transmitted simultaneously
over the same phone line by both modems at the same time without
interference. When information simultaneously flows in both directions
over a communication link, the communication is called *full duplex*. Some
modems only support information transmission in one direction or the
other at any given point in time and are called *half-duplex* modems. Still
other modems only receive or transmit information and never do both.
These types of modems and this form of communication is termed *simplex*.

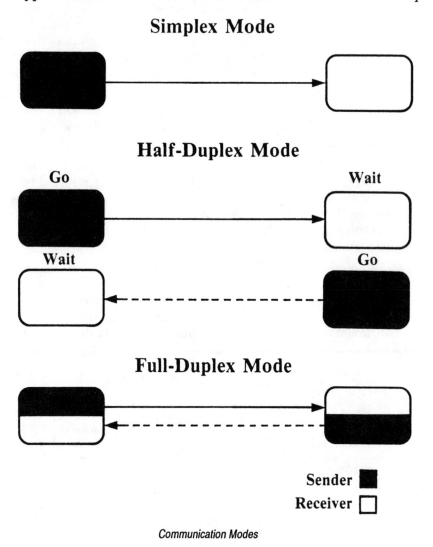

Communication Modes

We see that by changing the receive or transmit status of the modem and whether a one or a zero is being transmitted, the frequency transmitted also changes. Since both modems use the same link, all of their frequencies appear on the same connections at the same time. The modems separate the frequencies and only listen to those that apply to their needs.

Assume that the originate modem sends a 1270 Hz tone over the link. The receive modem determines that the tone is a valid frequency and converts the received analog frequency signal into a digital one which is transmitted over the RS-232 link to the DTE. The same process applies to a zero tone (1070Hz) that the receive modem senses. The reverse process occurs on the answer side.

This process of modulating and demodulating digital ones and zeroes into analog signals of specific frequencies is the process performed by a modem. Changing the frequency based upon received data (i.e., one or zero) is called *frequency shift keying*.

Of particular importance is the difference between the number of bits per second transmitted and the *baud* rate of the modem communication.

Baud rates refer to how many times a signal characteristic changes from one state to another in one second. For example, changing the frequency from one value to another 300 times in a second would represent a 300 baud communication rate.

A change in phase has similar consequences and also creates baud rates. A phase change is a change in the timing of one occurrence as related to another. For example, if a person is walking in a northerly direction and meets someone going in a southerly direction, we can think of those two people as being out of phase with each other. Since they are exactly the opposite of each other, they are out of phase with each other by 180 degrees. (See the previous discussion regarding degrees and sine waves.)

In computer or technology discussions, once we take any point as a reference, we can then monitor phase shifts of signals with respect to that reference. Those specific phase shifts occurring at a specific baud rate can be used to indicate data.

For example, assume that a modem can sense phase shifts in 45 degree increments. This means that phase shifts will occur in 45, 90, 135, 180, 225, 270, 315, and 360 degree increments and all of those given phase points can correspond to data combinations.

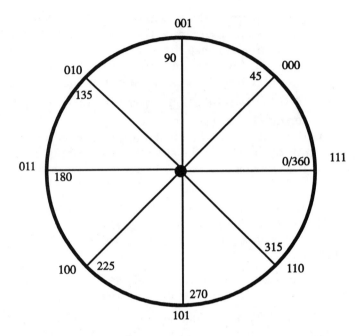

Quadrature (Phase) Modulation Encoding

Notice that this scenario provides for eight potential phase shifted transmission points. Any of those eight shifts has the ability to represent multiple bits of information. In fact, eight phase change points can be represented digitally with a sequence of three bits (000, 001, 010, 011, 101, 110, 111). This means that for each change in phase, information is transmitted regarding the status of the three bits that represent that particular change.

We now have the ability to transmit 3,600 bits per second (bps) on a 1200-baud communication link. It should now be clear that the baud rate and the bits per second of a modem are not the same. One is a measure of how often something changes state in a second (baud) and the other measures the total number of bits that were transferred.

A 1200-baud modem may transmit 2400 bits per second of information by using two bits, or four states, per signal change. Up to 9600 bits per second of information is possible using 2,400 baud modems with encoding schemes that support four bits, or 16 states, per signal change.

Many modems use a combination of amplitude and quadrature (phase) modulation to increase the number of available states. This technique is called *quadrature amplitude modulation (QAM)* and is used on modems supporting a full duplex transmission speed of 9,600 bps using a 1,200-baud modem. Modems using this technique comply with the Bell 209 and 2096 standards.

Asynchronous Communication and Modem Summary

Any communication path requires a transmitter, a receiver, and a communication link between them. The ultimate goal of any communication link is to transmit information from the transmitter to the receiver so that the transmitted information is accurately received.

This process is complicated in a technical environment by the need to make the transition from digital (DTE to modem) to analog (modem to modem using the telephone line) and then back to digital (receive modem to DTE). The link characteristics determine the technology used to change the form and representation of information to accommodate the different equipment and link components.

Computer equipment is digital. The current telephone network is predominantly analog and consequently directly incompatible with digital equipment. To transmit digital information over the analog telephone line, the one/zero bits of information must be encoded in a way that works over the analog telephone line. This is the function of a modem. Modems take digital information and convert it into analog tones that are transmitted from an originate modem, through the telephone network, to the answer modem where the tones are received and decoded.

The RS-232-C standard is the accepted method of communication between the modem (DCE) and the data terminal equipment (DTE).

Notice throughout this discussion that the answer modem must be able to understand completely the protocols and methods of transmission of the originate modem. If there is a disparity of any kind between the two devices, the likelihood of error free, effective data transmission drops substantially.

Notice also that even if there is end-to-end device protocol compatibility, the link itself may introduce errors and modify the information exchanged. Error correction schemes are embedded in the transmission protocols to address possible data changes.

RS-232-C is a well-known standard as are the modems that use it. Careful use will almost always guarantee some level of compatibility, but all of the details discussed in this section must be addressed before communication can occur.

Module Nine
The Merging of Voice and Data Communications

In dealing with communication systems, it is important to be able to discriminate between the information being transmitted and the method of transmission. The two are not necessarily the same.

The basic components of any communication system are the transmitter, the receiver, and the medium that links those two points. The ultimate goal of any communication system is for information from the transmitter to be provided to the receiver in a way that the receiver can understand it and use it. Much of the technology involved in current communications is involved with methods of transmission between the transmitter and the receiver. To better understand why these different methods of transmission are available, a brief discussion about information processing is in order.

Analog Versus Digital Communications

Until recently, most information was transmitted in *analog* form. It is called analog because what is actually transmitted electrically is a continuous electrical signal that looks like an analog or representation of the original information. If we look at the wave pattern of a person speaking, we see a continuously linked curve that at any given point and time represents the vocal inflections of the person speaking.

In reality, this analog wave pattern is a combination of many different sinusoidal wave patterns of varying frequencies, amplitudes, and relative phases. Each sinusoidal wave has a characteristic amplitude, frequency, and phase.

Frequency, in general terms, refers to how often something happens in a given period of time. In electrical signal terms we refer to frequency as the number of times a sinusoidal wave repeats itself within a second. If a wave changes from its positive amplitude tip to its negative amplitude tip and returns back to its positive tip, we say it has completed one cycle. The number of times that cycle repeats itself in one second is called the waveform frequency, which is measured in *hertz* (hz).

The amplitude of a wave is simply the height of the wave at its tallest point from a midpoint between the top peak and the negative peak, which we will call the zero amplitude reference point.

Phase is a more abstract concept which actually relates the timing of a given wave to a standard reference point in time. As the phase of something changes, its timing changes with respect to some other reference timing source.

Signal composition analysis is based upon the premise that a unique combination of sinusoidal waveforms of different amplitudes, frequencies, and phases can form any continuous analog signal.

It is intuitively accurate to think of sinusoidal wave forms as building blocks that can be assembled in the right combinations to form any signal structure. Although this technique is powerful, the information is still being transmitted in an analog, or continuous signal, form.

Another method of encoding information is using a digital format. Digital formats are combinations of one (1) and zero (0) electrical states called bits. The right combination of these one and zero bits can represent information such as letters or numbers. The most basic component of a digital signal is the bit. Eight bits form a byte, which is a common unit of measure used when determining the size of a particular sampling of digital data.

A standard method of encoding ones and zeroes to represent letters and numbers is the American Standard Code for Information Interchange (A.S.C.I.I.). This code was developed by the data processing industry to allow a constant standard for transmission of information between two different vendor's products.

Notice that if we want to transmit the information "Meet me in Chicago," we now have two different techniques for accomplishing the information interchange. The first is to transmit the message as an analog signal that would contain the voice information saying, "Meet me in Chicago." This is the mode used for telephone voice connections.

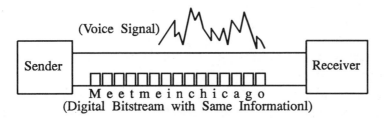

Digital and Analog Communication

A second method is to encode the letters M-e-e-t-m-e-i-n-C-h-i-c-a-g-o in a digital form and transmit the individual one and zero bits down a transmission line to a receiver. The receiver must understand the method of digital encoding so that the received bit streams are interpreted as the individual characters "M-e-e-t..., etc.. These characters are then assembled into the sentence "Meet me in Chicago."

The intent of the communication is the same. The transmitter wanted to let the receiver know that they were to meet in Chicago. The method of transmission over the transmission path was altered from analog voice to digital bits.

We see from this discussion that it is possible to transmit information in both analog and digital form. But even digital signals are composed of the different sinusoidal frequency components that make up any electrical signal. As long as the path supports transmission of all required frequency components between two points, there is the ability to transmit information. If any of the sinusoidal building block components are lost in the process, then some of the signal information will also be lost and the communication disrupted. These fundamental concepts form the basis of most communication systems.

It has been mathematically proven that *sampling* an analog signal (taking an instantaneous magnitude reading) at a rate of two times the maximum sinusoidal frequency contained in the analog wave form provides all the information required to accurately reassemble the initial wave. This two-times sampling rate is called the *Nyquist sampling* rate.

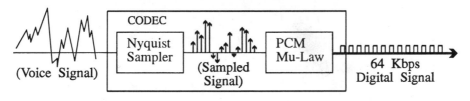

Voice Signal Digitizing Sequence

Encoding the sampled values into a sequence of one and zero bits allows for the initial signal information to be transmitted from one point to another but as ones and zeros. These digital bits can then be reassembled at the receiving end to accurately recreate the original analog wave.

The implications of this technique are profound. We now have the ability to sample an analog wave form at discrete points and code those discrete points into sequences of one and zero bits. These digital bits can be transmitted down a transmission line without any loss of information. The bits do not in any way resemble the initial analog wave, but the method of encoding/decoding their sequence allows for the re-creation of analog signal information.

On the surface, this may not seem a revolutionary development but it actually forms the basis for the replacement of most of the existing communication transmission systems of today. The ability to easily determine valid digital signal information from noise makes digital information more reliable than analog. This characteristic also provides a higher sound quality for voice communication. The popularity of the CD player for music indicates the public's acceptance of the high sound quality received from digitally recorded music.

A brief look at the characteristics of electrical noise assists in understanding the profound impact of digital technology on the communication industry.

The Nature of Electrical Signal Noise

All *noise* is analog in nature. Every time a signal is amplified or transmitted, a certain amount of noise (noise defined as unwanted signal) is injected into the original waveform. As the transmission distance increases, the number of times that the signal is amplified also increases. The more times the signal is amplified, the more noise is injected into the original signal.

Signal

Noise

Amp

Amplified Noise and Signal

This injected noise accounted for the poor sound quality experienced with long-distance telephone calls up until the early 1980s. A call from a neighbor did not have to be amplified as many times as a call from 2,000 miles away. Since each amplifying stage added noise to the voice information, the final signal received would have unwanted noise included with the desired information. Consequently, the long-distance call had a large amount of static, or noise, included with the normal voice information.

Digital technology offers an elegant solution to the analog noise problem. Remember that a computer sees only ones and zeroes. It is easy to automatically determine when something is either a one or a zero. It is difficult to automatically determine when something is analog signal and when something is unwanted noise.

Digitally encoded signals can more easily discriminate noise and tend to have less noise or unwanted signal contained in the transmission. This accounts for the high sound qualities of CD recordings.

Digitally modifying a digitally mastered original recording tends to introduce less noise to the music than analog processing and produces a much higher sound quality. A criterion for sound quality is the ratio of desired signal strength to the strength of the noise signal, and is referred to as the *signal to noise ratio*. A high-quality recording will have a much better (higher) signal to noise ratio than a scratchy, low-quality recording.

The same is true for communication links. The higher the signal to noise ratio for the link, the better the quality of information transmission and the less likely a digital bit error occurrence. This higher quality and lower error rate accounts for the rapid deployment of digital technology throughout contemporary communication networks.

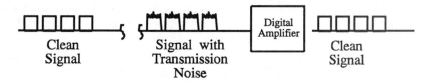

Digital Signal Noise Elimination

Adding Multiple Channels to the Same Link (Multiplexing)

Digitally transmitted information is easily manipulated by a computer. The computer is a device that can masterfully manipulate ones and zeroes at incredibly high rates of speed. In addition, computers have the ability to keep meticulous track of where specific ones and zeroes go. Therefore, it can divide multiple digital signals into their various one/zero subcomponents and transmit them over the same wire. This process is called *time division multiplexing*.

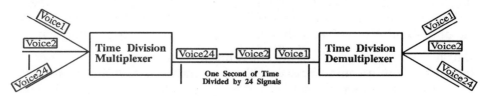

Twenty Four Voice Signal Multiplexing

Where previously a standard analog telephone line could handle one telephone conversation, we now have the ability to transmit over twenty-four telephone conversations down an installed communication link. The telephone company has gained twenty-four times the call carrying capacity from the same wire by simply changing the link termination equipment and the method of information transmission. In essence, the telco sees a 24:1 pair gain in this scenario.

Another method of transmitting multiple voice signals over the same communication link is a process called frequency division multiplexing. The frequency division multiplexing process superimposes the desired information signal upon another analog signal of a much higher frequency than the signal to be transmitted. Superimposing one signal on another is called *modulation*.

There are two types of modulation that most of us use every day. One of them is amplitude modulation (the radio AM band), and the other is frequency modulation (the radio FM band). These terms mean that a given analog signal, such as the voice of the announcer, is used to modulate the amplitude of a given carrier frequency, such as five hundred and ninety kilohertz. Frequency modulation uses the announcer's voice to modulate the frequency of the transmitting wave around a given center frequency, such as ninety-one point three megahertz.

Frequency division multiplexing divides the bandwidth of a particular communication link into separate smaller bandwidth segments, each with a center carrier of a specific frequency. This center carrier frequency is then modulated by the information signal being transmitted. In this way, many different information signals are transmitted over a single communication link. Even though there is only one physical path, there are many electrically created subpaths within the physical link.

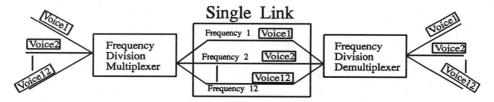

Frequency Division Multiplexing

Frequency division multiplexing was used substantially throughout the telephone industry until the acceptance of digital encoding. This technique creates *Base Channel* groups that contained 12 voice channels, *Super-groups* that contain 5 base groups (5x12=60 voice channels), and *Master Groups* that contain 10 Supergroups (10x5x12=600 voice channels). The value of this technique is easily seen when one considers installing 600 wire line pairs instead of a single high capacity line containing the frequency multiplexed groups and up to 600 voice channels.

The Telephone Network Wiring Plant and Pair Gain

The wiring plant of the telephone company is a major capital investment. It is much easier and less expensive to change the equipment at either end of a wire than to excavate underground conduits or uncover overhead cabling structuring and replace the wiring already in place.

Therefore, the telephone company is continually looking for ways to more efficiently use the installed wire plant. When more conversations can be transmitted over the same wiring plant than were previously available, the network has achieved *pair gain*. Transmitting two conversations on the same wire pair gains a wire pair since a second pair did not need to be installed and the second conversation is transmitted from one point to another.

The high data transfer rates possible with today's computer systems make digital transmission far more efficient and cost effective than the analog transmission. The first network segment to become digital was transmission between central office switching systems because it is expensive to add wiring over long distances. Simply replacing the endpoint equipment instead of replacing installed wiring was easily cost justified, and digital techniques were implemented to create the pair gain required to address increasing network traffic.

Once long-distance information was digitally encoded, the natural next step was to have the central offices become digitally based. As the central offices became more digitally based and more customers purchased computer equipment, it made sense to migrate on-site telephone equipment to a digital base.

As the site equipment and central offices became more digitally based, the only analog link left in the network was the link between the central office and the customer premises. This link is now progressively becoming digital with the implementation of digital interface standards such as Integrated Services Digital Network (ISDN).

Subscriber Telephones: Key, PBX, and Centrex Systems

The discussion regarding pair gain can also be applied to customer oriented telephone systems. The desire to minimize the expense and maximize the control associated with providing telephone communication spurred the migration of telephone switching equipment from the central office to the customer's premises.

The most familiar type of telephone service is the single line telephone connected from our home or small office to the telephone company central office. This basic line uses analog technology and has few features, which gives rise to the industry designation of it being *plain old telephone service (POTS)*.

Telephone service is usually billed on a monthly per line basis. If a company has 20 employees, POTS service would require that all 20 have their own line coming directly from the telephone company. This situation incurs 20 line charges even though all 20 people are not on the phone at the same time and consequently do not simultaneously need service.

In general, a telephone system only requires between 20 percent and 50 percent lines to the number of telephone sets. This ratio means that only 4-10 lines are needed, which substantially decreases the monthly line charges. The issue now becomes providing service to all 20 employees when only four lines are available. This is the function of key and PBX systems.

Most everyone has seen a *key system*. It is the telephone device that has several buttons, each of which correspond to a separate incoming telephone line. A user makes a call by pressing one of the buttons on the telephone, which causes the central key system controller, called the *key service unit (KSU)*, to go offhook, or *seize*, a line from the central office.

At this point, the caller dials the telephone number just like a normal telephone call. The ability to directly seize a central office connection by pressing a telephone set button is the major distinction of a key system.

When a call comes into a key system, the call is either routed to an operator who distributes the call to the proper party or the call rings all stations at the same time. Early key systems were mechanical and had limited functionality. Todays key systems are generally *hybrid*, meaning that signalling between the station set and the KSU is digitally routed to provide enhanced functionality but the voice channel is still analog. This combination of digital and analog makes a contemporary key system look a great deal like a private branch exchange.

Key systems are generally used by smaller organizations (under 75 stations and 30 central office lines) and where most call traffic is between the organization and the outside world.

Private branch exchange (PBX) systems are generally used in offices that require a great deal of telephone use within the organization. A typical PBX ratio calls for 80 percent of calls to occur between people within the organization, and 20 percent of calls to be with outside parties.

The 20 percent lines-to-station ratio mentioned for key systems is a good starting point for determining the number of lines required for a PBX system. If the company is heavily telephone oriented, such as telemarketing, then *traffic studies* are required to accurately predict the number of incoming telephone lines required to adequately address the customer demand.

PBX systems generally require that the caller dial a number, such as "8" or "9," to seize an outside line and make a telephone call. PBX systems also have extensive call processing features that allow their users to route calls over optimal routes (*least cost routing*) and also provide detailed records of telephone call activity (*call detail recording*).

Configuring a PBX or key system is a complex task and must be performed on an individual customer basis to ensure that optimal use of the product is obtained. Customers who are new to telecommunications are encouraged to use an independent source (such as a telecommunications consultant) for network and product evaluation since the vendors will all claim to provide the ideal solution and the most current technology for the least price. This application marketing approach by the vendors can be helpful in some instances, but it generally tends to confuse the uninitiated.

Centrex is a PBX type offering provided by the telephone company. The switch is located in the telephone company's central office instead of on the customer's premise as is the case with PBX and key systems. The customer is still billed on a per line basis but at a lower rate than telephone lines used for key and PBX systems.

Centrex service does not provide the rich feature set and high level of customer control seen with key and PBX systems, but it provides some distinct advantages. 1) Centrex equipment is owned and maintained by the telephone company. PBX and key systems are usually owned and maintained by the customer. 2) Centrex systems have virtually unlimited growth capacity since service is provided by the telephone company. 3) Centrex service is provided from the central office, which means that companies with offices in several locations around a city can easily tie them into one seamless telephone network. Remember, the telephone company has lines running in a star topology arrangement to virtually every premises in the U.S. For a PBX customer to accomplish this on his own, he would need to lease wire connections between the building from the telephone company which dramatically increases the cost of a noncentrex network. Customers with a campus type of environment should definitely consider the benefits of Centrex when making an evaluation.

Summary

The rapid increase in demand for telephone service forced the telephone company to implement technology that would allow them to transmit more information over the existing wiring plant. Changing endpoint equipment allowed the telephone companies to reap pair gain by transmitting more conversations over the existing wiring than was possible without the equipment. Frequency division multiplexing was the dominant technique until the introduction of digital technology.

Digital technology provided a versatile and noise free method for achieving pair gain and the technology was rapidly accepted for inter-central office communication. The network standardization on digital formats is driving the PBX and key system vendors to design digitally based, premises located equipment. Eventually, the network will be end-to-end digital meaning that a conversation will be carried as one/zero bits from one end of the connection to the other. ISDN is a digital standard that will allow for replacement of the final analog link between the central office and the customer premises. Digital technology allows for enhanced capabilities that were just not available in the analog world.

We now live in a primarily digital communications environment. A thorough understanding of the relationship between analog and digital signals is critical for understanding contemporary communication.

Module Ten
Powershift*: The Emergence of the Personal Computer

Perhaps no single event has caused a greater change in the technology environment of today than the personal computer. The development of the transistor and the integrated circuit laid the groundwork for the development of high-power yet low-cost digital processing devices. The development of the microprocessor, a micro or small version of a computer processor, is the breakthrough that changed mainframe computers into the stand-alone desktop processing units that are the personal computers of today.

The advent of the personal computer changed the way people do business. The data communications and data processing world started from a centralized main processor domain where few people were allowed access. There was an elite group of people in the management information system (MIS) department who had access to the processing power and the information contained on the large mainframe computer. Personnel needed to request information from the MIS department and were required to justify their request to someone who knew very little about the business significance of the request. The restricted availability of information also restricted the ability to make decisions to those people who had access to the needed information.

The personal computer now provides tremendous data processing power at a reasonable cost and provides the end user with direct access to information and processing power that was previously restricted. The increased availability of information and the increased speed of information processing provided by the PC shifted business decision making. Organizational decision making has expanded to more people and shifted organizational power as well.

---

* Adapted from Alvin Toffler's book *Powershift: Knowledge, Wealth and Violence at the Edge of the 21st Century.*

This shift in power has created a decentralized form of management that is becoming more the norm than the exception.

Looking back we see that the current changes from a centralized to decentralized form of management is directly related to the availability of information to people further down the organizational ladder. Now that these people have access to information, they have the ability to make credible decisions that previously were not feasible. This shift in decision-making power has been brought about significantly by the widespread business acceptance of the personal computer.

In 1980 a small percentage of business desk tops had some type of terminal equipment on them. Terminal equipment at that time was essentially split between two types of communication equipment: terminals based on the IBM 3270 communications protocol, and RS-232-C asynchronous communications terminals.

In 1980 local area networks (LANs) did not exist since these were designed to network together personal computers and the personal computer had not been introduced in early 1980; therefore, networking was not yet a major requirement.

Today the majority of business desk tops have some type of terminal equipment on them. This terminal equipment is either unconnected to other equipment (stand alone) or connected by modem, RS-232-C, local area network, 3270, SNA, or a variety of other communication protocols.

The number of desks with some form of information processing power on them has increased substantially. Processing power has shifted from centralized computer processing to decentralized computer processing and also shifted management power from centralized decision making to decentralized decision making.

The unwritten bylaws for the high-tech industry require that things get smaller, faster, cheaper, lighter, and more reliable. A quick look at the improvements in processing power available from personal computers shows that disk storage density (the amount of information storage per cubic inch) has increased 60-fold where the price per megabyte of storage has decreased by 40 times. Capability has improved by 60 times while price has been reduced by 40 times.

Today a person can buy a computer that has between 15 and 40 times the processing power of the original personal computer, yet sells for less money. Today a person can buy a portable notebook computer that is the size of a small textbook, has between 15 and 20 times the processing power of the original PC, yet sells for half the price. Personal computing is one of the best bargains available in American society.

If the last decade of improvement in processing power and reduction in size is an indicator of what the next decade will bring, we can assume that the developments will continue along the same lines.

The increasing importance of personal computers in our everyday personal and business life requires a basic understanding of their operation. This brief discussion presents microcomputer technical fundamentals and also gives an overview of the dominant personal computers on the market today — the IBM Personal Computer, its clones, and the Apple Macintosh computer.

Microcomputer Fundamentals

Microcomputer components can be divided into a few subsections. There is the muscle area which is called the processor and its related timing clock. There is the mass storage (disk storage) area and the internal memory random access memory (RAM).

Attached to any computer system are peripheral devices that augment system capability but operate on the periphery of the main computer. Typical peripheral devices include a display for showing computer information to the user, the keyboard used for input of information or instructions, and a mouse which is also used in conjunction with a graphical display for input of information to the computer. Printers are peripheral devices used for creating "hard" copies of computer generated information and modems permit transmission of digital information over telephone lines.

Additional devices becoming more prevalent are digital tablets that allow users to write on a pad which then translates their actions into computer language, light pens which are used for writing on digital pads and screens, and scanners which translate photographic images into computer information.

All of these input devices do nothing more than provide instructions or information to the computer. The computer then takes this information or group of instructions and performs the functions that it is designed to perform.

A crude analogy is possible between typical office operation and personal computer operation.

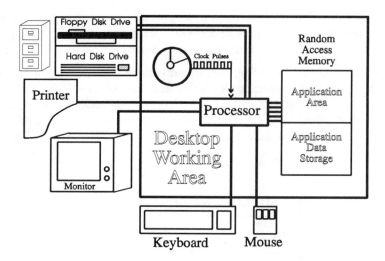

Basic Microcomputer Components

Mass storage devices typically consist of what are called hard disks and floppy disks drives. Hard disks are used for large amounts of storage with rapid data access, and floppy disks are used for smaller amounts of storage with slower access but provide portability of data.

Mass storage is like a typical office filing cabinet which contains files of information and also a file full of instructions. The internal workings of the computer, including the processor, the timing clock and the internal RAM memory, are like the center of a desk top which is the area where work is done. The display, keyboard, and mouse are nothing more than methods of giving instructions to the work area and those components that retrieve or display computer information.

In a conventional office environment, to perform a function at our desk we go to the filing cabinet, remove the file containing the pertinent information processing instructions, and return to our desk. In computer terms this action is the same as reading program instructions stored on the disk drives and transferring the instructions to the internal random access memory (RAM).

At this point, the instructions are located inside the computer work area, but no processing has occurred. All processing is done by the *central processing unit* (CPU) which is called a microprocessor when working with personal computers. Notice that all computer work is done by the processor. No processing is done on the disks or by the internal memory.

The instructions are transferred to the processor which performs the appropriate digital processing actions as dictated by the instructions. The specific instruction sequence determines which microprocessor actions will be performed in accomplishing the desired task.

Most co͟ ͟͟ ͟osses require some type of data for proper execu-
tion. Wh ͟ ͟ application process, the data is read
from tł ͟ ͟ ͟ ͟ ͟ ͟ RAM memory and then
transfe

Assum͟ ͟ght of students in a
class. ͟ eight of each student
and t͟ ͟dents included in the
samp͟ ͟ 30 students. It is only
the c͟ ͟s) that change.

In a͟ ͟le cabinet, remove the
fold͟ ͟n, and also remove the
file͟ ͟aging process. The files
are͟ ͟lication file details the
in͟ ͟les the necessary height
in͟ ͟performing the operation
w͟ ͟ventually determine the
c͟ ͟sult of the calculation is
͟ ͟folder, and returned to a

͟, the averaging application
͟stored in RAM for processor
͟tion is then read into another
͟s application instructions, it
͟AM section. Upon completion
͟r saves the resulting informa-
͟that is then stored on the mass

The physical equip͟ ͟instructions are stored and executed is called *hardware*. The sp͟ ͟struction sequence executed by
the computer is called *software*. Hardware is a physical reality and is not easily changed. Software, on the other hand, is a dynamic set of instructions that are relatively easy to change. The ultimate goal of using a computer is to improve productivity by automating repetitive tasks. Hardware cannot accomplish anything without software. Software running on a deficient hardware platform is frustrating and often less efficient than doing that task manually.

A proper blend of software and hardware is needed to make efficient use of computer systems. In addition, computers are only as valuable as the tasks they perform. If they cannot be used properly by the people who operate them, then the value of the system is decreased substantially.

This ease of operation criterion has been the subject of a heated rivalry between Apple Computer and IBM clone manufacturers. Apple users claim that the mouse/*icon* arrangement of the Mac makes the system more useful. IBM users claim that any system that is easy to use could not be very powerful. The fact is that both ease of use and processing power must happen at the same time for effective system use.

The following discussion takes a look at the background behind the PC versus Macintosh debate and provides a framework within which to evaluate the two options.

The Development of the Personal Computer Industry

The first microcomputer was introduced in the early 1970s by Altair. The name Altair came from a Star Trek episode in which Altair was the destination planet of the Starship Enterprise. The Altair computer essentially defined the "bus method" of transferring information between the microprocessor and different components of a personal computer. A *"bus"* is a multiple path conduit for transferring bits between the processor and the other computer components.

Altair also acted as the catalyst for development of the Basic programming language which was developed by Bill Gates and his partner in their Micro-Soft business, which later became simply Microsoft. Eventually, Microsoft became the standard computer operating system for the IBM personal computer and a contemporary application software giant.

The early days of the microcomputer were dominated by hobbyists and technology-oriented people with very specific applications. The entry of the IBM Personal Computer marked the PC industry with a huge stamp of approval in that "Big Blue" had sanctioned the industry by marketing their own PC.

IBM expected to sell only 250,000 PCs over the entire lifetime of the product. Some government orders for the original PC were in excess of 5,000 units. IBM obviously had no concept of the huge impact that their entry into the PC market would cause. The IBM Personal Computer (PC) became the industry standard for business computing. The software was lackluster by today's standards, and the system was difficult to operate, but the industry bought PCs with a vengeance and the market exploded.

The personal computer was initially introduced in 1981 with an Intel 8088 processor that ran at just over 4 megahertz speed, a 180 kilobyte floppy drive that quickly became a 360 kilobyte drive, and 64 kilobytes (thousands of bytes) of RAM memory. It was not very sophisticated, but it was IBM. That was enough.

In 1984 the PC/AT was introduced which had an Intel 80286 processor, 512 kilobytes of RAM memory, a 1.2 megabyte floppy drive (5 1/4 inch), and a 20 megabyte hard disk.

In 1987 IBM introduced the PS2 model 80 which had an Intel 80386 processor, 1 megabyte of internal memory, a 1.44 megabyte floppy drive (3 1/2 inch), and a 44 megabyte hard disk. Computers using the Intel 80386 microprocessor chip were introduced in 1990, and the Intel 80486 processor is the rage for "entry" level high power systems. Notice that major processor evolutions have occurred roughly every three years since the original PC introduction in 1981. When purchasing microcomputer equipment, believe that the system will last forever, or three years, whichever comes first.

The original PC processor by today's standards was inefficient and not very powerful. Its ability to effectively process large amounts of information was limited, which restricted its ability to enhance commands entered by the user. It is easier for a computer to interpret and understand commands entered in ASCII text (see prior section related to digital encoding of letters) than to sense a user action and translate that action into many different computer steps.

The text entered in a command structure required very little interpreting processing power on the part of the computer but required a high level of learning and skill on the part of the person operating the computer.

In addition, IBM designed the original PC by Engineers, for Engineers, and typically it took someone with a high degree of technical expertise to effectively use a personal computer or even read the manuals. The original operating system included on the computer was developed by Microsoft Corporation and was referred to as the "Disk Operating System" or MS-DOS. DOS is literally the program that allows the different components of the computers, such as the disk drives and display monitor, to operate in harmony with each other. People needed to learn to speak DOS before they could effectively run a personal computer.

IBM's initial intent was to create an industry standard processor platform upon which other companies could develop applications software. The goal was to foster industry evolution and growth around the PC seed planted by

IBM. The strategy worked. An enormous personal computer market and many young millionaires have been created simply by following the lead of IBM in its personal computer.

Computer hardware platform standardization and a lack of control over application implementation resulted in an explosive industry of micro-computer manufacturers and their respective IBM platform clones. Fierce competition resulted and a great deal of application software was developed. The big PC picture may have been defined by IBM, but the small parts were open to interpretation and improvement.

There was no standardized user interface. There was no standardized mode of operation other than MS-DOS. Software development was done for MS-DOS environment by companies such as Lotus and their 1-2-3 product and WordPerfect with their popular word processing package, but each package looked completely different.

Each developed software application looked different because it was per-sonalized to the designer. Learning a new DOS software application was like learning a new language along with all the associated pitfalls. Very little sensitivity was given to the needs of the ultimate end user.

Enter the Apple Macintosh Computer

This lack of sensitivity to the end user's needs was seen as an opportunity by Steve Jobs and the people at Apple Computer, a Cupertino, California, based personal computer company. Apple's initial 1983 attempt at creating a computer that was easy for the user to operate was called the Lisa, named after Jobs' daughter. The Lisa was introduced in the early '80s but met with limited market acceptance due to the newness of the approach and the high price tag of over $10,000.

The Lisa used the point-and-click mouse technology that has become synonymous with the Macintosh computer. In fact, the mouse technology was actually developed by XEROX Palo Alto Research Center (PARC) for use on the original Xerox Star System.

The intent of the mouse driven user operation was to allow users to input computer commands through the use of visual prompts and graphical symbols called icons. This approach represented a major breakthrough for users and for the computer industry in general. Instead of requiring users to learn new DOS-based computer languages, the Macintosh mouse user operated his system merely by pointing to a portion of the screen and clicking (pushing a button). From that point on, the computer knew exactly what operations to perform.

The intensive visual orientation and the ease of operation of the Macintosh, combined with its adequate processing power, made it very popular in graphic artists' circles. Even today, the Macintosh is the industry standard for desktop publishing and remains firmly entrenched in any of the visual or graphic arts industries as the computer of preference.

The basic processing components of the Macintosh are virtually the same as the personal computer model described earlier with one large difference. The Macintosh input/output mechanisms were tailored for easy operator use and the end user was considered as the principal component of a personal computer. The IBM PC was designed from the computer stand-point with the training and operation responsibility falling squarely on the shoulders of the end user. The difference may seem subtle, but the practical impact of the different design philosophies would cause a major industry revolution.

Some major benefits evolved from the Apple approach to the computer marketplace. The Apple standard graphical interface dictated that any Macintosh software developers had to develop software compatible with this graphical user interface. As a result, applications developed for the Macintosh all have a similar user look and feel. Operation of one Macintosh application was very similar to other Macintosh applications. End user training time was reduced substantially. People became less afraid to use the Macintosh and its users became more productive. Perhaps more than anything else, this end user operation sensitivity distinguished the Macintosh from the personal computer and its clones.

The original Macintosh was introduced in 1984 and had a Motorola 68000 processor running at 8 megahertz. By today's standards it was a slow processor but contained adequate processing speeds to perform most func-tions effectively. The Macintosh was not taken seriously in the early days simply because it did not come from IBM and there was minimal pain involved in learning its operation. ("I walked 10 miles through the snow, and so will you" syndrome.)

The ease of use factor allowed the Macintosh to substantially penetrate the business environment between 1984 and 1990. The Macintosh now owns a substantial portion of the microcomputer market.

Comparing the Two Systems

The major benefit provided by the IBM PC was its diversity of software applications and its wide acceptance in the marketplace. The intense competition from PC clone companies (companies that produced a product that exactly mimicked the IBM PC) kept PC prices low. Companies like Compaq and Texas Instruments promptly introduced products that competed directly with the IBM PC, but at a substantially reduced cost.

A major benefit of Macintosh was its graphical user interface and its standardized application development approach. The down side was the Macintosh's acceptance in niche markets only and the limited availability of software applications. The Macintosh also had no competition and consequently mandated a higher price tag than a PC.

The Macintosh was more expensive and easier to operate with fewer applications. The IBM PC was more difficult to operate, less expensive, but had a wider variety of applications that could run on it.

1990 brought with it the rapid processing power of the Intel 80386 microprocessor chip and clock speeds of 20 megahertz or more. 80386-based PC platforms can run productivity oriented applications and also present a graphical user interface. In other words, these PCs have the ability to run as conventional PCs or as computers that closely replicate the graphical operation of the Macintosh and without a major sacrifice in performance.

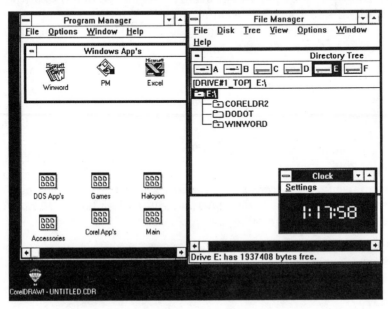

Microsoft Windows 3.0 is a graphical user interface that capitalizes on the PC power and the intense user desire for easy operation. Windows 3.0 was introduced in late 1990 and has rapidly become an accepted industry standard with over 10,000,000 copies shipped at the time of writing this book. Version 3.1 was released in early 1992.

Software application developers are rapidly standardizing on the Windows 3.0/3.1 graphical user interface in much the same way that Apple required its developers to standardize on the Macintosh user interface.

Windows 3.0/3.1 running on a 80386 powered PC seriously impacts the major Macintosh advantage: ease of use. The end user now has a graphical user interface on both the PC and the Macintosh with a large number of applications available for both systems.

There are still some differences between the operation of Windows and the Macintosh operating system, but the lines of differentiation are beginning to blur. Some analysts predict that by 1993 there will be no substantial operational difference in the end user presentation of the two systems. The end user will be able to transparently migrate from a Macintosh to a PC, or vice versa, with minimal operational disruption and complete data transparency.

Combined IBM and Apple Development

The recent press is writing a great deal about a project called "Pink" which is a cooperative software project between IBM and Apple. These two former rivals appear to have set their differences aside in the interest of developing an operating system that will compliment both of their strategic aims.

This project represents IBM's acceptance of Apple's market success and expertise in developing easily operated computers. IBM would typically turn to Microsoft for software development assistance, but a major falling out has occurred between the two companies over IBM's OS/2 operating system and LAN management software. The domain of microcomputers and software is dynamic and the IBM-Microsoft situation may change by the time you read this chapter. The only constant in this fast-paced industry is change, and microcomputer users should not rely on anything remaining as it is.

As the number of microcomputers increases, the need to manage the data and processing resources of these devices becomes more important. Information processing is the basis of the powershift discussed earlier in this section. Information processing capability is a valuable corporate resource that must be managed.

Current network operating systems require a high-level system administrator to keep them running. This environment is intimidating to many companies and precludes organizations from installing networks that tap into the combined processing power of installed personal computers.

The Pink project, as defined today, will develop an object-oriented operating system that will simplify network management. Using Pink, an administrator will have the ability to access and modify information related to different network components. The interface will probably be a graphical user interface similar to the point and click process of Windows and the Macintosh. When an administrator desires information about a particular network component, he will simply click on the object of interest as displayed on a network map and all information related to that object will be displayed.

There are major stumbling blocks in the way of Pink becoming an industry standard operating system, but with two major players like IBM and Apple driving the project, it is naive to ignore this networking development.

A final word of caution regarding the Apple Macintosh. The Macintosh is a powerful system but it is also essentially a sole source system. The IBM PC is an industry standard platform with various configurations available from many different sources. The Apple Macintosh can only be sourced from Apple and is viable only as long as Apple is viable. Although Apple does not show any signs of financial difficulty, neither did Wang Laboratories ten years ago.

This is an important point to consider when choosing a computer system and becomes especially important as they become increasingly more critical to company operation.

More companies are providing Apple compatible peripherals than ever before and the Macintosh may eventually become an open system with a public hardware architecture and software design. This will open the Macintosh clone market just as it occurred with the IBM PC.

This transition will be competitively driven primarily by the increased processing power of the PC combined with the popularity of Windows 3.0/3.1. Application developers such as Lotus and WordPerfect have rapidly jumped onto the Windows wagon, which increasingly adds credibility to the Windows-based PC approach.

Subsequent releases of Windows will include improvements and eventually the software will look very similar to an Apple Macintosh. When this happens, there will be no reason for Apple to maintain a proprietary hardware stance and Apple may see no loss in releasing the Macintosh architecture and software design.

PCs on LANs Compared to Minicomputers

Recall that a minicomputer is a centralized processor with many smart terminals connected through various types of communication links. Some processing is done by the terminal and some processing is done by the minicomputer itself. The result of the whole system is greater than the sum of the parts.

The popularity of the PC forced the industry to migrate away from centralized processing to distributed processing that connected PCs together with local area networks. A major local area network advantage is the ability to begin networking on a small basis and expand the network capabilities as dictated by organizational requirements.

Centralized processors required that the organization spend a large amount of money early in anticipation of organizational growth. Many times the technology would become obsolete before a justifiable amount of minicomputer capacity was used and the expected return on investment was never realized.

Today's local area networks have relationships between network clients and network servers. These client-server relationships are similar in many ways to the previous user/minicomputer relationship.

The local area network data server is essentially a central repository for application files and data that are accessed by smart PC terminals connected to a local area network. A minicomputer, on the other hand, is a centralized processing system that stores large amounts of information, which is accessed by terminal device users via some form of communication link.

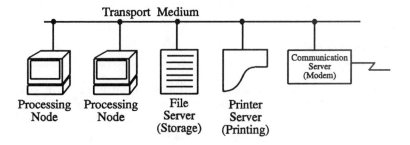

Transport Medium

Processing Node Processing Node File Server (Storage) Printer Server (Printing) Communication Server (Modem)

As minicomputers became more sophisticated, the processing power migrated from the central processor onto the desktop in the form of smart terminals. The minicomputer itself performs less of the processing function and acts more as a storage and print server for the powerful terminal users. In many ways, today's minicomputer network looks like distributed, very smart terminals connected to centralized storage devices. This description is essentially the same as a local area network.

Many companies are consolidating PC data and applications on centralized servers to ensure data security by limiting information access only to authorized personnel. Many of the nodes on a network do not contain disk drives, which means that no copying of network data is possible. These devices are referred to as *diskless nodes*.

Once again, the more things change, the more they stay the same. We started out with a centralized processing environment. The advent of the PC caused a migration to a decentralized processing environment. As the number of PCs in use increased, the need to share information contained on the PCs also increased and local area networks were created.

As the number of local area networks increased along with the geographic diversity of terminal locations, the need for networks that covered larger geographical areas created wide area networks (WAN).

As the network became more complex, the need to manage that network as a uniform resource also increased. Uniform network management became a paramount concern and appropriate products were developed.

As the number of people accessing the network increased along with the amount and value of available data, network security concerns arose. Local area networks migrated into a server-client relationship which is similar to the original minicomputer-smart terminal relationship of the late '70s and early '80s. The price of a minicomputer has also decreased substantially over the past decade while system modularity increased. A minicomputer is once again a cost effective alternative to LANs under specific circumstances and should be reviewed as an option when developing a new network.

The Parallel Universe

As the number of PCs increased so did the amount of total processing power available within local area networks. The problem with LAN processing power is that some computer terminal nodes are heavily used while others are virtually untouched. The heavily used stations are short on processing power, while the relatively unused stations have processing power to spare. Attempts are now under way to evenly distribute processing power over all LAN users.

Network operating systems are improving in quantum leaps and will eventually get to the point where the aggregate computing power of a network may actually be tapped by all members attached to the network. This scenario is called *parallel processing* because processing can occur in parallel on two distinct processing devices at the same time.

Instead of having one processor performing functions for its exclusive user, future networks may allow a function performed on one node to access processing power from another node. Likely, the processing power will be automatically allocated to the needy user by the network.

Instead of underutilizing some nodes and overutilizing others, future networks will have a more even distribution of processing power throughout the network. Networks will be multiprocessor based and allow complete utilization of processing resources on a national or international basis, independent of geography.

Summary

The introduction of the PC was a pivotal point in the history of information processing and communication technology. Rapid acceptance of the PC drove rapid improvements in communication technology to provide connections between the different devices and diverse geographic points where the PCs were used. As PCs become smaller, lighter, less expensive, and more powerful, the networks that route their traffic must also improve.

As graphical user interfaces become the standard instead of the exception, ASCII text transmission may become obsolete, and full graphic images will become the standard. Instead of transmitting a sequence of ASCII characters, a digital "picture" copy of the entire document will be sent.

The network will be the gating item and/or the facilitator of image technology adoption. Technological developments such as SONET, FDDI, ISDN, and broadband ISDN are destined to address this situation. These technologies may be solutions to the anticipated high bandwidth information conduit situation, but the need was driven by the introduction and acceptance of the personal computer in 1981.

Module Eleven
Tying Computers Together with Local Area Networks

The proliferation of inexpensive microcomputers and an increasing demand to collect, sort, analyze, and file information have spurred the development of integrated networks. An integrated network accesses, processes, and distributes information independent of the hardware, software, and communication systems that comprise the network.

The ideal network would allow a user to request information from any terminal or server (node) in the network and would return the requested information to the requesting user in its most usable form (i.e., report, chart, or graph).

There are several competing methods currently being developed to address this type of application. *Enterprise computing* is a relatively new attempt at making all points within an organizational data network appear transparent to the users.

The ultimate goal of enterprise computing is to provide information to the users when they request it. There are several methods competing for the top spot for making this information transfer. No matter what the final outcome of the marketing and technology battles, a mandatory first step to transparent computing is transparent *connectivity* to every affected network node. The LAN appears to be the backbone upon which this connectivity will occur.

Linking Micros to Mainframes

One established method for information distribution is to connect microcomputers to large *mainframes* so that the micro looks like, or *emulates*, an ordinary terminal. Notice that this terminal emulation is necessary for the micro to "talk" with the mainframe since the mainframe expects a specific terminal type to receive the transmitted information. Without terminal emulation, the mainframe to micro communication would look like binary garbage. The emulation essentially presents a familiar face to the mainframe and allows for understandable information transmission.

Together the micro and mainframe share information processing chores. The mainframe handles the big jobs requiring a lot of computer memory and disk storage. The micro user selects a smaller chunk of information from the mainframe and processes it further using local programs and disk storage in the micro. The result of the micro operation might be a spreadsheet report, a chart, or a graph that is created and stored on the micro, yet contains data obtained from the mainframe. This final result of the micro operation can then be sent to the mainframe for further processing.

This type of information processing scenario is typical of smaller remote offices of large companies. The corporate information database may be located on a centralized mainframe server in one city, and the field offices may retrieve (*download*) information from the mainframe into the micro. The mainframe data may then be processed using the micro capability, and the final computational results may then be sent back to the mainframe (*uploaded*). Once all field sites have reported their results, the mainframe can run a program that consolidates the information into a comprehensive report. Notice that the information transfer occurred in both directions, and that processing occurred both on the mainframe and on the micro.

Multiuser Systems

Multiuser systems (MUS) are another method for sharing information and processing tasks in an integrated environment. The heart of a multiuser system is a "super" microcomputer having enough memory and disk storage capacity to allow several users simultaneous access to the system from multiple work stations. Often, a MUS is composed of several microprocessors that share a common disk, all of which are enclosed in a single cabinet.

These systems are sometimes called minicomputers in that they perform many of the functions associated with mainframes but typically at a fraction of the mainframe cost. A minicomputer may have many "smart" and "dumb" terminal devices connected to it, and it serves the processing needs of each of these devices. There is usually no storage in the terminal devices unless a microcomputer is emulating a specific terminal type.

The major drawback with minicomputers and mainframes is that the constant centralized processing power gets divided between the number of users who are using the system at any given time. As the number of users increases along with the increased terminal activity, the response time of the centralized processor decreases. The time between user initiation of a system request and when the user receives the result of the request is called the system *response time*.

Response time is a critical factor with information processing systems because time is money, and most people get frustrated if they have to wait very long to receive their desired answers. Many networked systems are designed to provide a specific maximum response time under typical user inquiry traffic loads.

Local area networks have become attractive because everytime a microcomputer node is added to the network, another processor is also added. In this way, the processing power is distributed throughout the network at the nodes instead of centralized at one point. These types of systems are sometimes referred to as having a *distributed processing architecture*.

Local Area Networks for Microcomputers

Local area networks (LANs) allow microcomputers to exchange information and share common *peripherals* (printers, disk drives, etc.). For example, an office LAN that interconnects several microcomputers used as word processors might have only one printer on the network, but that printer can be used from any of the micros. Without the LAN, each user may have his or her own printer and disk storage device along with redundant software. Shared LAN disk storage is provided by a *file server* and shared LAN printers are referred to as *print servers*. When many users print to the print server at one time, their respective print jobs are placed into a *print queue* (defined printing order) which is managed by the *print spooler*.

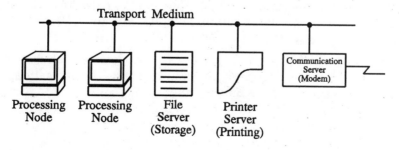

When LAN users require communication services, they access the *communication server* (i.e., a high-speed modem) connected to the LAN that transfers information over the appropriate communication links.

Another major feature of a LAN is the ability to share application and data files over all nodes attached to the LAN. For example, assume that common applications such as word processing and spreadsheets are used by every (i.e., 20) desktop computer user in an organization. Also assume that each node is attached to the LAN.

Instead of having a copy of the same application installed on each desktop computer (i.e., 20 word processing application packages), the LAN server can contain one copy of the word processing software that is accessible to each of the LAN node computers. This aspect alone minimizes the management headaches associated with many microcomputer organizations.

The LAN version of the application software generally costs more than the stand-alone version and requires a *site license* that authorizes the organization to use the software on a LAN. Pricing schemes vary widely between vendors, and the users are cautioned to get all the details on installation, maintenance, per user, and maximum number of users before buying a LAN-based software package.

This type of sharing also applies to the data used by each of the computer applications. Assume that each word processing station must modify the same group of documents. Without a LAN, redundant copies of the data would have to reside on each of the individual computer workstations. A LAN allows one copy of the data to reside on the file server, and all users are allowed access to the centralized data over their LAN connection. This procedure controls the access to sensitive data and also minimizes the likelihood of data being copied and distributed to the wrong people.

Many LAN users take advantage of the LAN sharing capability and purchase fewer peripheral devices but of a higher quality. This approach not only allows each user comparable access to software and peripheral devices but improves the quality of the final product and decreases the overall network price (i.e., instead of allowing ten users to each have their own $300 dot-matrix printer, administrators will allow LAN sharing of a single high-quality laser printer for $2,000).

The early days of LANs were focused on connections to each desktop. Now that many of the desktops are connected together, the security aspects of networks have become more important.

Local Area Network Design Considerations

Unlike multiuser systems, LANs allow computers and peripherals from many different manufacturers to be interconnected in a common network as long as the products conform to the proper industry standard specifications. Any LAN-connected micro with proper security authorization can access information on other LAN-connected micros or peripheral devices.

LANs fall into the two broad categories of *baseband* and *broadband*. LAN nodes may also be configured in any one of several well-accepted physical configurations or *topologies*: star, bus, and ring. Finally, there are three basic accepted media access techniques that have been adopted by the marketplace: CSMA/CD (Ethernet), Token Bus, and Token Ring.

Concepts of Broadband and Baseband Networks

Initial LANs were baseband, meaning that only one signal was on the LAN any given time. The signal in the case of baseband is the actual voltage levels associated with the digital information transmitted over the coax line. Since only one signal is allowed on the LAN, the entire bandwidth capacity of the baseband LAN is used in simply moving the digital bit from one point to another on the LAN. Broadband does not suffer this limitation.

Broadband LAN communication uses frequency division multiplexing to superimpose the digital bit information onto a carrier frequency that then carries the information through the LAN to the other nodes. The major benefit of broadband is that many different carriers can be used, which means that many different information paths are available from the same piece of coaxial cable.

Just as cable television carries many different channels, broadband LANs can simultaneously support many different data communications but not without a cost.

It is generally much more expensive to attach nodes to broadband networks, and the maintenance of the LAN is more complex due to the many different signals and generally larger size. In addition, if television, data, and manufacturing control is routed over the same LAN and the link is disrupted, then all forms of communication go out at the same time. The LAN can become a single point of failure for the organization. This aspect alone makes some users avoid using the full potential of broadband LANs.

Basic LAN Topologies

A *star topology* physical network is the most common configuration in use today. The standard telephone network is a fine example of a communication network configured in a star shape. Think of the central office as the center of the star and each communication link between the central office and the customer premise as a point of the star. Star topologies have a common center point and many "ray" end points.

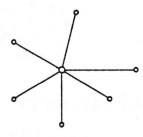

Star Network

A *bus topology* is the one chosen for the initial LANs based upon the Ethernet protocol. A bus has definite end points which are carefully terminated with specialized connectors. Bus topology LANs have maximum lengths and a maximum number of nodes (i.e., 2500 meters and 100 stations for Ethernet). Bus topologies are essentially multipoint networks, in that a single line extends from one point to another with many intermediary nodes attached. Each node has equal access to the bus, which means that there is no central failure point such as can occur with failure of the central hub of a star network.

Once the signal is sent by a node, it passes through the network without regeneration by the other nodes. *Cable terminators* are installed at the ends of a bus to absorb the transmitted signal and keep it from being reflected back onto the link and corrupting the new signal transmitted over the line.

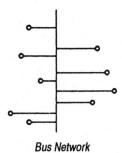

Bus Network

Ring topology networks have the beginning and end of the link attached so that the link actually forms a circle. Each node on the ring listens to data transmissions, receives and regenerates the signal, which helps to ensure data integrity. Notice that if any node fails on a ring network, the entire ring can be brought down. To address this potential problem, a second ring is generally installed to each node that allows for information transmission in the opposite direction (i.e., counterclockwise). The 802.5 token ring standard includes the second ring and a methodology for implementing the recovery of lost information.

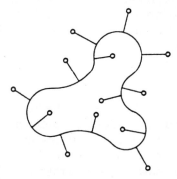

Ring Network

Hybrid networks are those that contain mixed topologies within the same network. The increasing need for data communication protocol transparency is making hybrid networks a common occurrence. Many people have ring or bus topology networks installed yet need to communicate using a contention or token passing scheme.

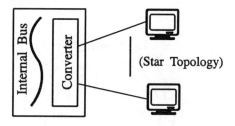

Hybrid Topology Equipment

Network Access Control Techniques

Network access refers to the way in which nodes gain use of the shared communications link. When a single pathway is used by many nodes, methods of controlling the information flow is critical. The methods used to control access to the network are generally classified as *polling*, *token passing*, or *contention* techniques.

Polling

Polling is a method for determining the order in which nodes may use the network. In *roll call polling* a centralized network node requests (or polls) status information from each node on the network. Only one device is polled at a given time and all polling is under centralized control. Because this technique specifically prevents direct conflict between nodes attempting to use the network at the same time, it is referred to as a noncontention method of network access.

Token Passing Access

Token Passing is a method for passing the use of the communications channel from node to node in a fixed, predetermined order. A *token* is a special "message" that continuously circulates around the channel, passing each node in succession. When a node has a message to send and the token is free, it changes the bit pattern on the token to show that the token is occupied and then transmits its message.

After the message is sent, the node changes the token bit pattern back to its "free" status and the token continues to circulate to the other LAN nodes. Other nodes now know that the channel is free and take control of the channel for sending their own messages. Since a node can send messages only when it has possession of the token, conflicts between nodes needing to send messages at the same time are avoided.

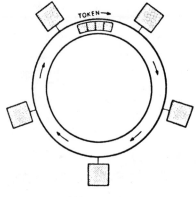

Token Passing

A major characteristic of token passing is its timing. Since the number of nodes on the network and the amount of time each node can hold the token is easily determined, the amount of time it takes for the token to pass around the network is also easily determined. This aspect makes a token passing LAN *deterministic* in nature and ideal for processes that require tight control of timing between nodal contacts, such as industrial or manufacturing process controls.

Slotted Channel Media Access

Slotted channel is a variation of the token passing method. Rather than a single token circulating on the communications channel, multiple message slots are used instead. Message slots merely reserve space on the channel for carrying messages. When an "empty" slot passes a node needing to send a message, the node "fills" the slot with its message and instructs the slot where to deliver it. When the slot and the message it is carrying reach their destination, the receiving node empties the slot, freeing it for use by other nodes as the slots continue the journey around the network.

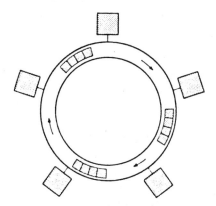

Slotted Channel Access Method

Contention Media Access: CSMA/CD and Ethernet

Contention techniques of communication channel access anticipate conflicts between nodes trying to use the channel at the same time and are actually designed to deal with the resulting *collisions* as part of the protocol for giving a node use of the channel. The *Carrier Sense Multiple Access with Collision Detect* (CSMA/CD) protocol is a commonly used contention technique for Ethernet and IEEE 802.3 compatible networks.

Although this is a mouthful, CSMA/CD is not very difficult to understand if the name is examined in pieces. You have likely used a technique similar to CSMA/CD when talking with a group of friends. If a person in the group wants to speak (and if no one else is talking), the person simply begins speaking. There has been no "collision" between two people wanting to speak at the same time.

If someone else is talking, the next person to speak waits for them to finish before speaking. Once again no collision has occurred since the second party follows proper protocol and waits for the first to finish.

Sometimes, however, two people, both noting that no one else is talking, begin to speak at the same time. If they continue speaking at the same time, then neither of them is understood. They both immediately realize they are interfering with one another and stop talking. Usually one party or the other begins speaking first and is allowed to continue.

The initial collision between parties was detected, and each party waited for a short but random length of time before trying to speak again. Eventually, one person begins speaking before the other and gains the floor.

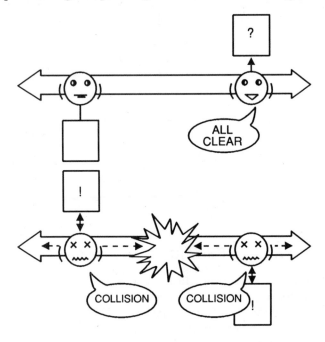

CSMA/CD Access Protocol

That is exactly how CSMA/CD works. Any node on the network can start sending messages anytime that it senses that the communication channel is free, which in LAN terms means that no "carrier" signal is present. When a node begins to transmit over the channel, it transmits a carrier signal that the other nodes detect, which instructs them to refrain from transmitting. This technique allows for access to the LAN by multiple nodes through sensing of the carrier signal. This accounts for the Carrier Sense Multiple Access portion of the name.

As in the case of a conversing group of friends, two nodes sensing that the channel is free may start sending messages simultaneously. When the messages collide, the energy level on the channel rises, signaling both nodes that they are interfering with each other. Both stop transmitting and wait a random period before starting again. Because each waits a different length of time, one node eventually gains use of the channel and sends its message. The other node may then gain control of the channel and transmit its information.

Ethernet, a contention protocol, was one of the first commercially popular LAN protocols. The groundwork for Ethernet was initially developed by XEROX Corporation in the early 1970s and became a commercial success when cooperatively developed with Intel and Digital Equipment Corporation (DEC) in the 1980s. DEC uses Ethernet to network its computers with each other and for connecting its terminal servers (devices that interface with the user terminals).

The IEEE 802 standards committee essentially adopted the Ethernet protocol as the basis for the IEEE 802.3 standard. There are some minor differences between the two, but for most purposes they are interchangeable.

The IEEE 802.3 standard defines a bus topology for its implementation. A bus is a configuration that has a distinct beginning and end. Nodes attach to the bus using some type of *media access unit (MAU)* or *transceiver* and share the same transmission medium which provides a 10 Mbps data conduit. The initial media option was a thick piece of coaxial cable sometimes simply referred to as "yellow" cable, since that was its characteristic color. There were consistent problems with effectively attaching the transceiver, and when it was installed improperly the entire network could be brought down. Alternate methods of implementing Ethernet were found.

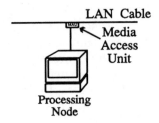

AT&T offers its Starlan product which follows the 802.3 standard but operates over twisted pair cable that only offers a 2 Mbps transmission rate. It is easier to install but offers more limited performance than a standard Ethernet LAN.

IBM even offered an 802.3 compatible LAN that they called PC Network. The product ran over thinner coaxial cable than a standard Ethernet but offered an additional benefit that Ethernet could not offer. PC Network was a *broadband* based system, where Ethernet 802.3 calls for a *baseband* system.

Summary of LAN Topologies and Access Methods

The amount of traffic that can be sustained on an Ethernet LAN is heavily dependent upon the number of active nodes and the length of each packet sent, once a node has control of the network. If more nodes are active, then the likelihood of two nodes desiring access at the same time (collisions) is higher, and the amount of network down time (while the nodes wait their random time period before retry) will increase. This increased down time means that no data traffic can occur during the waiting period and overall network traffic will decrease.

On the other hand, if the packet lengths are very long, then the number of times that a node desires access will decrease, which will reduce the likelihood of collisions and increase overall throughput.

This discussion is not designed to make you a network guru but simply to give you an idea of the tradeoffs that occur when designers select a topology and contention scheme for a particular application.

If the number of nodes is higher and precise timing between node access is critical, then using a token passing scheme is probably preferred. If the number of stations on the LAN is low (i.e., under 20), then an Ethernet LAN should be more than adequate.

In 1991 the average number of nodes on a LAN was under 20 stations. The mix of Ethernet to Token Ring LANs was 45 percent and 27 percent respectively, with the mix expected to even out at around 45 percent/45 percent within the next five years. The balance of the LAN market is taken up by other proprietary protocols, most of which are slowly fading into the sunset.

There are many Ethernet and Token Ring compatible products on the market. Both LAN networking strategies have their benefits, and solid arguments can be made for each in terms of being better than the other. As always, the user inherits the choice of which is best for his or her application. Sometimes the best solution is a combination of both. That topic leads to a discussion of bridges, routers, and gateways.

LAN Bridges, Gateways, and Routers

Bridges, *gateways*, and *routers* are loosely used data communication terms. Although they serve similar functions in terms of connecting networks, it is the level and type of function that they perform that separates them from one another.

Just as a bridge allows automobile traffic to flow from one side of a ravine to the other, a network bridge allows network traffic to flow from one network to another. Notice that a train cannot travel over a bridge designed for automobiles, and vice versa. Physical bridges are used to connect geographic points for the transport of specific vehicles such as cars or trains.

The same is true for communication network bridges in that they are used to connect networks that communicate using the same procedures (i.e., Ethernet) even though the physical media may be different (i.e., 10 Mbps coax to 10BaseT twisted pair). Notice that for both physical media types, the transmission type is still baseband and no baseband-to-broadband conversion is required.

Network bridges are generally used to extend the physical limits of a network or to increase the number of stations that are connected to the network.

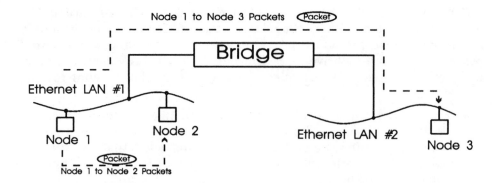

Gateways are used when the networks being connected are of different types (i.e., Ethernet and Token Ring). In this case the media access method and data transmission form is different on each network, and a terminal on the Ethernet LAN desiring to communicate with a terminal on the Token Ring LAN must have some form of interpreter in between. This is the function of the gateway.

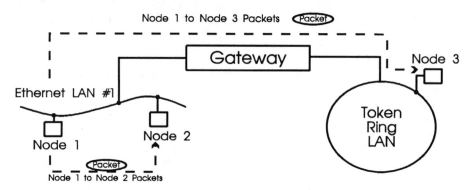

There are different types of commercially available gateways that can be used to accomplish the necessary conversions. They can come as dedicated boxes that perform a specific type of gateway function, or come as software that runs on a powerful processor platform such as a minicomputer or microcomputer.

An important point regarding the use of bridges and gateways is the ability of the device to transfer information from one network to the other without slowing down the communication process. The bridge is generally not performing a great deal of processing on the data it receives.

Assume that two Ethernet LANs are connected by a bridge. It monitors the information transmitted on LAN1 and LAN2. Information transmitted from a station on LAN1 to another station on LAN1 is not touched by the bridge, since there is no *internetwork* procedure required. Information transmitted from a station on LAN1 for a station on LAN2 is stripped from LAN1 and placed onto LAN2 for receipt by the appropriate LAN2 station.

Notice that the bridge can monitor the from/to addresses of the LAN traffic and select which information must be passed through the bridge. This means that LAN1 specific traffic stays on LAN1 and does not use transmission capability on LAN2 until LAN2 traffic is required. In bridge terms, this information transfer decision-making process is called *filtering*, in that packets on LAN1 are filtered to LAN2 as needed, and vice-versa.

Coming back to the performance issue, we can now see that the filtering process performed by the bridge takes time. If a lot of time is used, then the ability of the bridge to pass the information between LANs at the full Ethernet 10 Mbps speed would be hampered and network performance and response time would be eroded. Today's bridges are generally powerful enough to not negatively impact the information flow, but the concept of *throughput* (how quickly the translation process is performed) is important to understanding gateway performance.

Bridges also serve an important function in dealing with transmission of information between media operating at very different speeds. For example, assume that we need to connect a 10 Mbps Ethernet LAN in Dallas to one in Atlanta, and that a standard 1.544 Mbps T-1 telephone company line will be used for the connection. Also assume that a packet on the Dallas LAN is intended for a station on the Atlanta LAN.

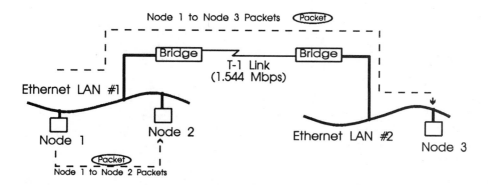

The Dallas bridge will sense the Atlanta address and strip the packet from the Dallas LAN at a full 10 Mbps rate. Notice that the T-1 can only accept the information in the Dallas bridge at a 1.544 Mbps rate (roughly 1/6th the speed). The Dallas bridge must have the ability to store, or *buffer*, the information for a brief time period while the information is transferred over the T-1 link to the Atlanta bridge. If another Atlanta packet comes into the Dallas bridge, then it must also be stored while the transfer of the first packet is accomplished.

It should be clear from this scenario that designing a network containing different network link types and protocols is a complex task which is heavily dependent upon the amount of information, or *traffic*, that will pass between the two networks. This speed conversion feature of bridges is valuable when dealing with larger geographical networks such as MANs and WANs.

Bridges are a specialized form of gateway. A gateway not only provides connections between networks, but also provides information conversion functions that allow information contained on one type of network to be passed through to another.

For example, assume that LAN1 is Ethernet and network 2 is an IBM SNA network. In this case, the information must be monitored on each side of the gateway but additional conversions must be performed to ensure that the information can pass transparently from one network to the other. This conversion process is the function of a gateway.

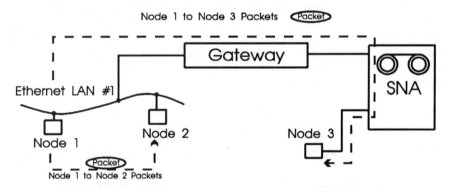

Notice that substantial processing may be involved on the part of the gateway in transferring information from LAN1 to the SNA network. The amount of traffic expected between the two networks is a critical design constraint to consider when designing gateways. The benefit of a gateway is that isolated networks can now communicate with each other between departments or across the country.

There is a network performance and financial cost incurred when gateways are used, but the benefits derived by the organization in being able to transfer data between previously isolated networks generally outweigh the equipment cost.

Routers are another class of internetworking products that allow information sent from one network to find its way to the intended receiver and pass through many other dissimilar networks. Different network types have their own method of addressing packet envelopes so that information can easily find its way from the sender to the receiver. When the information is sent and received on the same network, then routing of the information is not an issue.

Suppose that information is sent on a network in New York and is intended for receipt by a San Francisco user. The two networks need not be the same, and can even be connected by a number of different intermediate networks. The router in New York senses the information and selects a route for the information to follow as it makes its way to San Francisco. This routing information is added to the information being transmitted.

Static routing (always the same each time information flows between these two points) and *dynamic routing* (the optimal route is chosen for each communication) are two common routing formats. The router's function is to ensure that the information packet is labeled so that it flows from one point to another through various networks.

Source routing, commonly used by IBM, allows the sending station to specify the exact route that the information is to follow and is generally used when security or priority delivery is important.

Brouters, a combined bridge-router, are beginning to appear on the market. These devices combine the bridging and routing functions into one device.

Through proper implementation of bridges, gateways, and routers, *seamless networks*, where the network appears to the user to be without divisions, can be achieved and transparent connectivity is possible. A careful understanding of the network types and internetwork traffic involved can reduce the overall cost of the seamless network and increase overall network response time.

Metropolitan and Wide Area Networks

The IEEE Committee recognizes the expected increases in data traffic combined with the need for interconnection standards and is developing the IEEE 802.6 *Metropolitan Area Network (MAN)* standard. This standard is designed to interconnect data, voice and television data sources within a 5 and 50 km radius.

Smaller companies have seized the MAN opportunity and purchased high speed data transport capability (T-1 and T-3 over coax or optical fiber) from the established carriers. They then sell this bandwidth capability to users who require this type of high speed data conduit. The major benefit to the users is that they do not have to install their own network, they get lower prices than available from the telephone companies, and the MAN companies provide alternate routing of information and emergency backup plans.

Wide area network (WAN) is a general term used to describe networks that cover very large geographies such as national or international networks.

Summary

Just as the acceptance of terminal devices forced the computer vendors to develop different methods of networking terminals, so is the rapid deployment of LANs driving the development of methods for internetworking different LAN types.

The rapid increase in the number of LANs is testimony to the viability of the LAN concept. The expected decrease in microcomputer price combined with the increase in processing power are expected to increase the need for high power data networking.

At issue is the complexity of providing internetwork connection. The responsibility for providing the connection lies either with the user or with the network provider. The technical level of the network user is decreasing, now that the processing power is out of the domain of engineers. This means that the network must automatically provide the connections needed to accomplish the desired information transfer. This is best accomplished when standards are in place.

Finally, there is a new development on the horizon which could transform the way users access network information. IBM and Apple have joined forces in an attempt to develop a user friendly network access interface. At the time of this writing, it is still too early to determine whether this project will develop into anything substantial. One thing is for certain, any project that is jointly developed and marketed by these two industry leaders will have a definite impact on the networking industry.

Module Twelve
Circuit Switching Versus Packet Switching

In order for messages to travel across a network, a communications path must be established between the sender and the receiver to route them to their destinations. There are several modes of communication network transmission pathway switching: circuit switching, message switching, datagram packet switching, and virtual circuit packet switching. Each method has its advantages and disadvantages.

Circuit Switching

Circuit switching is the technique used by the telephone company to establish a connection between two telephones when a call is made. In circuit switching, the transmission path is established by providing the network with adequate information for the establishment of a connection between the two telephones. Usually, a new path is established every time a call is made between two telephones.

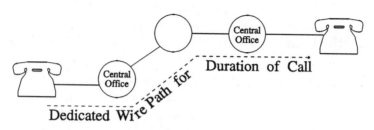

Circuit Switching

Calls are automatically routed to their destinations by the most readily available path as determined by the network routing software. The connection must happen before a call can go through. The short pause you experience between the completion of dialing and the first ring in a telephone call is the time required to complete the circuit switching connections. This pause is known as the *call setup time*.

A fundamental aspect of circuit switching is that the circuit switched connection appears as a solid wire connection through the network once the connection is established. The established transmission route stays constant once the connection is made. The path for information does not change. This facet is radically different from packet switching.

Message Switching

Message switching is a technique by which a message is stored in a portion of the network until the proper circumstances arise for retrieval. Conventional types of services that use message switching are voice mail and electronic mail.

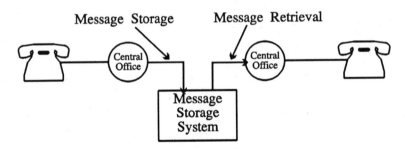

Message Switching Concepts

Notice that message switching services do not require simultaneous interaction between the sending and receiving parties. The message can be stored until the timing is right for delivery as determined either by the sender or by the network traffic situation.

Some other benefits associated with message switching are: 1) The sending and receiving parties need not be simultaneously available for message switching to function; 2) If a receiving terminal is inoperative, the message can be stored until it is back on line and able to receive the message; 3) Duplicates of the message can be sent to many stations with a single command from the sender (since time is not a critical factor); 4) Message logs can be kept to monitor the communications of each station; and 5) There is no call setup time involved.

The negative side of message switching is that interactive communication between sender and receiver is precluded. This type of system is sometimes called a *store and forward* system in that the messages are stored by the network for a period of time, then forwarded to the proper party.

Packet Switching General Concepts

Packet switching is a widely used method for exchanging data between computers (SNA), over local area networks (Ethernet/IEEE 802.3), and between diverse geographic sites and various communications networks (X.25). *Packets* are the containers in which messages are transported from their source to their destinations.

In concept, a data packet is similar to a standard post office letter envelope. To ensure proper delivery the envelope contains a return (sender) address, a deliveree (receiving station) address, and some type of letter (data) contents. Notice that as long as the addressing is in a form that is understandable by the postal service, the letter will be delivered even if the letter contents are in a foreign language.

The bits contained in a packet "envelope" may be formatted in a way not understandable to the delivery system, but it does not matter as long as the bits are delivered in the right sequence. The device that ultimately receives the packet of information must be able to decipher the bit streams and create the transmitted information. Constructed by the computer, a data packet contains an informational data message, a from and a to address. In this sense, a data packet is like a conventional envelope with letter contents.

Packets generally have a maximum length (generally a few thousand bits) which is determined by the transmission characteristics of the network, such as speed and the number of bit errors per thousand or million bits transmitted, referred to as the *bit error rate*. If the total message sent exceeds the length of one packet, several packets may be sent with each packet carrying only part of the message.

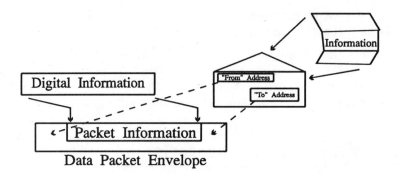
Data Packet Envelope

Packet switching is the transmission process by which packets are routed through the communications network as they travel to their destination. A routing network is a fully connected network, except every node is not necessarily directly connected to every other node. Transmission paths are typically determined on a dynamic basis for each packet that is sent, depending upon the busy status of the network links at the time of transmission.

Datagram Packet Switching

Assume that we want to send a message that is 3,000 bits long and each packet on the network is limited to 1,000 bits in length. This means that three packets are required to complete the transmission from sender to receiver. Each of these individual packets is called a *datagram*.

The significance of dividing the message into smaller pieces is that the separate packets may take different routes through the network from sender to receiver. This allows for dynamic allocation of overall network capacity and causes the overall traffic flow to be more even. In addition, should one node in the network fail, the packets can sense the failure and take a route to the receiver that does not include that node. Notice also that no call setup time is involved with this technique since the network dynamically determines the optimal path.

Notice that each packet may not take the same route as the others. This means that each node in the network must make a routing decision for each packet it receives. This places an additional processing overhead burden on the nodes but increases routing flexibility. Also notice that the packets may not arrive in the proper sequence if packet one takes a long route and packets two and three take shorter routes.

The receiving side must be able to determine the proper packet sequence so that the original message can be properly reconstructed. This is the function of a *packet assembler/disassembler* (PAD). The sending PAD divides the original message into separate packets and transmits them over the packet switching network. The receiving PAD reads the information embedded in the packet envelopes and reassembles the received packets in the proper order to accurately create the original message.

Special codes are embedded in the packet envelope that indicate the sequential place in line for the data contained in each particular packet. This information coding is all part of the packet switching protocol used by the network.

Virtual Circuit Packet Switching

The concept of a packet still applies to virtual circuit packet switching, but the path used for routing packets is defined at the beginning of the communication and stays constant for all packets that follow.

The basic procedure is as follows: 1) The sending station sends a *Call Request* packet into the network, which defines the sending node's identification number and the intended receiving node's identification. 2) The network defines the optimal route for packet transmission between the two stations and sends the packet to the receiving node. 3) Sender and receiver now exchange packets in a similar way to the datagram procedure except the pathway is not dynamically determined for each packet. All packets follow the route defined by the first packet. In essence, the network has defined a simulated or *virtual circuit* between the two stations. 4) One of the stations sends a *Clear Request* packet through the network to have the virtual circuit connection removed from the network.

Virtual circuits have benefits if two stations intend to communicate for a long period of time. The benefits are derived because each node in the network that receives a packet no longer needs to make routing decisions once the virtual circuit is defined. The packets containing the proper addresses will follow the virtual path defined, which decreases the amount of overhead processing required to maintain the communication path. Some networks provide additional services such as error correction and transmission speed control since the sequence and routing of the packets is well defined.

A negative aspect of virtual circuits is that the path is defined and inflexible. Should one of the nodes in the defined routing fail, the entire path is affected and the communication will fail unless the network has an automatic recovery capability. Also notice that the network must determine the optimal path to reserve for the communication, which means that call setup time is involved with virtual circuit switching.

Switching Technique Performance Discussion

Each switching method has its advantages and disadvantages. The basic criteria for decision making are 1) the amount of time involved with setting up the call, 2) delay of transmission during communication process, and 3) communication reliability should a network link break down during transmission.

The following table outlines the relationship between the methods discussed with regard to these criteria.

Circuit Switching	*Message Switching*	*Datagram Switching*	*Virtual-Circuit Switching*
Setup time required	No setup time required	No setup time required	Setup time required
No delay	Large delay	Routing delay	Minimal delay
Fixed route	Dynamic routing	Dynamic routing	Static per call routing

Module Thirteen
Communication
Standards Models

There is no way for technical communication to occur without complimentary standards for information transfer. If the sender transmits information in a form different from that used by the receiver, then the communication will not occur (i.e., a French-speaking person talking to someone speaking Chinese). Standards committees such as the American National Standards Institute (ANSI) and the Consultative Committee on International Telegraphy and Telephony (CCITT) continually work to create standards that guide future equipment and software development.

There are also *de facto* standards which the market accepts. Usually these standards have been in place for a long time, and a great deal of equipment has been installed around this standard. The users incur a substantial cost when this equipment is replaced, so the standards tend to remain. In addition, when the market demands a solution to a technical problem, a solution is generally found. Many *de facto* standards are adopted simply by this market need fulfillment.

The bottom line on standards is that whatever the market is using or plans to use is a standard. Committees may create what they think is right, but if the market does not adopt it as a solution, the standard will die.

There are several basic user motivations for adopting standards. 1) There are risks involved with networking equipment from different vendors using different protocols. Standards minimize the risk that something will not work as planned. 2) The use of standards insulates the user network management function (higher level) from lower level changes. 3) Standards allow sharing of information from different sources and even over different network types. 4) Large network management is a complex task, and standards assist in keeping systems under control and promote unified network management schemes.

The essence of a standard is the acceptance by all parties involved that communication is to occur as agreed. When that happens, there is a standard. The International Standards Organization (ISO) seven-layer Open Systems Interconnection (OSI) model and IBM's System Networking Architecture (SNA) are briefly presented.

Application
Presentation
Session
Transport
Network
Data Link
Physical

OSI Model

The Seven-Layer OSI Model

This model was proposed by ISO in 1978 as a framework for product development. It is not itself a model for a specific product or standard offering. Instead, it provides a standard model for use in development of functional product standards.

The communication industry has focused on making products OSI compatible. Even the federal government announced its intention to purchase large amounts of OSI compatible equipment under its Government Open Systems Interconnection Purchase (GOSIP) plan. The importance of OSI is that it allows vendors and customers to discuss product relationships in a compatible framework.

OSI divides communication into a seven-layer process: 1) physical link control, 2) data link control, 3) network control, 4) transport control, 5) session control, 6) presentation, and 7) application. When people discuss products, they refer to a product as working at "level three" or as being "transparent to everything above level three." These statements mean that the product in question is designed to perform functions at the OSI level three (network control) layer of the OSI model. Level one is considered the lowest level and level seven the highest.

The lower levels of the model deal with the details of communication such as physical dimensions of connectors and specific voltage levels. The higher levels deal with items specific to the ultimate user application. Each layer of a communication procedure will have its ISO standard associated with it, but the overall communication procedure may have a commercial trade name.

The physical link control level (1) defines the physical and electrical characteristics of a standard. It typically includes connector dimensions, specific voltage levels, and pins used for information conduction. RS-232-C is a level-one standard.

The data link control (2) level is used for ensuring the accuracy of information transferred between two network points. This level also defines methods for properly accessing the network, such as CSMA/CD and Token Passing. Error detection and correction is also part of level two.

The network control level (3) is responsible for addressing and routing of information through a network. Packet switching level three takes a large block of information received from level four and breaks it into smaller components that are then routed through the network. Specific routing decisions are made at level three. Level three on the receiving side reassembles the packet into its original large block form that is then passed up to its respective level four.

The transport level (4) makes the decision regarding which route is best for the information being transmitted. For example, assume that a particular network has both a packet switched and dedicated leased line connection between two points. The network manager may define one path (i.e., packet switched) as best for particular types of traffic. The transport level converts the user defined network address (i.e., Chicago System) into the appropriate binary address (some bit string that describes Chicago System to the network software). Level four then passes the overall information block to level three for subdivision as described above. Level four also ensures that the overall block of information (the total message) is received intact and asks for retransmission if message content errors are detected.

The session level (5) controls the specifics of a particular "conversation" between two network nodes. Notice that levels 1-4 simply deal with the accurate transport of information from one point to another within the network. They do not control what actually occurs during the time of connection, or session. Level five deals with issues such as half or full duplex, who will transmit first, and also recovering the connection should it be broken for some reason. It may even deal with automatic recovery of the connection at a later, predefined time. The session layer tells level four which node is desired for connection, and level four sets up the network transport.

The presentation layer (6) establishes the operations performed on the bit stream once it is properly received, or properly orients the data for transmission. In other words, level six controls how the information is presented to the receiving user. Encryption is a common level-six activity. Assume that the bit stream is rearranged in such a way that receiving the bit stream without understanding the rearranged pattern will only yield garbage. This is called encryption. Once this bit stream is received, level five passes the encrypted bit stream to level six which then rearranges the bits into their proper pattern. Level six also handles formatting of information for proper display on the specific data terminal in use.

The application layer (7) controls the final outcome of the entire process. The successful completion of the level-seven activity is the net reward for the user. Typical level-seven applications are file transfers from one device to another and electronic mail. Notice that the ultimate goal is to send a message between two points, but a careful definition of the underlying six layers is needed to provide the required network connection and ensure the information is transferred properly.

Systems Networking Architecture (SNA)

IBM introduced *Systems Network Architecture (SNA)* in 1974, and by 1990 there were over 36,000 SNA compatible networks installed. The high penetration of SNA warrants a quick look at some aspects of the standard. Many of IBM's competitors have installed SNA compatible networks but used their own equipment instead of IBM's. This is a classic example of how *de facto* market standards benefit an industry and the end user.

SNA divides the network into *physical units (PU)* and *logical units (LU)*. Terminals, printers, computers, and specific processor devices are examples of physical units. A person logged onto the network at a terminal is a logical unit. Notice that a physical unit (i.e., terminal) can support many different logical units (i.e., users). A *session* must be established before two logical units can communicate. Sessions can occur between users, devices, and computer programs.

Each SNA device has a specific 24-bit-long network address, and all devices typically communicate using IBM's Synchronous Data Link Control (SDLC) protocol, but other protocols are supported within SNA networks. IBM traditionally isolated itself from any other market protocols but has made substantial progress in opening up their networks and systems to other market standards such as X.25.

SNA also uses a seven-layer standard model, but the activities performed at each of the layers does not exactly match those defined in the preceding OSI discussion. For example, the OSI network (OSI 3) and transport (OSI 4) layers are combined into a single SNA path control layer (SNA 3), but the single OSI session layer (OSI 6) is divided into data flow (SNA 5) and transmission control (SNA 4). Care must be used when comparing OSI and SNA layers.

SNA networks are usually designed to maximize the network feeding into the centralized processing mainframe computer. Little intelligence exists in the network surrounding the mainframe. In the IBM world, the mainframe is where processing takes place. Some industry analysts contend that this firm IBM mainframe dominant perspective has caused IBM's market share erosion.

Module Fourteen
Modems: A Detailed Discussion

A modem used to be considered an exotic and expensive peripheral used by experienced "hackers" only. This perception was accurate when modems were temperamental and required a lot of "fiddling" to use effectively. Early modems were dumb devices requiring knowledgeable users to make them work. The explosion in *bulletin board systems (BBS)*, *electronic mail*, and *on-line databases* coupled with advances in modem technology have improved modem performance and ease of use while reducing costs. A modem is now a valuable and easy-to-use addition to any personal computer system.

Today's modems are "smart" enough that even the most inexperienced novice can enjoy *telecomputing* (computing from one computer to another over telephone lines). In recent years, the smart modem market has grown by leaps and bounds and so has the number of inexpensive smart modems available to the PC user. As a result, the prospective modem buyer faces a bewildering array of features and options when making a purchase decision.

Deciding which modem is best for your needs requires an understanding of the various features and which options really enhance a modem's usefulness. This module examines the advantages and disadvantages of smart modem features.

What Are Smart Modems?

Smart modems, or intelligent modems, contain a microprocessor chip that is built into the unit itself. This processor performs high-level functions such as automatic dialing and answering normally associated with a smart modem. Furthermore, the built-in microprocessor also interprets commands from the user's computer to control the operation of the modem. For example, to dial, a user might type "ATDT5557777" which is interpreted by the modem as a command instruction (ATDT) followed by a telephone number. The modem microprocessor interprets this command, goes off-hook, and dials the 555-7777 number.

If the remote system answers with a modem, the receive (answer) modem transmits a carrier signal which is received by the sender (originate) modem which signals the user by displaying "CARRIER DETECTED" on his monitor.

Earlier "dumb" modems were controlled using separate wires in a cable between the computer and modem. Each wire had a specific control function which required a large number of lines and limited the number of commands. Commands to a smart modem, on the other hand, are sent along the same wires used for data transfer between computer and modem, transmit and receive.

Modems have two basic modes of operation: command and data transfer. Command mode is used to instruct the modem regarding the specific operations it is to perform, such as dialing and going on-hook. Data transfer mode is used for transmitting the actual binary bits that comprise the information to be transmitted.

The modem is instructed as to which character strings make up modem commands and which strings are informational data to be transmitted. A unique sequence of characters that is unlikely to occur in normal data transfers is used to change the modem from command mode to data modes of operation. This sequence of characters is called the *attention command*. When in the command mode (also called the local mode), the modem treats character strings as commands and attempts to perform them. When in the data mode, character strings are treated as data received from or sent to a remote system.

Smart Modem Features

When choosing a modem, look for one that is easy to connect to both your telephone and your computer and one that fits within your budget. Don't go out and spend hundreds of dollars until you have decided what you are going to do with a modem. There's absolutely no sense in buying a souped-up sports model if all you're ever going to do is drive it around the block on Sundays. Here are some things to look for.

Data Transfer Rate

Perhaps the biggest single decision in buying a modem is choosing the data transfer rate. The most common choices are 300, 1200, and 2400 bps, although there are special commercial grade modems that transmit at 4800 and 9600 bps speeds. These higher speed modems generally must be *matched*, meaning that both ends of the communication link must have the same modem type from the same vendor. This discussion will concentrate on the 2400 bps and lower modem types. Price is heavily dependent on transmission speed. Not surprisingly, you pay more for a higher speed.

Most 1200 bps modems are really 300/1200 bps modems. That is, the 1200 bps modem can transmit data at either rate so that you can use it to communicate with on-line databases and other services that limit you to 300 bps operation. At 1200 bps, data is transferred four times faster than at 300 bps. A 2400 bps modem is twice as fast as a 1200 bps model. It is difficult to find modems that only transmit at 300 bps. The most common modem available today is a 1200 bps model that also communicates at 300 bps. 2400 bps modems are rapidly becoming the industry standard. The cost of the higher speed nearly doubles between 1200 bps and 2400 bps.

If you can easily afford it, go with the higher speed — it offers you more flexibility in the long run. Remember that the higher speed is more efficient only when you send and receive large chunks of data at a time, such as a full-screen menu. If, however, you carry on an on-line conversation with someone through one of the "CB" simulator services so that you are continuously reading text as it scrolls across your monitor and responding with your own typed messages, then the advantage of the higher speed is lost. A less expensive modem would be quite satisfactory for this latter application.

The commercial modems that operate at 4800 bps, 9600 bps, and higher speeds may require specially conditioned, private (leased) telephone lines for reliable data transmission and usually contain some type of proprietary error correction protocol.

Connection to the Telephone

Acoustic couplers are early modems that are coupled acoustically to the telephone system. The user places a telephone handset into the cradle of the unit containing a microphone in one rubber cup and a speaker in the other cup. In this way data tones produced by the acoustic coupler are picked up by the telephone transmitter (the speaking end of the handset) and sent to a remote system. Data tones sent by the remote system are sensed by the modem (DCE) through the telephone receiver (the listening end of the handset) and converted into the proper binary bit streams, then sent to the local computer (DTE).

Acoustic Coupler

Acoustic couplers are useful when portability is important and a standard modular telephone connection is not available. They are easily connected to the telephone system for transmitting data where a direct connection is impossible, such as in a hotel room or when traveling. They are also used in conjunction with systems that use digital signalling between the telephone station set and the central communication system. Remember that telephone systems have traditionally been analog and a standard connection was enough.

The acoustic coupler method of connection is subject to noise interference and is therefore less reliable than direct-connect methods. Acoustic couplers were initially designed to work with round handsets, and many of the newer telephone handsets are square. It still does not work well to put a square peg into a round hole.

Direct-connect modems attach to the telephone system using a standard telephone company modular plug that fits into a number of standard jacks. A cable either plugs directly into a wall-mounted modular jack, entirely eliminating the telephone instrument, or plugs into both the wall jack and the telephone so that the phone is an integral part of the connection.

There are several different kinds of modular telephone jacks. The *RJ11C* is a four-wire modular jack commonly found in the home for use by residential and business telephone systems. The center two wires (green and red) are the tip and ring lines.

RJ12W, RJ12C, RJ13W, and RJ13C are other standard jacks of varying number of lines and different physical dimensions which are used for other applications such as multiple phone line systems. If your site is not equipped with modular phone jacks, the telephone company will install them for you or you can easily install them yourself. There are also adapters that convert nearly any type of telephone outlet into any form you may require.

 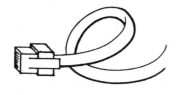

Modular Telephone Accessories

The direct-connect method electrically couples the modem to the telephone system, so the Federal Communications Commission (FCC) requires modem manufacturers to conform to standards that prevent possible damage to telephone company equipment. Only direct-connect modems that meet with FCC approval should be used, and the telephone company requests that modem users register with them before connecting to the phone system. Registration instructions are generally included with your purchase.

The telephone company generally bills higher rates for modem connected lines than for standard voice lines, even though the type of line to them is the same. Their justification for the increased price stems from the average duration of a voice call (3-5 minutes) versus a modem call (perhaps several hours).

Notice that each call uses central office switching equipment, but the voice call only uses it for a short period of time where the modem uses it for 20 to 60 times longer. The increased duration means that the central switching equipment associated with a single call is not available for use by 20 to 60 other customers, and the size of the switch must be increased to accommodate the increased traffic. The cost of this incremental equipment is then passed onto the consumer in the form of higher rates for modem lines.

Typical Modem Configuration

Originate/Answer Operating Modes

Some modems have a switch that allows you to change between originate and answer modes of operation. Most smart modems, however, provide you a command for changing the operating mode.

The reason for designating an originate mode and an answer mode has to do with the way modems communicate. Modems convert digital data to analog "tones" when communicating with another modem across a telephone line. In order for both modems to "talk" at the same time (as in full-duplex), each must use different tones; otherwise, it would be impossible for the modems to tell who said what. Modem standards are set up so that the modem that starts (originates) the communication uses a specific set of tones, while the modem that answers the call uses another.

For any communication between two modems, one must be in originate mode and the other must be in answer mode. Whenever you initiate the communication, such as when you dial into an information service, your modem must be in originate mode. If someone calls your modem to initiate a file transfer to your system, then his modem must be in originate mode and yours must be in answer mode.

Auto Dial/Auto Answer Capability

Some very inexpensive modems require you to manually dial the telephone number when making a data call. Others, however, are able to dial the number for you using the smart modem features discussed earlier.

Auto dial is the feature that gives a modem the capability to automatically dial telephone numbers. When coupled with the right software, auto dial simplifies the dialing procedure. From your PC keyboard, you merely type the proper command for dialing and the telephone number. The computer and modem do the rest, even telling when the call has been completed.

When shopping for an auto dial modem, keep in mind the kind of dialing method required by the telephone company equipment in your area. Older telephone company equipment uses pulse dialing, while newer systems use tone dialing. The phone companies are gradually replacing their old equipment with tone systems and will eventually become fully digital. If you are presently using a rotary dial telephone, then you are on a pulse dialing system. Push button phones can be either pulse or tone. If you have any doubts, a quick call to your local telephone company customer service representative will identify your type of service.

Some auto dial modems do pulse dialing only and some do tone dialing only, but most do both. To be safe, you should stick to those that do both. If you choose a modem that uses one or the other, make sure it is compatible with your local phone company. Another good reason for choosing a modem that has both capabilities is that you never know when you might move into an area where a different dialing method is used.

Auto answer is the feature that gives a modem the capability to automatically answer the telephone when it rings. Some auto answer modems can be set up to answer after a specified number of rings. Others can signal the computer that the phone is ringing without actually answering it.

This feature has limited usefulness because both modem and computer must be on and running the proper communications software when the incoming phone call is received. In most cases, you probably won't be leaving your computer running unattended for long periods. But when you know that you are going to be sending data to your system from a remote location or, likewise, requesting data from your system from a remote location, leaving your computer and modem running in auto answer mode definitely has advantages.

Most bulletin board systems use some form of auto answer modems to automatically accommodate the large number of incoming data calls.

Combined Voice and Data Modem Use

The ability to switch between voice and data provides a convenient way to use the same telephone line for voice and data communications. On some models, the flip of a switch quickly changes to one or the other mode when the need arises.

Suppose you want to send data between your computer and a remote computer using the telephone line. The initial setup requires some coordination between the two sites. Assuming that you have only one phone line, you normally do the coordination by talking to each other over the phone, and then, if your modem doesn't have voice/data switching capabilities, hanging up and calling back to start the data mode transfer.

The voice/data switching feature lets you do all of the above with only one telephone call. With the modem set to "voice mode," you call the remote site and verbally prepare for the data transfer. When everything is ready, instead of hanging up, you merely flip the modem switch to "data mode" and your computer starts communicating with the other.

Call Progress Detection

Call progress detection is used to follow the progress of a call after it has been dialed. It gives you the reassurance that your call has been placed and that the phone on the other end is either ringing or is busy. Most modems include a tiny built-in speaker over which you can hear your modem dial a number, the phone ring or busy signal from the other receiving phone, and the carrier signal once the other modem answers.

Some of the more sophisticated modems actually interpret the telephone signals and display on the computer monitor in words what happens, such as "RINGING" or "BUSY." Some modems even recognize when a human voice rather than another computer answers the phone and prompts you for instructions. This is a particularly useful feature if your modem lets you switch between voice and data. You could turn your computer and modem into an *attack dialer* or *power dialer* that retrieves telephone numbers from a computer data file and then automatically dials your voice calls and can redial a busy line until your call goes through.

Modem Switches and Indicators

Modem manufacturers differ widely in the kind and number of switches and indicators they put on their products. In general, switches are used to turn power on and off, change from data to voice mode, and to set up basic operating parameters. In the latter case, *DIP switches* (Dual In-line Package) located on the modem circuit board are set either "on" or "off" to select operating parameters or to enable or disable options. The instruction manual supplied with your modem shows you where the DIP switches are located, what each switch is used for, and how to set the switches so that the modem operates properly with your computer. DIP switches derive their name from the integrated circuit chip design that they resemble. They are a common type of switch used in most computer systems.

LED indicators (Light Emitting Diodes) are tiny lights, usually visible from the front of the modem, that allow you to tell at a glance whether power is on and whether the modem is on-line to a remote system. Their use varies between manufacturers. Some manufacturers don't use any at all. Table 14-1 describes the LED indicators used on Hayes Smartmodems which is the accepted industry standard.

Modem Ready (MR) is illuminated and remains illuminated whenever power to the Smartmodem is on. The remaining indicators operate only when power to the modem is on.

Terminal Ready (TR) is normally illuminated whenever the modem and computer are properly connected and the computer is on and ready to send or receive data. By changing a DIP switch behind the front panel, the Terminal Ready indicator will light up whenever the Smartmodem is on, regardless of whether the computer is also on.

Send Data (SD) blinks on and off when data is sent from the computer's serial port to the Smartmodem, such as when sending the Smartmodem a command or transmitting data to a remote system.

Receive Data (RD) works like Send Data only in the opposite direction. Whenever data is received from a remote system, the Receive Data indicator blinks on and off.

Off Hook (OH) indicates when the Smartmodem has "picked up" the telephone receiver. It is lit whenever the Smartmodem is using the telephone line and is off otherwise.

Carrier Detect (CD) shows when the Smartmodem has established a connection with another modem and has detected its carrier signal. When the Smartmodem recognizes a carrier signal, the Carrier Detect indicator lights and remains lit until the remote modem hangs up the telephone.

Auto Answer (AA) shows whether the Smartmodem is in the auto answer mode. This mode is set by a Smartmodem command or by a DIP switch setting behind the indicator panel. The Auto Answer indicator is lit when the Smartmodem is in auto answer mode. Each time the telephone rings, the light blinks off, then on again until, after a specified number of rings, the Smartmodem answers.

High Speed (HS) is another common indicator which shows that the modem is operating in its higher bps transmission mode versus the slower mode.

When the Smartmodem is not in the auto answer mode, the Auto Answer indicator is off. Then when the telephone rings, the Auto Answer indicator lights during each ring to let you know that there is an incoming call.

Table 14-1 Typical Smart Modem LED Indicators

Indicator	Description
Modem Ready (MR)	On when modem is turned on
Terminal Ready (TR)	On when computer is ready to send or receive data
Send Data (SD)	Flashes when data is sent to the modem by the local computer

Receive Data (RD)	Flashes when data is being received from a remote modem
Off Hook (OH)	On when the modem has "picked up" the telephone line to dial a number and remains on until the modem "hangs up" the phone
Carrier Detect (CD)	On when the modem has set up a telephone connection to, and has received a carrier signal from, a remote modem.
Auto Answer Mode (AA)	On when the auto answer feature is enabled.
High Speed (HS)	Used to indicate higher bps transmission mode operation.

Internal and External Modem Types

Modems are either *external modems* that attach to the computer through a standard cable connected to the serial interface port (RS-232 port) of any computer, or are made to fit directly into a computer bus slot and are called internal modems. An external modem is portable between a number of different computers and only requires a serial port and a cable for attachment.

An internal modem is usually around $100 less expensive and consumes less desk top work space, but it is attached to its computer and not easily moved from one machine to another. Should you decide to buy a different computer, the internal modem needs to be transferred to the new machine. Furthermore, an internal modem takes up a bus slot in the computer, thus limiting the number of future accessories that you can add to the system.

Pre-Purchase Considerations

Buying a modem can be a confusing experience, but with a little preparation you can make a wise choice. In this module we have discussed the major features and what each can do for you. But before you make a decision, you need to determine how you will use the modem.

If you will be a casual telecomputer, only occasionally checking up on your stocks through the Dow Jones News/Retrieval service or reading and leaving messages on a local or national bulletin board, then you don't need to spend a lot of money on a high-speed, full-featured modem. You should be able to get a reasonable 2400 bps smart modem for under $200. For under $100, there are several fine modems available which are not as capable, but serviceable nonetheless.

For frequent telecommunications use, you should buy the best you can afford. A 2400 bps modem with lots of time-saving features will save you some future frustration. The 9600 bps modems (V.32 compatible) have dropped in price to become affordable for most communication intensive modem applications.

Look for "Hayes-compatible" modems since Hayes is the *de facto* personal computer modem industry standard. Hayes developed a modem command set that allows software to deliver communication instructions instead of requiring that the user continually set DIP switches. This feature becomes important when considering the software used to instruct the modem.

There are many excellent Hayes compatible communication software packages on the market that relieve the user of most lower level modem commands. These software packages translate the user commands into the proper Hayes compatible commands and make the modem perform the functions you need. The modem type is important but using the proper software is critical to productive and convenient modem use.

Many of the newer integrated operating systems such as Windows 3.0 include a communication software program that can speak to your modem and not require you to learn a new language. If you are a sharp shopper, you should be able to find a good modem and communication software combination for under $300.

If you are going to start out casually but plan to become a heavy user and are on a tight budget, you should consider buying a less expensive modem now and plan to replace it later as the need and your wallet warrant. Regardless of which modem you buy, first determine what capabilities you need, then try it out before you buy.

Modem Types and Accepted Standards

There are many manufacturers of modems offering a wide range of features, standards (Bell 103,212,etc.), and prices from which you can choose. Software suppliers and communications programs are even more abundant. It is easy to get confused when faced with so many choices, especially when the choices change so rapidly.

Modem manufacturers and software suppliers are continually improving their products. As the technology improves you will be able to buy better or faster products at a lower price.

If you can wait six months or even a year to buy a modem, for example, you'll get more for your money. A smart 2400 bps modem that today costs between $150 and $300 should sell for between $49 and $150 a year from now. Of course, two years from now, the same modem will cost even less. You can carry this line of thinking too far, however. Modems get cheaper every year, but they will never be free! So if you are ready to buy now, do it and don't worry too much about what you can get tomorrow.

9,600 bps modems appear to be the next vanguard in commercially available modem products. Of particular interest at the 9,600 bps speed is compatibility with other modems operating at the same speed. Modem manufacturers have traditionally used their own proprietary information encoding schemes to increase bit transfer rates. This worked well when the same modems were on each side of the link. When the two modems were different, there were problems.

The days of 9,600 bps modems being proprietary appear to be over. The 9,600 bps modem manufacturers now provide products that are compatible with the V.32 standard, which implies that modems from two different vendors should communicate well at 9,600 bps.

The venders are also promoting V.42bis compatibility which allows them to encode bits on the modem transmission and ideally communicate at up to 38,400 bps on a dial-up line. Once again, the standard does not ensure that modems from different vendors will communicate with each other. There is a four times speed benefit derived from running at 9,600 bps versus 2,400 bps. 38,400 is that much more exciting, but at a higher cost.

A word is due here regarding the relationship between the CCITT standards and their relevance to the end user. The Bell 103 standard covers transmission at 300 baud (BPS). 1200 baud is covered by the Bell 201A standard. 2400 baud is covered by the CCITT V.22 standard. V.32 and V.32bis cover the 9,600 baud and 14,400+ baud transmission rates, respectively.

These standards only cover the baud rates of the transmission and do not necessarily specify the method of encoding bit information or detecting/correcting errors. Earlier accepted standards for error detection and data encoding were the Microcom MNP-4 and MNP-5 standards. Using these techniques in conjunction with a particular modem could double the data transmission rate.

The newer CCITT standards for error detection and data encoding are V.42 and V.42bis, respectively. This combination provides up to a tripling of data transmission rates.

Notice that it is possible to run a 2400 modem and use the V.42/ V.42bis error detection and data encoding schemes to increase data transmission speed. Understanding that some of the standards deal with baud rates (the number of signal changes in a second) while others deal with error detection and data encoding assists greatly in understanding contemporary modem equipment.

What follows is a small sampling of available products. It is by no means complete, nor is it intended to be. There are several fine books on the market that present exhaustive surveys of current modem and communications software offerings. The following reviews are included only to provide a glimpse into the prices and features available. Features range from those found on the simplest modems and communications programs all the way up to "fully loaded" modems and programs.

The modem manufacturers provide a variety of modems that comply with the *de facto* industry standards and generally provide proprietary modems for very high speed communication. Many other manufacturers build modems to be "Hayes-compatible."

Hayes Computer Products

The Hayes Smartmodem family includes a variety of freestanding as well as internal modems. Information on these products is readily available at any computer store.

Hayes is currently promoting its recently announced Optima 96 external modem which sells for around $450 including their Smartcom EZ software. The product provides data transmission speeds from 300 bps (CCITT V.21 of Bell 103 compatible) up to 9,600 bps (CCITT V.32 compatible). 1,200 bps, 2,400 bps, 4,800 bps speeds are also provided in the same unit. It connects to the microcomputer through a standard RS-232-C port. Naturally, the product supports the Hayes standard modem interface language.

Smartmodem OPTIMA 9600, a high-speed, inexpensive, V.32 modem.

U.S. Robotics, Inc.

Founded in 1976, U.S. Robotics is a marketer and manufacturer of data communications hardware and software. The company's roots are as a supplier to companies such as Apple and Zenith for sale by them under their respective label. Today U.S. Robotics is a full product line modem equipment supplier under its own name.

Its product line includes the Courier commercial model modem, the Sportster line designed for small business or home use, the WorldPort modem designed for portable use, and modem management software systems.

Courier 2400

Manufacturer	U.S. Robotics
Introduction Date: 1985	
Standard:	Bell 103, 212A, and CCITT V.22 compatible
Operation:	300/1200/2400 bps
Size:	1.33" x 6.375" x 10.25"
Computer Interface:	Connects to standard RS-232 serial interface port
Telephone Interface:	Direct connect RJ-11
List Price:	$499
Features:	

- "Fallback to 1200 bps" in originate mode
- Auto-dial/Auto-answer
- Automatic speed selection in answer mode

- Call duration reporting
- Call progress detection
- Built-in speaker with volume control
- LED status indicator front panel

This product was introduced in 1985.

The Courier 2400 is a fully Hayes-compatible, freestanding modem that operates at 2400, 1200, and 300 bits per second. It may be used with any computer or ASCII terminal equipped with an RS-232 serial interface port.

In addition to the Hayes command set, the Courier 2400 offers several unique functions and commands for enhanced ease of use and efficiency. The unit records and stores the duration of calls in hours, minutes, and seconds and allows you to display this information on your screen or to keep a printed log of your calls.

The call progress detection feature shows (on your terminal or computer screen) the status of calls in progress, indicating a connection, a busy signal, ringing, or a dial tone. The modem automatically disconnects upon reaching a voice line or a busy signal. The current operating status of the modem, such as communications parameters and result code messages, can also be displayed.

The commands for instructing the modem to perform these operations are described in a detailed user's manual, on a handy reference card, and on the underside of the modem enclosure.

Other useful features include a built-in speaker with volume control for monitoring the telephone line (not really necessary with the call progress detection feature), diagnostic self-test, externally accessible option switches, and a 9-function LED display panel.

The Courier product line also includes 1200 baud ($349), 2400 V.42bis ($599), V.32 bis ($995), and computer rack mounted models costing over $1,000.

The U.S. Robotics Sportster product line offers similar basic communication features, but at a lower price. Sportsters come in both internal and external models. Products range from the Sportster 1200/PC ($139), 2400 models ($179 to $229 w/V.42 bis), and V.32 compatible ($649).

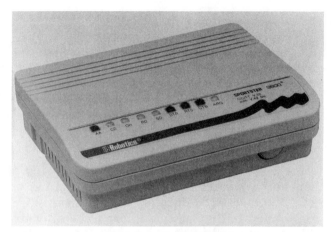

U.S. Robotics Sportster 9600

The WorldPort product line was obtained in the 1991 acquisition by U.S. Robotics of Touchbase Systems, Inc. of Northport, N.Y. The WorldPort portable modems are designed for use with notebook and laptop computers. They are battery operated and do not need an AC outlet. In addition, the WorldPort products also operate with acoustic couplers but only at 1200 bps. Battery life is expected from 1.5 hours (9600 bps) to 10 hours (1200 bps) and the unit automatically turns itself on and off.

The WorldPort product line includes several 2400 baud units with varying data encoding protocols which yield higher bit transfer rates. Product comes in either internal or external configurations, and prices range from $299 to $499. The WorldPort 9600 is an external V.32 compatible modem and sells for $699.

The WorldPort 9600, a fully portable 9600 bps V.32 modem with MNP 4 error control and MNP 5 data compression.

Everex Systems, Inc.

Everex is a company that produces a complete line of computers and associated peripheral devices. The company went through severe financial problems in 1991 and restructured its entire upper management team. Certain areas of the company have been scaled back and others eliminated completely. The good news about Everex is that they have a high degree of customer satisfaction, and their products are available through almost every retail location and easily purchased. Caution is recommended because the company is in flux.

The product line is relatively simple. It consists of the Evercom 24 and 24+ model, the EverFax 24/96 (fax modem), the Evercom 96+ (V.32 with V.42 capability), and the portable 24/96 Carrier modem.

Evercom 24 and 24+ modems come in external and internal styles. External units have an "E" suffix. The speed of both modems is 2400 bps, but the 24+ also supports MNP Class 5 data encoding to increase bit transfer rates. Pricing is $129 (24), $269 (24E), $249 (24+), and $299 (24E+). Actual retail prices for these units are less expensive if you shop around.

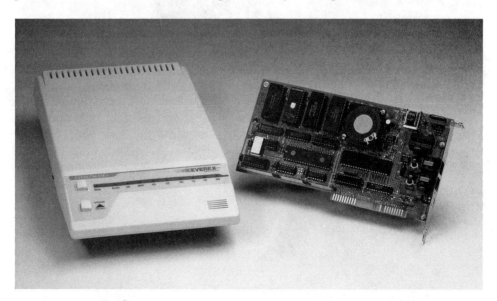

Everex EVERCOM 24+ & 24E+

The EverFax 24/96 comes in both internal ($399) and external ($499) models. This unit allows the computer to transmit data at 2400 bps over standard communication links but also allows for faxing of information at 9600 bps for fax machine compatibility.

The Carrier 24/96 ($399) external modem provides the same capability as the EverFax 24/96 except in a portable style. This unit connects to the laptop/notebook computer on one side and the telephone line on the other. This fax feature is becoming more important as mobility increases along with fax machine use. It allows the PC to send information, such as ASCII text files, to a fax machine. Fax communication software is required in addition to the fax modem.

There is also a standard Carrier 24 model which transmits at 2400 bps and costs $299. Both Carrier models support battery or AC power.

Everex Carrier 24/96

Getting On-Line

Beware the communication hardware and software sales demonstration. It all looked so easy when the salesman was demonstrating everything in the store. But now you are the owner of this equipment and it is up to you to put it together and make it work. There was a time when this was the most frustrating part of any computer system purchase. The instructions packed with the equipment were often confusing, perplexing, and so vague that you would soon be cursing Alexander Graham Bell and wondering why nothing seemed to work.

Fortunately, the situation is improving as more "user friendly" products that use the same communication standards appear on the scene. Connecting a modem, loading the software, and making the first call can be done quickly if you take the time to do a little preparation first.

It is always a good idea to read the vendor's instruction manual before doing anything, but in today's hectic world it is hard to sit down and read a 100+ page manual. One way around this problem is to understand in advance the basic steps that are required to properly connect a communication system.

Connecting the Modem and the Computer

There are two basic ways that a modem connects to the computer. An internal modem plugs into a bus slot inside the computer and an external modem connects to the computer using a cable.

Internal modem installation can be complex and computer configuration specific, so it is not practical to give a general procedure for installing board modems. Follow the instructions that come with the unit.

Some personal computer manufacturers design and build external modems (or plug-on modules) for their systems and supply the proper cables for connecting them to the computer. All you have to do is plug the cable into the proper port in the side or back of your computer.

RS-232 Serial Interface

The RS-232C serial interface is the standard interface used for data communications between computers and modems. It is an industry standard reached by agreement among the Bell Telephone Companies, the Electronic Industries Association (EIA), and various interested hardware manufacturers. The "C" represents one revision of the standard and is usually dropped in normal usage.

The RS-232 Cable

Problems occasionally arise when the modem is connected to a computer using a standard RS-232 cable. Usually the cable is not supplied as part of the modem and you have to buy it separately. It helps to know how many and which of the 25 signals in the DB-25 connector are used by your computer, your modem, and your communications software.

See Module Eight for more information on RS-232 Connection.

Modem Setup Options

Option switches establish certain default operating parameters whenever your modem is first turned on. If you own a smart modem, then many of these operating parameters can be overridden by commands to the modem once power is turned on.

Configuring the Hayes Smartmodem

All modems come with option switches that are either directly accessible or accessed after a panel is removed. There is usually a DIP switch pack containing eight configuration switches numbered from 1 to 8. Each switch controls a different option.

Hayes Smartmodem Configuration Switches

Switch Number	Default	Function
1	Down	Turn on DTR signal to enable the Smartmodem.
2	Up	Turn on English word result codes.
3	Down	Send result codes to computer or terminal.
4	Up	Turn on echo of Smartmodem commands.
5	Down	Turn off auto-answer feature.
6	Down	Turn on carrier detect signal.
7	Up	Configure Smartmodem for RJ11 (single line) modular telephone jack.
8	Up or Down	Switch 8 is not used.

Switch 1 controls the data terminal ready (DTR) signal supplied to the Smartmodem by your computer. When switch 1 is in the UP position, the Smartmodem responds to the DTR signal given by your computer and communications software. This allows you to hang up the phone or to ignore (not answer) an incoming call by giving a command.

If your computer or communications software cannot control the DTR signal, then by setting switch 1 DOWN, you tell the Smartmodem to ignore the DTR signal given by your computer and assume that your computer is always ready. Check the instruction manuals supplied with your computer and communications software. If the manuals indicate that you can control DTR, then set switch 1 UP.

Switch 2 controls the way the Smartmodem acknowledges results of commands that you have given. When switch 2 is in the UP position, the Smartmodem gives results back as English words that describe what happened. When switch 2 is in the DOWN position, the results are given as numbers.

Switch 3 turns the result code option on or off. When switch 3 is in the UP position, the Smartmodem does not send results of command actions back to the computer regardless of the position of switch 2. In the DOWN position, switch 3 causes the Smartmodem to send either English word or numeric results depending on the position of switch 2.

Switch 4 tells the Smartmodem that you want it to echo commands back to your computer screen so that you can see what you typed. UP turns echo on; DOWN turns it off.

Switch 5 controls the Smartmodem's auto-answer feature. When switch 5 is in the UP position, the Smartmodem automatically answers the telephone on the first ring. If you do not want the Smartmodem to answer the telephone, then switch 5 must be set in the DOWN position.

Switch 6 controls the carrier detect signal sent to your computer by the Smartmodem. When in the UP position, switch 6 causes the Smartmodem to tell your computer when a communications link has been established between the Smartmodem and another system. If switch 6 is put in the DOWN position, then the Smartmodem assumes the carrier is always present.

Switch 7 tells the Smartmodem what kind of telephone jack the modem is connected to. The UP position is for a typical single-line household telephone that uses an RJ11 jack. The DOWN position is for multiline telephone systems that use RJ12 or RJ13 jacks such as those found in office buildings.

Switch 8 is a spare switch that is not used. Therefore, it can be set in either position without altering the operation of the Smartmodem.

Connecting the Modem to the Telephone Line

Connecting the modem to the telephone line is a simple procedure. In the case of an acoustic coupler there is no permanent connection at all. Each time you use the unit, you fit the telephone handset snugly into the coupler's specially designed rubber cups. There is usually a notation or an arrow on the coupler that shows you the correct way to insert the handset. The connection to the telephone lasts only as long as you are communicating. When you finish, you remove the handset from the rubber cups and hang up the telephone.

Direct-connect modems are usually permanently (or at least semipermanently) connected to the telephone line. This is done in one of two ways.

On some modems there is a single jack for connecting the modem to a modular telethon wall jack using a cable like that used for plugging a common telephone into the wall jack. The cable is usually supplied with the modem. If it is not, you can find modular telephone cables of varying lengths at a local hardware store. Using this method of connection, the modem takes the place of the telephone instrument.

The disadvantage to this arrangement is that it dedicates the wall jack to data communications only. If you want to use the jack for voice communications, you must first unplug the modem and them plug in a telephone. Modems connected in this manner must have auto-dial capability so that you can dial the telephone number through your communications system. A dual RJ11 plug adapter is recommended because it allows connection of both the telephone and the modem into the same outlet.

Federal Communications Commission Restrictions

The Federal Communications Commission (FCC) requires that you observe a few simple rules when using your modem on the public telephone network.

You must call the local telephone company and give them your modem's FCC registration number (found on the unit) before connecting it to the telephone line. The telephone company also requires the telephone number the modem is being connected to and the *ringer equivalence* of the unit (also found on the unit).

The FCC also requires that the manufacturer of your modem make any necessary repairs to the unit that are required to maintain valid FCC registration.

Module Fifteen
Communications Software and Electronic Mail Services

As the personal computer becomes more commonplace, the terminal and modem will replace pencil and paper as the primary means for nonverbal communications. Electronic communication has already become a major part of today's automated offices. The expected increase in mobile computer systems (i.e., notebooks and laptops) will increase the demand for nationally available electronic mail and file transfer services that are not tied to a specific geographic location.

The rapid adoption of computer communications by general commercial markets is mainly due to the improvements in communications software. The packages are easier to operate and the end users derive benefits from use in a short period of time. The on-line services have also heavily stressed ease of use, and the payback to them is rapid increases in subscribers.

Most of the communication packages provide the same basic capabilities but vary widely in the way they interact with the user. The best way to determine which package is best for your needs is to determine the level of data communication expertise you bring to the transaction along with how often and with whom you plan to use it.

Communications Software Features

Communication software packages provide automation and intelligence to the operation of your personal computer communications system. A look at some of the features that a communication program offers will help you choose from the many programs that are available. Some basic features to consider include the following:

- Command-Driven or Menu-Driven Operation
- Terminal Emulation
- Data Capture
- Help Files

Command-Driven or Menu-Driven Operation

The way you interact with a communications program falls into two categories: *command-driven* or *menu-driven*. Command-driven programs require you to type short command words that tell the program to perform specific actions. Some commands also require you to type parameters that affect the way the action is performed. Menu-driven programs require you to pick an action using a simple keystroke or two from a menu of actions presented on your computer screen.

Of the two, menu-driven operation is easier to use for those who are new users and not familiar with program operation. Command-driven operation, however, is faster and more powerful once you have learned the operation of all the commands. A good communications program combines both modes of operation. That way, you can use the menus while you are learning the system, then switch to the commands when you are comfortable with them.

Terminal Emulation

Many communications programs allow your computer to emulate a variety of popular smart terminals. This feature is useful if you are using your personal computer communications system to communicate with various mainframe computers that expect your system to conform to specific terminal formats. Attempting communication with an incompatible terminal type can meet with data garbage being streamed across your data screen.

Some typical terminals emulated include ADDS Viewpoint, Data General D200, Data Point 3601, DEC VT-100, Hazeltine 1400, HP 2622A, as well as terminals from Honeywell, IBM, Lear-Siegler, and Televideo.

Data Capture

Data capture is the feature that allows information exchanged during interactive file transfers to be stored temporarily in RAM, then on disk so that you can review it later. This operation can be automatic, or it can be initiated by command.

File Transfer

Transferring files from one PC to another or between a PC and a central computer is a major operational component of communication software. There are many different file transfer protocols in common use today, and it is important that the devices on each end of the connection are communicating using the same protocol.

The basic differences between the protocols is their ability to detect and correct errors and what type of data they are designed to transfer.

Each communications vendor provides its version of the best transfer protocol, but it is probably proprietary to that vendor. The methods most commonly accepted for universal transfer between PC devices is *XMODEM*. Variations of XMODEM are *YMODEM*, which allows for transfer of many files at once, and *ZMODEM*, which provides fatal communication disruption recovery. If the communication link should go down before the communication is over, this protocol allows the transfer to start where it left off instead of from the beginning. It also verifies that a redundant file is not transferred from one system to another, which increases overall transmission efficiency.

KERMIT, named after the frog, was designed by Columbia University and is used primarily for transfer between different types of computers. KERMIT uses a packet transfer scheme and gives the user a great deal of flexibility over how the information is packetized and sent. The binary form of transfer is used for sending program files (i.e., xxxx.EXE) and the text mode is used for ASCII text files.

Help Files

Help files are on-line aids that remind you when and how to do particular communications functions. These prompts are displayed on the computer screen and provide helpful information about program operation. A program can often be run simply by reading the information shown on the screen and following the instructions.

Some help features merely show a complete list of all commands and parameters the program uses. After you are familiar with the operation of the program, this list is probably enough to jog your memory for the command you want. Other help facilities are more sophisticated. They show only those commands that are available to you in a particular situation, such as when you are in the middle of a file transfer, and ignore those that do not apply. This is called *context sensitive* help.

Communications Programs

Modems are expensive paperweights without the communication software that makes them work. The files transfer or interactive bulletin board type of communication is the ultimate goal of a modem, and the communication software makes that process enjoyable and productive. While it is important to use a compatible modem, it is critical to use communication software that is well designed for your needs.

The software packages listed here are the most commonly used in the industry and give a good introduction to the basic features of effective communication software.

Crosstalk Mk.4, Version 2.0

Supplier: DCA
1000 Alderman Drive
Alpharetta, GA 30202-4199
(800) 348-DCA1

Computers:	Variety of IBM compatible personal computers
Operating System:	PC DOS of MS-DOS version 2.0 or newer, Windows or DESQview and other windowing programs
Communication Devices:	Hayes, Intel, U.S. Robotics, and other Hayes compatible modems
Speed:	300 to 115,200 bps
Street Price:	$140 (Crosstalk Mk.4, Version 2.0)
	$122 (Crosstalk for Windows Version 1.2)
	$28 (Crosstalk Communicator)

Crosstalk is one of the pioneers in microcomputer communications software. Almost every mid-1980s PC with communications capability ran a copy of Crosstalk.

Crosstalk Mk.4 is a data communications program that supports most intelligent modems. It uses a command language called Crosstalk Application Script Language (CASL) to perform operations that include setting up operating modes and parameters, dialing telephone numbers, sending and receiving data, and terminating (hanging up) calls.

CASL is a full programming language with over 350 commands, so there is a lot of flexibility included with this feature. Unfortunately, someone must learn the new programming language to effectively use CASL's power for customizing applications. If you have the time to learn it, CASL can add a lot of functionality to your system. CASL allows users to create customized scripts and user interfaces that automate the communication process for the end user. This customized scripting feature is particularly attractive in environments where the users are non-computer literate and a technical staff can support them with CASL applications.

Terminal emulation is provided for 21 popular terminals including IBM 3101, DEC VT100, VT102, VT220, TeleVideo 910, 920, 925, and 950, ADDS Viewpoint, Hazeltine Espirit III, and others. Since DCA also makes the IRMA 327x terminal emulation cards, the system also supports IBM 3270 communications when used in conjunction with the IRMA products.

File transfer protocols are a critical component of any communication software. Crosstalk Mk.4 supports 11 file-transfer protocols including KERMIT, XMODEM, YMODEM, ZMODEM, and others.

On-line help is just a keystroke away. By typing Alt-H, you can look at a list of all Crosstalk commands that relate to the current operation. Information about specific commands, including CASL commands, is available by highlighting with a cursor or pressing Ctrl-Page Up.

The package comes already configured to communicate with several information and electronic mail services but allows you to add bulletin boards, databases, and other services of your own choosing.

Crosstalk Communicator is a stripped down version of Crosstalk Mk.4. The speed is the same along with the basic system requirements. The major difference is the number of terminals supported (13 instead of 21), the number of files transfer modes (8 instead of 11), and the overall ease of use. This package is designed for the casual user or executive that needs to perform basic communication functions such as electronic mail or basic file transfers. Predefined scripts for the most commonly used information services are included to make it easier for the user to get up and running.

On-line help is provided along with a subset of the CASL software. More sophisticated scripts created with Mk.4 CASL can still be run on the Crosstalk Communicator software, which is ideal for larger corporations that have an internal MIS department that does development for field personnel. The street price of $28 makes Crosstalk Communicator a good starting point for people wanting to test the communication software waters.

Procomm Plus

Supplier: DATASTORM TECHNOLOGIES
P.O. Box 1471
Columbia, MO 65204
(314) 443-3282

Computers:	Variety of IBM compatible personal computers
Operating System:	PC DOS of MS-DOS version 2.0 or newer, Windows or DESQview (see notes below)
Communication Devices:	Virtually any modem, Hayes-compatible or not, external, internal, and at any speed
Speed:	300 to 115,200 bps
Street Price:	$69 (Version 2.01)

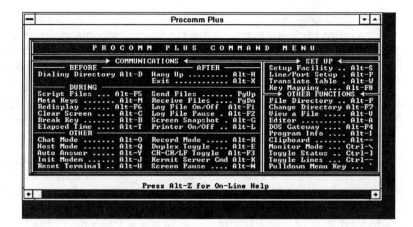

Procomm is another pioneer in microcomputer communications software. It started out as a shareware product in the mid-1980s and is now marketed by Datastorm. It is also in wide use as both the shareware and Datastorm supported product.

Procomm contends that it supports "virtually any modem."

It uses its own command language called ASPECT to allow scripting of user operations that include setting up operating modes and parameters, dialing telephone numbers, sending and receiving data, and terminating (hanging up) calls. Their example of a useful script file is to have your computer automatically call a particular information service during the evening while you are away from the office and even print it on your printer. The same cautions regarding the time involved with learning a new programming language apply here as they did with Crosstalk's CASL.

Procomm Plus also allows for host mode connection to a PC from a remote site. For example, assume that your office-based PC is configured as a host and you carry your laptop with you when you travel. You arrive in a different city and realize that you forgot an important file back on your office PC. Host mode allows you to access your office PC and download the file to your laptop without anyone's assistance on the office side.

Password security is provided to keep unauthorized persons from logging onto your system, but serious security issues are raised by leaving your PC unattended and available for hackers to access.

Terminal emulation is provided for 33 popular terminals including IBM 3101, DEC VT102, VT220, TeleVideo 900 Series, ADDS 60 and 90, Heath/Zenith 19, Wyse 100, and others. Procomm also provides 132-column operation to allow viewing of more data on the screen.

File transfer protocols are a critical component of any communication software. Procomm Plus supports 15 file-transfer protocols including KERMIT, XMODEM, YMODEM, ZMODEM, and others. In addition, Procomm Plus allows for definition of three external protocols that are not covered in the standard ones provided. These are user definable.

On-line help is just a keystroke away. By typing Alt-Z, you can look at a list of the Procomm Plus commands that relate to the current operation.

Procomm Plus may be run with Windows or DESQview multitasking systems, but some special configuration issues must be addressed when running with Windows 3.0. Procomm Plus can only be run in a window in the 386 enhanced mode of Windows. It can only be run in full-screen mode in Real or Standard Windows operation mode. It is also recommended that the "background" box on the PIF file be set to allow Procomm Plus to reside in memory if another application is started. This is helpful because it allows the user to perform other operations while Procomm Plus performs a file transfer in the background.

Windows 3.0 Terminal Option

Microsoft Windows 3.0 provides a terminal operation as one of the standard accessories. This is a very basic communication facility and not on a par with Crosstalk Mk.4 or Procomm Plus. It is briefly mentioned here because of the wide popularity of Windows 3.0, and many of the readers may already have Windows 3.0 on their system.

Windows divides the file world into text and binary files and provides send and receive transmission facilities for both. Selecting the Text Transfer option under the Settings menu initiates the steps to performing a text file transfer. Selecting Binary Transfers from the Settings menu brings up an option for transfer in KERMIT or XMODEM protocol form.

Windows also provides a selection between three terminal emulation types: TTY (Generic), DEC VT-100 (ANSI), and DEC VT-52. The default is VT-100 unless set otherwise by the user.

Windows does allow the user to define specific numbers, configurations, and transfer modes for specific communication tasks. These configurations can then be stored under that party's name and recalled at a later time. This feature minimizes the amount of setup on the user's part when he wants to perform the same function again later.

Windows 3.0 Terminal is functional on a basic level, and it is a good way to get acquainted with communications software. The major downside is the poor documentation and lack of clear explanation provided in the manual. If you try this and get frustrated, purchase Procomm Plus or Crosstalk and take advantage of their expertise and clear documentation.

pcAnywhere IV

A brief note is due a new technology offered by Symantec's DMA company as *pcAnywhere IV*. This software package provides some limited communication capabilities similar to those mentioned in the Crosstalk and Procomm sections, such as VT-220 terminal emulation and XMODEM file transfer support. This software is unique in that it allows a remote user to interact with a host PC as though the remote were actually running the host PC software. In other words, a remote computer user in Chicago that is connected using pcAnywhere IV to a host computer located in Dallas can see everything that the Dallas user sees on his screen. The opportunities for communication that this capability presents are tremendous.

For example, user training can be done over the telephone. A remote trainer can watch the actions of the student over the pcAnywhere IV link and verbally instruct them over a standard telephone line. Software can be downloaded, configured, and installed remotely and may not even require a visit by the software developer. Indeed, the end user may never receive a disk-based copy of the software. It was delivered and installed over the telephone line.

The product's most current version at the time of this writing is 4.01 and its street price is $125. The price is modest and certainly within the range of users who may need this type of capability. This technology may even be the norm in the next decade.

Installing Communication Software

The final step in putting your communications system together is installing the communications software. The procedure for doing this varies from communications package to communications package. For some packages you need only to make a working copy of the disk before loading and running the software. Other packages require you to run a configuration program that customizes the software for your particular computer. The configuration program generally presents series of questions or menus about special features of your equipment, such as the hardware address of your RS-232 port (found in the user's manual), and uses your answers or selections to modify the software to take full advantage of your hardware.

Look for an "install" of "setup" program on the communication software disks. Simply run these programs, and the rest is question and answer.

Bulletin Board Services

A bulletin board system (BBS) is an electronic nerve center, collecting and organizing messages that are exchanged among its users. In addition, many bulletin boards provide public domain software libraries, magazines, news, and stock market information. Users often form discount purchasing clubs or use the service to discuss topics ranging from the latest computer hardware and software to such diverse topics as politics, psychology, health, and education.

There are more than 1000 public bulletin boards operating in the United States. These are constantly changing as old boards cease operation and new ones spring up to take their places. Most users know each other only through their electronic communications, but, like CB radio operators, they have become a relatively large subculture having their own manners, ethics, and jargon. A bulletin board is an excellent source of friendly advice and technical assistance as users share information and personal experience.

Some hardware and software vendors now distribute their software upgrades over bulletin board systems like those provided by CompuServe. This procedure is beneficial to both the end user and the vendor because software is available at the user's discretion and the vendors have a more uniform distribution of software within their user base, which makes supporting that base easier and less expensive.

How a Bulletin Board System Works

A public bulletin board system is usually a one-person operation. The system operator, called the *sysop* by users, usually runs the board as a hobby, charging little or nothing to callers for using the service. A BBS is composed of a personal computer, modem, and bulletin board program. Bulletin board programs are similar to communications programs. They perform many of the same functions; however, the bulletin board program also controls user access to the system, organizes incoming messages, and responds to user commands for information. The entire system can be put together for less than $3000.

Many bulletin boards use menus similar to those found on the information utilities. When you call the board, it displays a menu of commands for performing specific functions. Typical functions include user assistance (help), message exchange (read or reply), and software library access (download). By choosing one of the menu items, you tell the BBS what you want to do.

Some bulletin boards do not use menus, requiring the user to type simple commands instead. For example, to scan the current messages on the board, you type **S**. This displays a summary of message numbers and topics. After you have found a topic of interest, you type **R** to read the message. A message usually begins with a title, the date it was posted, who sent it, and in some cases, to whom it was sent. This is followed by the text of the message. To enter a message, you type **E**. This command activates the editor and lets you compose a message to be posted for others to read. Messages are usually removed from the bulletin board by typing a delete command such as **K** (kill).

Nearly all bulletin boards provide a "help" feature to guide new users in the operation of the board. Help commands explain the general features of the system as well as the meaning of each command.

How to Access a Bulletin Board System

Your computer, modem, and communications software (and the telephone number of one or more boards) is sufficient entrance fee for most hobbyist bulletin boards. When the bulletin board computer answers your call, it first asks some questions about the equipment you are using (speed, number of lines and columns on your monitor, etc.). If you get a busy signal instead, try again later. Most hobbyist bulletin boards are low budget operations and may only have one telephone line, which means that only one user can access the system at a time.

Once you establish connection with a bulletin board and log on (some boards require you to enter a password), the board responds with the following kind of information:

>   You are caller number 12345
>   You last called on 12/25/84
>   Number of messages is 215
>   Highest message number is 767

Caller numbers are assigned sequentially to each new caller. For BBSs that use passwords, the system keeps track of the last time you signed on. In this example, there are currently 215 messages on the bulletin board. Each message is identified by a message number sequentially assigned by the

BBS when the message is posted — message 767 in our example is currently the highest message number.

Once you are signed on, you can scan, read, and post messages. On some boards you are allowed to *download* files (transfer files to your PC) from the software library.

Searching BBS libraries for *public domain software* often turns up real treasure. Experienced users are always contributing valuable computer programs and tools for all who use the board to share. When you find a program you want, you can download it to your computer using a file transfer protocol provided with your communications software package. Likewise, if you write a program that you think may be useful to others, you are encouraged to *upload* it to a BBS. Generally, a software contributor also writes and transfers a file of instructions to help others run the program.

Nearly all bulletin boards that allow users to swap files and programs use the XMODEM protocol. XMODEM was written by Ward Christensen to allow users of his Chicago Computerized Bulletin Board System (CBBS) to send files back and forth. It has since become a BBS standard for file transfer. If you plan to sift through public domain software, make sure your communications software includes XMODEM protocol. Most communications packages do, but it's always best to check before you buy.

When swapping public domain software with other BBS users, keep in mind that it is illegal to transfer copyrighted software. For example, you should never upload a program to a BBS that you purchased from a retail store. Not only is this theft, but transferring copyrighted material over the public telephone network is also a federal crime. A program in the public domain can also be copyrighted. The program's donor only needs to add a copyright notice in the program itself. In this case, however, you can download the program to your system and distribute it to others as long as you do not remove the copyright notice or sell the program.

Computer viruses have become a problem with some public domain software obtained over bulletin board systems. A virus scan is recommended before using the software you download.

Sending Mail Electronically

When you open your mail in the year 2010, chances are pretty good you will find an electronic letter. Although nationwide electronic mail is still relatively new, the service may soon be as common as the telephone and the post office.

Using an electronic mail service, you write a letter using either your computer's word processing software or a text editor provided by the service. Preparing your letter off-line using your own word processing software, however, will save you connect-time charges. Once the letter has been entered into the service's central computer, you can route the letter to an electronic mailbox where it can be read on-line by the addressee. If you prefer to send a printed copy, the letter is sent to a printer near the desired destination. From there it is delivered to the addressee either within hours, overnight, or by ordinary first-class mail and all for a reasonable fee.

MCI Mail is a popular electronic mail service. CompuServe is a combination bulletin board and information services. Other services such as Prodigy offer services similar to CompuServe, and for a flat monthly connection rate, but do not offer the diversity of services.

MCI Mail: The Nation's Newest Postal System

MCI Mail offers a wide range of capabilities at competitive prices. You access the service by using your modem to dial a local telephone number or an 800 number. Letters, memos, contracts, and reports can be electronically sent to anyone in the continental United States and many international destinations. If you desire, the memos can be printed on private letterhead produced by the system's laser printer, by fax or telex.

MCI Mail Features

As an MCI Mail subscriber you are given a user name and password that allow access to the central computer. After logging on, you can compose, edit, and send documents (letters, reports, etc.), read incoming mail, or organize and store data on the system. As an added incentive to new subscribers, MCI Mail even provides a free subscription (no initiation fee) to Dow Jones News/Retrieval, but there are still usage fees. Access is provided directly through MCI Mail. Unfortunately, when dialing through MCI Mail, you must pay the Dow Jones prime-time rate until 9 p.m. Eastern time, whereas regular Dow Jones subscribers pay the prime rate until 6 p.m. local time. For West Coast users, this presents no problem, but users in other time zones are penalized anywhere from one to three hours.

Dow Jones rates are billed between $1 and $3 per minute depending upon the services accessed and the speed of the modem used. 2400 baud modems are also charged a fee for each information unit (1,000 characters) of information accessed. These fees can add up quickly, so be cautious of the time if you plan to use this service.

Menus and a help facility guide the new user through basic MCI Mail operation. Simple commands are used to scan messages, read documents, and gain access to Dow Jones.

Suppose you want to create a memo to send over MCI mail. Type CREATE and the system responds by displaying a formatted screen that resembles a blank memo form commonly used in business. After entering your text, type a slash (/) to end the document and return to the menu. If you want to edit the memo, you can instruct the system to EDIT TEXT. Another command lets you send the document when you are satisfied that it is correct.

When you want to send an urgent message, you can use MCI Mail Alert to notify your recipient that a message is waiting. Once you request an Alert, up to three attempts are made by an MCI Mail Alert Operator to notify the recipient by telephone. You can also specify a time to begin calling. If you send a message between 9 a.m. and 5 p.m. Eastern time, the recipient is called the same business day. When you post an Alert after 5 p.m., you specify a time to begin calling on the next day.

You are kept informed every step of the way by the Alert Operator who posts a notice to your MCI mailbox letting you know if the recipient has been reached or if all attempts have failed. An automatic receipt appears in your MCI Mailbox once the recipient has read the message.

Another nice feature of MCI Mail is "mail waiting" notification. With this feature, the system tells you when you have an "unopened" piece of mail waiting in your electronic mailbox as soon as you log on to the system. You can open your mailbox and get a summary of who sent mail, when it was sent, and what the topic is. Several options are available for disposition of any piece of mail, including reading it, storing it, deleting it, or answering it.

An excellent service provided by MCI Mail is the ability to send a specific memo to a group of people. You establish an MCI Mail distribution list and specify that the memo just created is to be sent to the members of this list. This single action on the part of a user can create mail for a large number of people. Indeed, some companies that have a large number of travelling people use MCI Mail as their communication medium. Nominal discounts are offered to those people who send the same paper mail to many different people.

MCI Mail recently added a FAX delivery service that works either domestically or internationally. Your return fax and telephone number can be included on the delivered fax's coversheet if you desire. You can also specify the intervals between delivery attempts. As a last resort, you can also specify an alternate delivery method (i.e., telex) should the delivery attempts fail.

MCI Mailing Fees

There is a subscription fee of $35 paid annually for each individual. MCI Mail fees are a bargain. Fees are determined by the number of characters and whether the mail is to be delivered electronically or in paper form.

An Instant Letter delivered to an electronic mailbox on the system costs $1.00 per 7500 characters. Other rates apply to letters with fewer characters. An Overnight Letter up to 6 pages in length costs $9.00 domestically and between $12 and $30 internationally. MCI Letter service is also provided and delivers your message through standard first class mail.

MCI Mail also offers a preferred pricing schedule which costs a flat $10 per month and waives the annual fee after the first year. This service allows the subscriber 40 free messages per month. One message unit is charged for each instant letter up to 7500 characters in length and one message unit is used for each additional 7500 characters.

CompuServe

CompuServe initiated the first nighttime service to computer enthusiasts in 1979. These early hobbyists blazed a trail through the CompuServe computers, swapping programs and information with each other through on-line user groups. With the explosion of home computers, however, the number of novice users created a demand for more consumer-oriented services. CompuServe responded in 1980 and again in 1983 by revamping its structure and adding a host of new features having broader consumer appeal.

Today the CompuServe Information Service is the largest worldwide communications provider to modem equipped personal computer users. It offers its members electronic mail, personal computer support, news services, personal investment information, home shopping, entertainment, and computer games. Over 1,500 databases can be accessed from CompuServe. CompuServe has over 890,000 subscribers in the United States and over 100 foreign countries.

Principle areas of activity for CompuServe users are the special interest forums, CompuServe Mail, and the travel related functions.

The forums allow users to attend on-line conferences and exchange information through interaction with other users who share similar interests. There are over 300 CompuServe forums on topics that range from humor and rock music to medicine and specific types of personal computers. The forums are also used for downloading public domain software, and software companies such as Borland, Microsoft, and Lotus provide customer support through the forums.

CompuServe Mail is similar to MCI Mail. Electronic messages can be sent to any of the subscribers, and the message can be delivered in either electronic or paper mail form. CompuServe has established a corporate E-Mail (electronic mail) system for private use by corporations and also provides access to AT&T mail, AT&T Easylink, MCI Mail, and the Internet.

The CompuServe Official Airline Guide (OAG) and EAASY SABRE features are popular with CompuServe users. These and other travel related services allow users to check airline fares, make reservations, and book hotel reservations. Over 750 worldwide airlines and over 68,000 hotel properties are accessible through this service.

CompuServe operation is made easy by the use of the Information Manager software product. It is a series of pull-down menus that lead the user through operation of the major CompuServe services. The menus items are accessed using easily learned keystrokes. Cautions regarding the use of a mouse are included in the documentation. The mouse related installation procedure must be followed carefully, or unexpected things can result.

In short, CompuServe provides a wide array of information and correspondence services that truly expand the reach of any computer user.

Signing Up with CompuServe

To sign up for CompuServe there are a number of starter kits available from your local computer dealer at a retail cost of $49.95. Membership kits are also available directly from CompuServe (800-848-8199) for $39.95 and include a $25 credit toward future usage. This is a one-time membership charge, but a $2-per-month membership support fee is charged against your account even if you do not use it.

The kits include a user ID, password, a basic reference manual, Information Manager software for PC and Macintosh computers, and a subscription to the monthly members magazine.

CompuServe Charges

After the initial $25 usage credit is used, users pay hourly connect rates based upon transmission speeds of their modems. Connect time is billed in one-minute increments, with one minute being the shortest connect time possible. 300 baud modem users pay $6.00 per connect hour (10 cents per minute). 1200/2400 baud modem users are the most common and they pay $12.50 per hour (21 cents per minute), and 9600 baud modem users pay $22.50 per hour (38 cents per minute).

Additional communication surcharges are added to the per minute billing. These are 30 cents per hour for CompuServe networked calls, $10.50 for CompuServe Gateway connections from Canada, and $9.00 per hour for WATS carried connections. In addition to all these charges, there are also special fees for certain premium services. There are no more daytime and evening rates for connect time charges.

Once you get past the connect charges, many services can be accessed at no additional charge. Access to some information, however, requires that you pay an additional monthly subscription fee or an hourly surcharge for use of the information.

Logging On to CompuServe

Logging on to CompuServe requires a few simple steps that connect you to the service and identify who you are. Once you reach the CompuServe computer, it asks you to enter your User ID. This is a number like 54321,123 that CompuServe issues to you to identify your account just like a department store issues you a credit card number when you open an account.

After entering your User ID, the computer asks for your password. Your password is your "key" to "unlocking" your account. When you enter the correct password, the CompuServe computer allows you to access the service and charges your account number for the time and services you use. Because your password protects your account from unauthorized users, you should always keep it secret.

Because CompuServe is continually changing, it is a good idea to check the on-line SERVICES menu option frequently for the latest offerings.

Once you are logged onto CompuServe, simply follow the menu instructions to accomplish your communication goals.

Citizens' Band Simulator

CB is a popular citizens' band radio simulator that equips users with their own multiple-channel transceivers and scanning monitors for going "on channel" across the entire country. 72 CB channels are provided 24 hours per day for continual conversation.

Signing on for the first time can be a bewildering experience for the uninitiated. All you need is a "handle" (CB jargon for the name you want to use while "on the air") to sign on. Immediately, fragments of conversations begin scrolling across your screen. You have to just jump in. The interaction seems chaotic at first with everyone frantically typing messages to everyone else. But with a little practice and on-line help from other CBers (they love to come to the aid of a new user), you soon get into the action yourself.

Module Sixteen
Future Trends

One Phone Number Per Lifetime

The early telephone network was established before the concepts of electronic digital computers and packet switching were even a conceptual reality. The numbering plan established for the telephone network was based upon the central office being physically connected to a subscriber's premises, and with all other central offices inter-connected through a fixed wiring network.

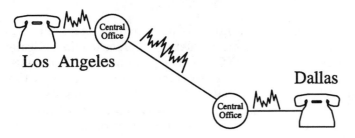

Wired Connections

Area codes and prefix numbering schemes were developed to allow network switching equipment to accurately direct the call setup request over the proper wiring paths to the proper receiver and complete the call. The route was determined by the physical connection between switching centers. The switching center end points were determined by the ten-digit telephone number. Packet switching technology has put call setup and routing into a completely new perspective.

Voice communication can be digitized, which means that conversations can be transmitted through the network as one and zero binary bits. Bits of information are now transmitted inside of data packets which are routed through the network over multiple paths and are essentially pathway independent. The only information of interest to a packet switched network is the sending and receiving locations.

A packet from Los Angeles to Dallas may actually go through nodes in Chicago and New York before arriving at its end location. The wire path is not the critical item it once was, and the implementation of high-speed fiber-optic links and high-power digital processors makes the transmission time delay essentially route independent.

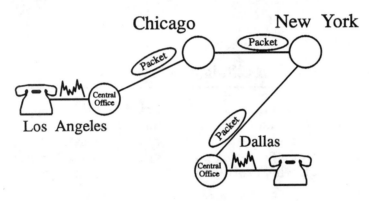

Packet Switching

This scenario makes the associating of a particular telephone number with a particular geographic region obsolete. A person could be issued a 312-555-1717 telephone number in Chicago and then move to Dallas and retain the same telephone number. The only modification is to notify the network that 312-555-1717 is now located in Dallas and that packets should now be routed there instead of Chicago. In this way, a telephone number could be issued to a person, and they could retain it indefinitely.

This scenario also opens up other possibilities regarding distribution of telephone numbers. Assume that some geographic areas such as Los Angeles are running out of telephone numbers and have implemented new area codes to increase number plan capacity. Assume that another geographic region, say Boise, has a surplus of telephone numbers.

Today's wiring-based network precluded Los Angeles from using the surplus Boise telephone numbers to service Los Angeles customers. The fully packetized network would remedy this situation by allowing the high need areas to designate Boise numbers as Los Angeles termination points and all calls would simply route to Los Angeles instead of Boise. The implications of this are interesting.

Many companies today trade EPA pollution credits as commodities. A company is issued a certain number of pollution credits per year. If they have extra credits, they sell them to companies that need more than they were allocated. The same could happen with telephone numbers. Boise's numbers could be sold or leased to Los Angeles and telephone numbers could become a commodity item traded on stock exchange boards.

This eventuality may sound a little farfetched, but notice that the cellular carriers are already implementing bypass numbering schemes that already accomplish this on a smaller scale. We may eventually end up with our Social Security Number as our telephone number.

One thing is for sure. The concept of telephone traffic being routed between two points based upon geography will eventually become obsolete. The implications regarding long-distance charges will also be affected by this development.

We are now charged for long distance based upon the length of time on the phone and the distance. This made sense when the wiring between two points (i.e., Dallas and Denver) had to be economically justified based upon the traffic between the two points. Now the packets may not even travel directly from Dallas to Denver. Network decision may route the packets from Dallas to St. Louis to Minneapolis and then to Denver.

This routing has no relevance to the wiring between Dallas and St. Louis, and the economic recovery schemes currently in effect will probably be obsolete. We may eventually be charged for the percentage of the aggregate network traffic capacity that our calls use. Instead of being billed for message units, we may be billed on a per packet basis and long distance will become a function of packet sizes instead of miles.

The world of telecommunications is changing quickly. The 100+ years it took for the system to evolve from Bell and Watson's invention of the telephone will probably be completely transformed by 2005. We live in exciting times, and the ability to communicate economically and effectively over longer distances is an important ingredient in this exciting mix.

Integrated Services Digital Network (ISDN)

Integrated services digital network (ISDN) has been a topic of substantial debate and indecision since the early 1980s. The common joke about its state of constant flux was that ISDN stood for "I still don't know." Luckily, this situation has turned around and ISDN is becoming a communication reality.

ISDN is basically a fully digital network including information transmission and network control. It is more than a digital transport strategy. It is intended to provide a new level of overall network services since the network, including the party receiving the call, can know everything about the inbound call such as its number, etc. This information allows the receiving party to automatically retrieve information related to that number before moving on with the call processing. The implications for inbound service organizations is profound. Fundamental to providing these services is an end-to-end digital link between sender and receiver.

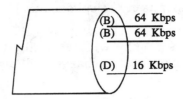

ISDN Basic Rate Interface

The digital connections come in two flavors: the *basic rate interface (BRI)* and *primary rate interface (PRI)*. These two interfaces are composed of various combinations of 64 Kbps *bearer (B)* channels that are used for the actual information transmission and either a 16 Kbps or a 64 Kbps *delta (D)* channel used to control the operation of the connection.

The basic rate interface is a two-wire digital connection that supports two 64 Kbps B channels and one 16 Kbps D channel. Notice that this arrangement allows for standard digitized voice to be transmitted along with 64 Kbps data. The primary rate interface includes 23 B channels and one 64 Kbps D channel. Notice that the speed of the primary rate interface matches the 1.544 Mbps rate of the standard T-1 line.

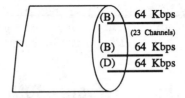

ISDN Primary Rate Interface (1.544 Mbps)

The major benefits associated with ISDN is the ability to connect a fully digital terminal device to any telephone outlet in the country and transmit digital information to any other ISDN outlet on an as needed, dial-up basis. The interface standard at the wall outlet will be universally accepted, which means that the information provided by any ISDN compatible terminal device will be readable to the ISDN network.

FAXes become digital and up to seven times faster with substantially reduced error rates and increased quality. 2400 bps modems become a thing of the past since an ISDN data terminal can now send data over a circuit switched connection at 64 Kbps. It is now a struggle to get 19,200 bps data transmission rate over a standard dial-up telephone line.

The primary rate interface also presents other capabilities that were previously not available. Should the entire 1.544 Mbps bandwidth be needed only for a short time, the PRI will provide the full rate as needed, then allocate the residual bandwidth to other functions until the full bandwidth is needed again. This method of modifying the bandwidth allocation to different communication functions is called *dynamic bandwidth allocation*.

This is of particular interest when transmission of video information is considered. ISDN also provides a H0 (384 Kbps) channel and an H11 (1.544 Mbps) channel. These channels are useful for transmitting large amounts of data like that required for video (television). While transmitting digital video information, the PRI bandwidth can be allocated to provide 384 Kbps (6x64Kbps) with the balance used for other communication such as voice or data. After the video communication is completed, this 384 Kbps can again be subdivided into its six B channels for additional voice and data communication capacity. Instead of needing separate lines for the video and voice, one line can be used for all with minimal loss of performance.

ISDN does raise some interesting issues regarding personal privacy since the caller's telephone number is now accessible to the person receiving the call. Does the receiving party have the right to that number, and what are they allowed to do with it once they have it. 800 numbers could be used for prequalifying persons with certain demographic characteristics, and those lists could be sold to third parties. Many states, such as California, provide the subscribers with the option of blocking their number from traveling through the system. This approach is being adopted by many states, and since it is controlled by the local PUC, uniformity of implementation is not likely.

The *European Community* (EC) may actually end up leading the U.S. in ISDN implementation. Their primary rate H12 interface has 32 channels and transmits at 2.048 Mbps. In 1991 estimates were that eight of the European countries will support 14,665 BRI and 2,665 PRI lines. By 1994 Belgium, Denmark, France, and the United Kingdom expect to have 100 percent ISDN availability to their subscribers. There is still a problem in that the ISDN in one country may not match the ISDN of another. There are multiple standard issues to reconcile before ISDN becomes universally accepted by the EC, but they appear intent upon finding a solution.

Fiber Distributed Data Interface (FDDI)

As the number of LANs increases along with the heavier dependance upon graphical information, the amount of networked data traffic will increase substantially. To address this situation, a fiber-optic based standard was developed by the American National Standards Institute (ANSI). This *Fiber Distributed Data Interface (FDDI)* operates at 100 Mbps and has two counter rotating rings to ensure network reliability in a similar way to that discussed with token ring. In addition, FDDI allows for synchronous and asynchronous data transmission and can cover a distance up to 200 km with no more than 2 km between stations.

Media access is similar to token passing except that special priorities are included that allow a station to hold the token for a longer period of time should its transmission needs require it. In essence, if an FDDI node has not used all of its allocated time, that time can be used by another node with a higher transmission priority. This allows for more dynamic allocation of the FDDI backbone bandwidth.

Several vendors have introduced full 100 Mbps FDDI compatible networking cards that route information over twisted pair wiring. Their transmission distance is limited to under 100 meters, but the speed over twisted pair is an indicator of where the industry is going. In 1984 the general marketplace assumed that it was impossible to transmit more than 4 khz of information over twisted pair. The confusion between the telco adopted bandwidth constraint and the electrical limit of twisted pair has now been eliminated and more high-speed data is routed over twisted pair every day.

An FDDI-II standard is under investigation by the ANSI committee. This standard helps define methods of accessing the FDDI rings and should allow for time-sensitive traffic, such as digitized voice, to be routed over the FDDI ring.

Broadband ISDN, Fast Packet Switching, and SONET

Broadband Integrated Services Digital Network (BISDN) is a proposed service designed to transmit conversations, multimedia (i.e., video) transmission and messaging services, and generalized high-speed network access. It is still under investigation and development, and a debate is currently raging about whether fast packet or frame relay is the best option to pursue.

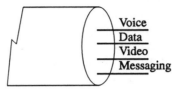

Broadband ISDN

The use of the broadband term with respect to BISDN should not be confused with broadband technology used for LANs other than that they are both techniques for transmitting tremendous amounts of information.

The LAN broadband is actually a frequency division multiplexing technique, where the ISDN broadband is simply very fast digital information transmission. Two things are the major driving forces behind the intended deployment of BISDN: the advances in the commercialization of optical fiber and the increasing need to link together high-speed LANs.

LANs operate at 4, 10, and 16 Mbps transmission rates. LANs in separate geographic locations need to connect over some form of telecommunications network. Some companies install their own private networks to achieve high data transmission rates. This process is expensive and potentially dangerous in light of the rapid technology changes. Other companies rely upon the public network but typically have to sacrifice speed and performance, since telephone lines typically operate at 2.4 Kbps (dial up), 9.6 Kbps (dedicated leased or dial up), 56 Kbps (dedicated leased), or 1.54 Mbps (dedicated leased).

Notice that even at the maximum data transfer rates, the telephone network speeds are substantially lower than the LAN speeds. In addition, many times these leased lines are chosen of a higher speed to simply accommodate the peak traffic rates (1+ Mbps) and the overall speed of the connection is wasted at other low traffic times (64 Kbps).

This wasted bandwidth is paid for by the consumer even though it is not used. This is mainly because the connection between the two link end points is typically a physical one and not easily modified for various traffic rates.

Conventional ISDN is designed to address this issue by providing dynamic bandwidth allocation on an instantaneous, as needed basis. Broadband ISDN simply takes that concept to a higher speed but modifies the underlying technology.

BISDN information is divided into subsegments before being placed onto the network. Each of these information segments is placed into a data envelope of sorts that contains network overhead information regarding the network path that the data is to follow, the specific data channel with which this particular packet is associated, and some basic error detection. These fixed length packets are more commonly referred to as *cells* and contain both user information and network routing overhead.

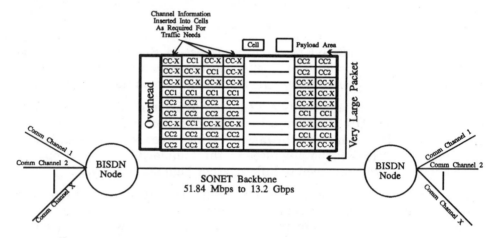

Asynchronous Transfer Mode Graphical Description

Each of these cells is then placed into a spot on a much larger transport packet and transmitted over the fiber-optic link. This larger transport packet also has large groupings of fixed length cells within it, and the number of these cells that is used for a particular transmission is determined by the needs of the data connections. In other words, different data types receive different levels of priority. This is important to a network that intends to route voice, data, and video traffic.

Digitized voice traffic is consistent in nature. 64,000 bits of information need to go from one point to another within one second or the communication gets distorted. The 64,000 bits are divided into 8,000 separate 8-bit segments that are transmitted at regular intervals.

Just in case there were not enough eccentric telecommunication terms, the ANSI committee defines time-sensitive data, or data with a constant bit rate, as *isochronous* network traffic. Data transmission happens in spurts, or bursts, and is called *bursty* in nature.

A characteristic of bursty data transmission is that it happens quickly and then is over. It also generally does not matter when the burst happens, within reasonable computer oriented timeframes. Consequently, if the voice channel needs a few more of these cell slots in the larger packet, then the data traffic can wait while the voice channels use the data channel's bandwidth. When the next larger packet comes by again, the data traffic that waited is inserted into the proper number of cells to complete the data communication. Notice that the bandwidth of the larger packet has been dynamically reallocated. This is a primary goal of BISDN.

This method of inserting and holding smaller cell packets to best utilize the larger packet's bandwidth is a principle characteristic of the proposed broadband ISDN standard and is referred to as *asynchronous transfer mode (ATM)*. ATM inserts the smaller cell packets into the larger frame in whatever order is needed to optimize the connections.

This means that one larger packet may contain a few of the smaller packets for a particular communication channel while the next may be completely occupied by that channel's smaller cell packets. It is the responsibility of the equipment on either end of the connection to reassemble the cells into the proper sequence to recreate the original transmission.

This process of subdividing the information and inserting it into a larger high-speed data transport frame is called *fast packet switching* and is based upon the CCITT I.361 standard.

BISDN networks are expected to operate somewhere between 150 Mbps and 600 Mbps and some user access ports are being defined at 155 Mbps.

SONET (Synchronous Optical Network) is expected to become the underlying backbone upon which these high-speed data transfer systems will operate. Its major contribution, aside from raw speed, is the ability to insert and remove cells from the larger frame without having to take the entire frame apart. Instead of having to process the entire frame to simply remove one cell, SONET protocol allows for the removal of a single cell on its own.

This process is much faster and contributes greatly to the overall transmission rates by decreasing the network overhead. The technique is used by some proprietary vendor products, but SONET is the accepted standard that accurately defines how the accepted process is supposed to occur.

Expected SONET operating speeds range from 51.84 Mbps to a theoretical upper limit of 13.2 Giga (billion) bps. The CCITT official name for SONET is *Synchronous Digital Hierarchy (SDH)*.

Frame Relay

This technology is a virtual circuit packet switching scheme that has been adopted by many of the IXCs such as Sprint and MCI and some of the RBOCs. Its concepts should be familiar to you at this point, but its implementation is unique. Frame relay technology is very similar to conventional packet switching, except that many of the overhead items such as error correction and generalized routing information have been dropped. This streamlined packet can be processed much faster by the networking nodal components. The network sets up a virtual circuit link and then a large frame (or block) of data is sent between the two points.

A good conceptual way to think of this arrangement is to imagine a letter being sent across the country. After you address the envelope you can either place it in a mailbox and leave the delivery method to the discretion of the post office (conventional packet switching), or you can place it into an airplane that is going to your intended destination. The envelope on the plane will arrive at its destination faster than one placed into general delivery.

In essence, by placing the envelope on the plane you created a defined path for the envelope to follow (or a virtual circuit connection in data terms). Few decisions needed to be made to complete the transfer. In fact, if the letter were coded for routing so that the address did not need to be read, then it would travel even faster. This is the essence of frame relay transmission.

Frame relay transmission speeds are today shown at up to 2 Mbps, with some talk about increasing the speed to 45 Mbps. At these speeds, and with the bursty nature of LAN traffic, frame relay makes a good choice for inter-LAN connections.

Switched Megabit Data Service (SMDS)

This is another technology under investigation as the ideal highspeed data transport standard. SMDS is based upon the IEEE 802.6 metropolitan area network standard and uses a packet switching technique to transmit data over a dual bus fiber-optic network.

Of importance to the Broadband ISDN (BISDN) discussion is that SMDS is data cell compatible with the asynchronous transfer method (ATM) used in the BISDN standard. This aspect alone makes SMDS a prime candidate for the transitional technology that will take us from the T-1 days of today to the BISDN of the late 1990s. Equipment installed today may not have to undergo tremendous changes to become compatible with the final BISDN standard.

The use of SMDS is more complex than frame relay because SMDS does not use the virtual connection methods employed by frame relay. Each SMDS packet has to find its own way through the network, and many packets from the same communication may take different paths. This is inherent in the nature of the connectionless packet switching techniques employed by SMDS.

Video Conferencing and TeleMedia

Perhaps no industry stands to benefit more from the recent and expected increases in networking speed than the video conferencing industry. The high data transmission rates required for effective video information transfer have previously prohibited widespread adoption of video conferencing equipment. That appears to be changing quickly.

The two basic means of video conferencing in use today are via a satellite uplink and a general broadcast downlink. Although this method does allow a certain amount of interaction, it is generally a one-way communication path in that only one party can see the other. Remote educational programs are typically implemented in this way. These systems use a satellite link to transmit the professor's lecture to the remote locations, but use a standard telephone link to connect the remote sites back to the lecture lab for student questions.

Another method causing excitement is video conferencing over land-based high-speed digital lines. For this to become a reality, either the speed of the national telecommunications network needed to increase or the amount of bandwidth required to transmit acceptable video signals needed to decrease.

In fact, both requirements are occurring at the same time.

Video Telecom, a Texas-based video conferencing equipment supplier, contends that acceptable video signals can now be transmitted over 56 Kbps lines vs the 1.5 Mbps required in 1980. The information contained is the same, but technology now allows for *compressing* that information into less bandwidth. This development now allows for 56 Kbps lines to connect video conference sites on a circuit switched basis. Not surprisingly, the billing rates for switched 56 Kbps lines has decreased dramatically since 1988.

The cost per hour for 56 Kbps in 1988 was around $45. In 1990 the cost had decreased to around $5 per hour.

Video conferencing involves no travel by the participants, and electrons know no international boundaries. Workers become more productive if they do not spend three days traveling for a two-hour meeting in another city. Video conferencing will become a more accepted business tool as decreasing per-hour connection time charges combine with improvements in compression technology.

Module Seventeen
Regulatory Issues in Telecommunications

The heavy dominance of the American telecommunications industry combined with the critical nature of telecommunications to the prosperity of society have caused the telecommunications industry to become heavily regulated.

The industry did not start out heavily regulated. It was through the rapid acceptance of the telephone by the general public; the initial licensing/financing strategy taken by Bell, Watson, Hubbard, and Vail; and the market free-for-all caused by the expiration of the original patent that industry regulation became necessary.

Providing telephone service is a capital intensive process. It requires many years of providing service to recover the initial financial investments. The first few years are particularly precarious since there is generally a large outflow of cash and minimal cash inflow. Established carriers can drop prices during this period of time, as is allowed in any free market economy, and drive the new companies out of business.

In many cases, these established companies then purchase the equipment of the failed company for a fraction of the initial cost. These predatory business practices are more possible in a heavily capital equipment intensive industry such as the telecommunications industry. Regulations are in place to minimize the likelihood of this happening.

Regulation is also designed to prevent a carrier from using its dominance of the *local loop*, the connection between the subscriber's site and the telephone company, to its own advantage and to the disadvantage of its competitors. If a telephone service provider, or *carrier*, controls the access to the network and also the network, it is likely to provide pricing incentives that induce subscribers to use that particular carrier's services rather than those of a competitor. The carrier may even introduce technological barriers to network access in the form of proprietary access codes, custom signalling, or physical constraints that would not allow competitors to provide quality equipment at a reasonable price.

This type of preferential use of the local loop by the carriers would restrict free trade and impede the free market economy process.

On the other hand, it is also in the best interests of the economy to promote an effective telecommunications system. As we saw earlier, standardization is a critical ingredient in providing universal communication service. If every equipment vendor was allowed to introduce its version of equipment along with a unique set of technological standards and pricing structure, the industry could quickly fall into disarray just as happened with the data industry.

It is along this tightrope that the regulatory bodies and the telephone suppliers must walk. They must ensure that the benefits of a free market economy are passed along to the consumer while also maintaining the highest communications system possible.

Let's start in the beginning and see how the regulatory environment of today developed. From this historical perspective we can understand the critical importance that regulation plays in the telecommunication industry and lay a framework for understanding where it may evolve in the future.

The Beginning of the Telephone System

The National Bell Telephone Company was established to sell licenses of the Bell telephone patent to those companies who wanted to provide service. These companies were allowed to use Bell in their name. National Bell later became American Bell in 1880 when Western Union sold its telephone operation in response to losing Bell's patent infringement suit. AT&T became the parent company to the Bell system in 1899.

During the early days while the patent was still in effect, a telephone company had to receive a license from Alexander Graham Bell to use his telephone technology. There were a number of Bell-owned telephone companies in place, along with a great number of licensees, who legally had purchased the right to sell the product and services.

The original patents expired in 1893/1894. The technology was now generally available to anyone who wanted to begin their own telephone company, and a rash of smaller companies sprang up across the nation.

Many of these companies were undercapitalized and went out of business after they had already induced subscribers to use their service.

In the early 1890s there were over 125 telephone companies in place with many of them offering duplication of service in the same area. Many of these companies concentrated their attention on the major urban areas since they could reach a larger number of subscribers with less wire and stood the best chance of financial success. Unfortunately, when many companies are after the same consumer, a price war occurs which drives the profit margins for each competitor to such low levels that the service provided is eventually lost. This occurred in many cases and is happening today in the personal computer market.

Additionally, the intense concentration of service in the urban areas also meant that the rural areas were essentially being neglected.

AT&T was initially created as a long-distance service provider whose charter was to provide connections between New York and the rest of the world. The lofty intent of the charter is above reproach, but the implementation may have been questionable.

Many of the Bell companies were allowed access to the AT&T long-distance network, but the independent companies were denied access in many cases. In other words, a subscriber to telephone service from a smaller independent company was only able to call other subscribers to the same small company's service. They were not allowed access to the long-distance network and could not call outside of their local area. These smaller companies accused AT&T of preferential treatment, which it indeed appears it was.

To further complicate matters, AT&T was also aggressively purchasing many of these smaller carriers and consolidating them into a larger network. AT&T was seen as applying negative leverage pressure by denying long-distance service to the smaller local loop providers. The lack of long-distance service meant that the smaller company needed to install its own long-distance network or survive in a very competitive industry with a less competitive service. AT&T was accused of diminishing a particular company's market position, then buying the company for inclusion under the Bell umbrella. This is a classical predatory business strategy.

The Bell system had been in place a full decade ahead of most other providers and naturally had a stronger market presence and more established capitalization. It was without question the strongest telephone provider of the time.

The smaller companies began to apply pressure to the federal government to intervene on their behalf. USITA was formed in 1897 as a representative body for the independent telephone companies to lobby against AT&T. It still exists today as the U.S. Telephone Association and includes the RBOCs as members.

In 1910 Congress passed the Mann-Elkins Act which put regulation of interstate telephone company business under the auspices of the Interstate Commerce Commission (I.C.C.). The primary purpose of this act was to create a uniform billing system between the various telephone companies so that persons calling from one point of the country to the other could be assured of proper billing of their telephone calls. This might have helped the situation for specific companies, but the industry as a whole was still in a struggle with AT&T for equal service.

The AT&T 1909 purchase of Western Union may have been presented as altruistic on AT&T's part but indeed was construed by the independent telephone companies as predatory, offensive business tactics on AT&T's part. Their claim was that AT&T was now going to dominate the telecommunications industry and drive the independents out of business, which would stifle competition and preclude the American consumer from a free market for telecommunications services.

AT&T was actually in the process of buying up many of the independent telephone companies thus curtailing the competition, so there appeared to be some basis to the claims.

In 1912 a formal complaint against AT&T was filed with the federal government, which then informed AT&T in 1913 that the United States Department of Justice and Interstate Commerce Commission were both beginning an investigation into the charges. The legal basis for the allegation was that AT&T's practices were in violation of the Sherman Antitrust Act regarding monopolization of an industry.

In 1913 AT&T disposed of its Western Union operation as the first of a sequence of commitments known as the Kingsbury Commitments, named after Nathan Kingsbury, an AT&T vice president who wrote the agreement. This sequence of commitments were made on AT&T's part to avoid a full-scale government investigation into its operations.

The Kingsbury Commitments were that AT&T would divest its Western Union stock, would get approval from the I.C.C. before purchasing any additional independent telephone companies, and would provide a uniform interconnection to its facilities for use by any of the nationwide telephone companies that needed such service for its customers. This is really when Vail's vision of universal telephone service started to become a reality, and it happened only seven years before his death in 1920.

President Wilson nationalized the telephone & telegraph operations in 1918 in response to World War I. Both were put under the auspices of the post office department. Vail worked with Albert Burleson, the postmaster general, and convinced him that the telephone company could work more effectively in support of the U.S. government's efforts if left on its own. In July of 1919 the government gave AT&T back its autonomy.

Congress passed The Graham Act in 1921, which officially recognized AT&T as a monopoly and exempted it from Sherman Antitrust regulations or restrictions. It also allowed independent telephone companies to become monopolies in their own areas. The rationale at the time was that monopolies in the independent areas would free the companies from competitive pressures and allow the companies to provide a higher level of service to their subscribers. It also precluded local subscribers from having to contact multiple companies for telephone service. Standardization was now starting to enter the industry.

The *Federal Communication Commission* (F.C.C.) was created by Congress with the Communications Acts of 1934. The Interstate Commerce Commission was in place to regulate the transport of product between states and was not really set up to manage information flow. The critical value of communications was finally recognized, and the F.C.C. was created to control the flow of communication and information from one state to another.

The F.C.C.'s charter is: "for the purpose of regulating interstate and foreign commerce in communication by wire and radio so as to make available, so far as possible, to all the people of the United States a rapid, efficient, nationwide and worldwide wire, radio, and communication service with adequate facilities at reasonable charges." Notice this also is closely in alignment with Vail's vision of AT&T becoming the telephone service company for the public.

In 1949 the United States Department of Justice sued AT&T for violations of the Sherman Antitrust Act again. Specifically, they were concerned about Western Electric Company, which had become the manufacturing arm of the Bell system. The contention was that Western Electric would produce telephones in such volume that it could undercut other domestic manufacturers and impede their ability to produce comparable products at competitive prices. In addition to this market advantage, Western Electric had the ability to leverage its position with the Bell system to facilitate entry into other industries.

The basic problem was that Western Electric was funded by the regulated arm of the telephone companies and consequently funded by public monies, yet it was able to leverage that publicly funded position to the detriment of other industries. This issue was resolved by the 1949 AT&T consent decree that allowed AT&T to retain control of Western Electric but precluded it from manufacturing noncommunications related equipment. In addition, Western Electric was ordered to limit its sale of product to Bell companies and the federal government. This was not seen as a major sacrifice by AT&T since the fledgling computer industry was not much of a market opportunity and the domestic telephone industry was essentially owned by AT&T.

In 1968 a major decision was handed down by the F.C.C. in favor of a small Dallas company called Carter Electronics Corporation. This company wanted to connect a rubber coupling device between the telephone and the AT&T network. No electrical signals were transferred, yet AT&T claimed that this device could harm the public network and as such should not be allowed. They refused to allow attachment of the Carterfone product to the network.

Tom Carter, the president of Carter Electronics Corporation, sued AT&T and won this landmark case, which is commonly referred to as the Carterfone Decision. This event basically opened up the telecommunication industry to a huge multibillion dollar industry which is now referred to as the interconnect industry. Prior to the Carterfone decision, all equipment was available only through AT&T on a leased basis. Carterfone allowed other suppliers to provide comparable equipment to subscribers on either a lease or purchase basis. The sole source supplier of station equipment now had competition for consumer purchased equipment.

In 1969 another decision was handed down in favor of Microwave Communications, Incorporated (MCI), which was interested in providing inter-city telecommunications over satellite links. This service would directly compete with AT&T long lines (long-distance) service. The technology proposed by MCI was not new, but having that technology provided to consumers by an independent company was new. As soon as MCI won its suit, the highly competitive long-distance industry we know today was spawned, and a new group of carriers called *Other Common Carriers (OCC)* or *Specialized Common Carriers (SCC)* was created.

In the initial stages, the OCCs typically took the high profit routes, such as communications between major cities, and channeled their attentions in direct competition with AT&T. Access to these OCCs was provided to consumers by dialing a complex set of access codes that greatly increased the number of digits dialed by the consumer to make a simple long-distance call.

These extra digits were a constant point of contention between the OCCs and AT&T, and it was resolved recently with the introduction of the Equal

Access regulations. Prior to equal access, AT&T had the exclusive advantage of *One Plus* dialing (any number preceded by a "1" digit would automatically go over AT&T long-distance facilities). The OCC's subscribers needed to dial as many as 18 digits to make the same long-distance call. Equal access now allows a consumer to choose which long-distance carrier will carry his calls after the "1" is dialed. The other carriers are still available, but additional numbers must be dialed to make the same long-distance call over the non "One-Plus" carrier.

The 1971 Computer Inquiry I decision handed down by the F.C.C. stated that the data processing industry was not subject to F.C.C. control. This left the data processing industry unregulated and essentially without imposed standards but still maintained that telecommunication was critical to the national good and would stay regulated.

In 1971 the F.C.C. also handed down its open skies policy which stated that anybody could get into the satellite business if they could afford it. This decision allowed companies to provide communication links for transmission of information and spawned several new companies such as American Satellite and Satellite Business Systems.

In 1981 Computer Inquiry II was handed down by the F.C.C. To contemporary communications business in America, this is probably the single most important event in recent history. In Computer Inquiry II, the F.C.C. decided that computer companies would be allowed to transmit data on an unregulated basis and that the Bell System companies would be allowed to participate in the data processing market, which previously had been restricted to them. Customer premises equipment and enhanced services would be deregulated and be provided by completely separate entities from the regulated basic voice service common carriers. The telecom network was divided into several parts: basic and enhanced services along with deregulated customer premises equipment and regulated network equipment.

Basic telecommunication services would still remain regulated and consisted essentially of the ability to provide an end-to-end connection. They did not include the ability to take or modify, in any way, the contents of the information transmitted over that link. Anything that was not a basic service was considered enhanced and under the jurisdiction of the unregulated entity.

AT&T was required to provide regulated communications services and maintain the level of telecommunication services expected by the American consumer. In addition, AT&T was now allowed to provide unregulated communication services and did so under the name American Bell, but the two organizations were not allowed to fund each other. Long distance, which was unregulated, was separated from the company that provides local telephone service, which was regulated. A deregulated arm of AT&T could now provide computer and telephone equipment for sale to the general public, but this deregulated entity's operation could not take advantage of or be funded by any of the activities of the regulated AT&T entities. AT&T has not divested itself of the operating companies at this point.

The modified final judgement handed down in 1982 by Judge Harold Green stated that AT&T must divest itself of its twenty-two operating telephone companies by January of 1984. So companies such as Southwestern Bell, Bell Atlantic, Pacific Northwest Bell, Pacific Bell, Illinois Bell, all of which were previously arms of AT&T, would now be stand-alone organizations providing local communications services. These companies, previously referred to as Bell operating companies, would now be referred to as the Regional Bell Operating Companies (RBOCs) and would each have their own regulated and deregulated arms.

AT&T was also prohibited at this point from using the Bell name since that was restricted to exclusive use by the local operating companies. So American Bell, which was part of AT&T, changed its name to AT&T Information Systems (ATTIS). Regulated network services are sold by AT&T Communications (ATTCOM).

This transition from a regulated to a deregulated industry was traumatic for the people who worked within the regulated Bell entities. It was also traumatic for the customers.

What was previously a uniform connection from a telephone on one person's desk through the network to a telephone on another person's desk had now been subdivided into separate entities. The telephone and the wiring on the premises was now considered premises equipment and under the control of the customer. The connection into the local telephone loop was now considered the domain of the Regional Bell Operating Company and was considered a regulated service and subject to tariff control.

The connection from one Regional Bell Operating Company to another was opened up to competition between AT&T and other common carriers such as Sprint or MCI.

A new geographical division called a *Local Access and Transport Area* (LATA) defines the area over which an RBOC can transmit calls without requiring the services of a long-distance carrier. If the call termination point is within the same LATA, then the RBOC can transmit the call. If it must pass from one LATA to another (even if the two points are across the street from each other), then the call must be passed to a long-distance or *interexchange carrier* (IXC) for inter-LATA transmission.

Where before the customer only dealt with one company that provided all of these services, they now had to deal with multiple vendors competing on multiple levels. Vendors were occasionally confused about their particular level of authority.

The key point at this time was that AT&T and the other B.O.C.s were prohibited from offering enhanced and regulated services through the same entity. Also important, regulated services revenues could not be used to fund deregulated services. This became cumbersome for AT&T, and eventually the Justice Department realized the extent of the financially negative impact on AT&T. In 1986 they allowed AT&T to combine AT&T Information Systems and AT&T Communications into one organization called AT&T Communications Services and lifted most of the restrictions.

AT&T is still a dominant carrier in the United States. It still receives preferential and restrictive treatment from the Justice Department. Computer Inquiry III (C.I.III) was a 1987 study carried out by the F.C.C. It allowed the Bell operating companies and AT&T to offer unregulated and enhanced services if the companies agree to provisions that allow interconnection through a group of publicly sanctioned interfaces called the *Open Network Architecture (ONA)*.

Under ONA if a telephone company offers a deregulated service, it has to provide competing vendors equal access to that deregulated service. This precludes the regulated entity from unfairly leveraging its position to the exclusion of other competitors. C.I.III and O.N.A. are still under some public debate at the time of this writing.

A heated debate was also under way in 1991 regarding the recent FCC decision to allow the regulated arms of the RBOCs to provide cable TV services over the telephone lines. The service is being dubbed *"video dial tone,"* and it can also include information services such as yellow pages, directory services, and general information. Once again, this service cannot be subsidized by profits from the regulated side of the business, but the accounting safeguards currently proposed are relatively lax and hard to monitor. The ruling will probably also allow the cable television companies to provide telephone service.

The danger here, once again, is that the telcos will take advantage of their strong network position and install proprietary technology or pricing schemes that will negatively impact competition. The cable television industry along with the newspaper industry are fighting the rulings for obvious reasons. At the time of this writing, the entire issue is under appeal.

Some believe that this new regulatory environment will provide the incentive for the RBOCs to invest in fiber optics to the American household curb. This is not necessarily a trivial issue. Current estimates are that this migration to a fully fiber network would cost between $100 and $200 billion and take five years.

Video dial tone would allow the RBOCs to provide "video on demand." The corner video store would be replaced by an RBOC service. Conceptually, the consumer would sit at home, select a video from a menu on his TV screen, and the video would be played at the viewer's discretion. Not bad if it keeps us from having to go to the store on a cold winter night, but not good if it drives up the cost of telephone service by 400 percent. By the time you read this, the issue might be resolved, but looking at the situation in 1991 there was a lot of uncertainty about the outcome and the ultimate net user benefits.

Other issues under debate are the various new tariff offerings from AT&T. They are currently Tariff 12 and Tariff 15. Tariff 12 allows AT&T to provide particularly attractive reduced pricing for its select customers who have special needs. At issue on Tariff 12 is the definition of "special." AT&T wants everyone to be "special" so that their prices can be less expensive than the competition. Tariff 12 is the topic of ongoing debate.

Tariff 15 is probably not going to live very long. This Tariff is designed to allow AT&T to offer pricing that is comparable to its competitors, but after the fact. In other words, if AT&T is going to lose a customer to a competitor due to comparable service for a lower price, then AT&T wants the option of matching their price.

The FCC contends that there is no benefit to the customer since AT&T is not beating the competitor, only matching the price. In addition, the practice appears discriminatory in that it is only being offered to customers who are in jeopardy. Why is it not available to the general customer base? The debate goes on, and it probably will as long as there is an AT&T, an RBOC, a PUC, and an FCC. The topics may change, but the essence of the debate remains the same.

Regulatory Issues Summary

The difference between regulation on the state level and regulation on the federal level is the difference between the FCC and this federal charter, and the Public Utilities Commissions (PUC) and their charter on a state basis.

In essence, the FCC's charter is to control interstate communications and also control radio and airwave communications through licensing of radio and television stations in separate areas. The FCC also becomes involved with regulation and licensing of frequency bandwidth allocation of the airwaves. The PUCs on the other hand, are responsible for communications and tariffs within a state. Consequently, there is a struggle going on between the PUCs and the FCC on who will have jurisdiction over specific types of telephone calls.

There is an ongoing debate over who has the right to regulate a telephone call that starts in Texas, goes to a satellite, and arrives in a foreign country. Satellites are under the FCC regulation, but regulations within the state between the telephone set and the satellite link-up are handled by a local PUC regulation. Who is to have jurisdiction over that telephone call? These issues are constantly under debate and constantly under revision.

In light if this, the individual consumer must make informed decisions about what is happening in the industry. Hopefully, this chapter has indicated to the reader that the types of services available to the reader user and subscriber are heavily dependent upon the regulatory environment of the time and the regulatory structure of the organization providing the services.

Regulatory Issues Time Table

Date	Regulatory Issue
1880	National Bell becomes American Bell.
1893/1894	Bell's original patents expire.
1897	USITA formed to represent independent telephone companies.
1899	AT&T becomes parent company to the Bell System.
1909	AT&T purchases Western Union.
1912	AT&T investigated by federal government.
1913	AT&T disposes of Western Union to avoid further investigation.
1921	Congress recognizes AT&T as a monopoly and exempts it from anti-trust laws.
1934	Federal Communications Commission (FCC) created.
1949	Federal government sues AT&T for violations of Sherman Anti-trust Act.
1968	Carterfone Decision opens up the market for other companies to lease or sell equipment to consumers.

1969	MCI wins decision for competition in long-distance service.
1971	Computer industry not subject to FCC rules.
1971	Satellite communications opened up by FCC.
1981	Computer companies would be allowed to transmit data on an unregulated basis.
1991	Debate over cable TV services and reduced pricing is ongoing.

Glossary

ACK   See acknowledge.

Acknowledge (ACK)   In a communications protocol, a message indicating an error-free transmission of data. In XMODEM protocol, for example, an acknowledge message tells the originating computer a transmitted character was successfully read by the receiving computer.

Acoustic coupler   A device for transmitting and receiving data over a telephone line through a standard telephone handset.

Analog   A method of coding data that uses continuously variable physical quantities.

Answer mode   The operating condition of a modem set up to answer the telephone and to receive data from another system. Also used to determine the one/zero transmission frequencies used in some modem transmission schemes.

ASCII   American Standard Code for Information Interchange wherein letters, numbers, and special symbols are represented as unique 7-bit codes. This ensures standardization of information encoding as bit streams.

Asynchronous transmission   A method for sending and receiving a serial stream of data with a variable time interval between successive characters. With this technique, each character is delimited by a start bit and a stop bit used to synchronize the transmission. See also start bit, stop bit.

Auto-answer   Feature that allows a modem to automatically answer an incoming telephone call.

Auto-dial   Feature that allows a modem to dial a telephone number. The number is part of a command sent to the modem (under communications software control) by a user.

Balun   A device used to connect twisted pair wiring (*bal*anced wiring) to coaxial cable (*un*balanced). Frequently used to minimize the use of coaxial cable.

Bandwidth   Measure of information-carrying capacity of a communications link transmission medium.

Batch mode	The technique of running a set of computer programs sequentially, without user intervention, so that each program is completed before the next one of the set is started.
Baud	A measure of transmission speed roughly equaling bits per second for low speed modem transmissions. The number of times that the amplitude, phase or frequency of a sinusoidal signal changes in one second is the baud rate, and specific bit sequences can be encoded into the baud changes.
Baudot code	A 5-bit character code used for transmitting data on the Telex network and also used extensively with telecommunication devices for the deaf (TDD).
Binary-state signal	A digital signal that can assume a value of 0 or 1 only.
Bit	The smallest quantity of data for encoding information. A bit can assume a value of 0 (space) or 1 (mark) only.
Bits per second (bps)	Measure of information transfer rate expressed as the number of bits transmitted or received each second.
Block	A unit of information composed of a group of data. Blocks usually have special characters at the beginning and end to designate the start and finish of the block since blocks may be of differing lengths.
Board (internal) modem	A modem built on a printed circuit board that plugs directly into a bus slot in the computer.
bps	See bits per second.
Broadcast mode	Technique for simultaneous, one-directional transmission of messages to all nodes in a network.
Bus network	Network in which nodes share a common communications link over which information is transferred from any of several sources to any of several destinations. Bus topologies have a definite beginning and end point.
Bus slot	One or more locations in a computer where additional circuit boards can be inserted.
Byte	A sequence of eight adjacent binary digits (bits) operated upon as a unit of data.
Call forwarding	Telephone company feature that allows the automatic transfer of incoming phone calls to another number.

Call progress detection	Modem feature that allows user to monitor the progress of a telephone call from dialing through answer or busy.
Call setup time	The elapsed time between dialing the last digit of a telephone number and hearing the first ring or busy signal. Represents the time required for the network to establish an end-to-end connection.
Carrier	A continuous signal (tone or frequency) capable of being modulated with a second (information carrying) signal. See also modulation.
Carrier detect	Modem circuitry that detects and indicates the presence of a carrier signal on a communications link.
Carrier sense multiple access with collision detect (CSMA/CD)	Network access protocol that allows transmitting nodes to contend for a shared communications channel. This is the media access scheme used by the Ethernet protocol. See also contention techniques.
Carrier wire	The central signal carrying wire in coaxial cable.
Cathode ray tube (CRT)	An electronic vacuum tube, such as a television picture tube, that can be used to display character and graphic images.
Cellular mobile telephone	A portable telephone that communicates directly to cellular telephone carrier receivers and transmitters using radio signals only. Geographies are divided into cells that can each "hand off" a conversation to a neighboring cell if the mobile parties move between cell boundaries.
Central processing unit (CPU)	The part of a computer that controls the interpretation and execution of instructions. Also called the microprocessor.
Channel	The communications path over which information is transferred. More than one channel can occupy a single physical communications link if proper multiplexing techniques are employed.
Character	The smallest unit of useful information in an ASCII data set. These units include decimal digits (0-9), letters (A-Z), punctuation marks, and other special symbols. See also ASCII.

Check bits	Special bits added to data to help ensure error-free transmission. The parity bit added to each character of ASCII data prior to transmission is an example of a check bit.
Circuit	Physical link (copper wire, etc.) used to carry electrical signals (information) between two or more points.
Circuit switching	Switching technique used in telephone networks where the connection (circuit) between two stations (telephones) is completed only when a call is made from one station to the other. A dedicated path is established only for the duration of the call. This techniques requires call set-up time but also allows for a single party to connect to many others on an as-needed basis.
Clear to send (CTS)	An EIA RS-232 control signal used by a terminal or computer to detect that its local modem is ready to send data.
Coaxial cable	A cable consisting of a central carrier wire enclosed within and insulated from a conducting sheath, often copper braid, and encased in a protective covering. Used in higher frequency applications.
Command-driven	Mode of user interaction with a computer program that requires the user to type short command words and parameters that tell the program to perform specific actions.
Command prompt	Indicator written to the CRT showing that the computer is waiting for command or data input from the keyboard.
Communications link	The physical connection between communicating nodes used for transmitting and receiving data.
Communications satellite	A satellite orbiting the earth and acting as a communications relay station. Communications satellites usually occupy geosynchronous orbits meaning that they appear to remain stationary over a single point.
Computer bus	Shared communications link for transferring data between different parts of the computer (CPU, memory, etc.)
Conditioned line	Leased telephone line enhanced by special equipment to allow higher data transmission rates and lower bit error rates.

Connect time	The amount of time that elapses while the user of a remote terminal or microcomputer is connected to a time shared system. Connect time is usually measured by the duration between log-on and log-off.
Contention	Conflict between two or more devices trying to access a common communications channel or other network resource at the same time.
Contention techniques	Rules used to resolve conflict between devices trying to access a common communications channel at the same time. See also carrier sense multiple access with collision detect.
CPU	See central processing unit.
Cross Connect	Connecting one set of contacts on a distribution frame to another set of contacts that eventually terminate at the end user's location. Cross connects are usually done at the MDF or IDF.
Crosstalk	Noise or interference between communications circuits that degrades transmission quality.
CRT	See cathode ray tube.
Crystal oscillator	A quartz-crystal controlled circuit that regulates timing in a computer, modem, or other electronic equipment where critical timing is important to the proper operation of the device.
CSMA/CD	See carrier sense multiple access with collision detect.
CTS	See clear to send.
Data base	Computer files that organize and store information for later retrieval by users or programs.
Data capture	A feature of communications programs that allows information exchanged during both interactive and file transfers to be saved in memory and stored on disk for later recall.
Data communications	Movement of information between remote systems over a common communications medium.
Data communications equipment (DCE)	Device that provides all the functions required for connection to telephone company lines and for converting signals between telephone lines and data terminal equipment.

Data set ready (DSR)	An EIA RS-232 control signal used by a terminal or computer to detect that its local modem is connected and ready to send or receive data.
Data terminal equipment (DTE)	The end-user machine (terminal or computer) that plugs into the termination point (DCE) of a communications circuit.
Data terminal ready (DTR)	An EIA RS-232 control signal that tells a modem when its local terminal or computer is connected and ready for operation.
DB-25 connector	Standard 25-pin connector used for terminating cables connecting EIA RS-232 serial devices.
DCE	See data communications equipment.
Demodulation	The process of retrieving an information signal from a modulated carrier wave.
Dial-up line	A circuit-switched line that is accessed by dialing a telephone number. See also circuit switching.
Differential phase shift keying (DPSK)	Technique for modulating an information signal onto a carrier wave. Used in high-speed data communications.
Digital	A method of coding data that uses discrete, integral numbers to represent measured physical quantities.
DIP switch	A group of switches enclosed in a plastic case and mounted on a circuit board. Each switch in the package may be individually set on or off to control a particular operating mode or parameter.
Direct-connect modem	A modem that is electrically connected to the telephone system via a modular phone cable and jack.
Distributed processing	The simultaneous use of multiple, geographically distributed computers to cooperatively retrieve, analyze, move, and store information.
Download	The process of transferring data files from a remote, time-shared system to a local smart terminal or computer.
DPSK	See differential phase shift keying.
DSR	See data set ready.
DTE	See data terminal equipment.
DTR	See data terminal ready.
Dumb modem	Modem that uses hard-wired signals from an external device such as a computer to control the operation of the modem. The intelligence required to operate the modem comes from outside the modem.

Dumb terminal	Terminal that uses hard-wired signals from an external device such as a computer to control the terminal's operation. The intelligence required to operate the terminal comes from outside the terminal.
EIA	See Electronic Industries Association.
Electronic Industries Association (EIA)	Association responsible for drafting standards to be followed in the manufacture of electrical and electronic equipment.
Electronic mail	A data communications network used for sending correspondence to other network user terminals or for sending printed mail to off-network users.
Emulation	See terminal emulation.
External modem	A self-contained modem enclosed in a metal or plastic housing that connects to the computer or terminal with a special interface cable.
FCC	See Federal Communications Commission
Federal Communications Commission (FCC)	U.S. government agency responsible for regulation of the communications industry.
Fiber optics	A communications transmission technology that uses light as an information carrier, producing high data transfer rates, high immunity to electrical or electromagnetic interference, and low error rates. See also fiber-optic cable.
Fiber-optic cable	Thin glass or plastic fibers that "conduct" light waves that have been modulated with information signals. The cable is small and light, and has a higher information-carrying capacity than conventional twisted-pair wire or coaxial cable.
File transfer	The process by which data files are transferred intact and error-free across a communications link.
Frequency shift keying (FSK)	Frequency modulation of a carrier wave by a modulating (information carrying) signal to produce a digital signal.
FSK	See frequency shift keying.
Full-duplex	Mode of operation between two communicating devices that allows them to send and receive data simultaneously.
Fully connected network	Network in which each node is directly connected to every other node in the network.

Geosynchronous orbit	A circular orbit made by an artificial satellite along the earth's equatorial plane 22,300 miles above the equator. Because the period of a satellite in a geosynchronous orbit is exactly 24 hours, the satellite will remain stationary over one point on the earth's surface.
Ground clutter	Buildings, hills, and other obstructions that block or interfere with the transmission of microwave signals.
Ground station	Earth-based station for relaying satellite transmission signals between earthbound communication networks.
Half-duplex	Mode of operation between two communicating devices such that only one of them can send or receive data at a time. The result is alternating, one way at a time, independent communications between the devices.
Handshaking	The exchange of control signals required to establish a communications channel between two devices.
Help file	A feature of computer programs that provides on-line aids to remind you or instruct you how to perform a particular command or function. Serves as an adjunct to the user's manual.
Host computer	The primary or controlling computer in a multiple computer operation. See also mainframe.
Hybrid	A special device used to provide full duplex telephone connections over two wires, when four wires would be required without the hybrid.
Interactive terminal	An electronic device composed of a display (CRT or printer) and keyboard used to converse with a host computer for the purpose of running programs and storing and retrieving information.
Interactive transfer	The process by which commands and information are transferred across a communications link between an interactive terminal and a host computer. See also interactive terminal.
Intermediate Distribution Frame (IDF)	A wiring distribution point located between the main distribution frame and the endpoint where telephone equipment is connected. IDFs are used to make wiring changes easier.
LAN	See Local Area Network.
LATA	See Local Access and Transport Area.

LED	See light emitting diode.
Light emitting diode (LED)	Small indicator lamp used on modems and other electronic devices to show status (power on, off-hook, carrier detected, etc.).
Local Access and Transport Area (LATA)	There are 161 distinct geographic areas in the U.S. that were established to determine when a call must use an interexchange carrier (IXC). Intra-LATA calls are generally handled by the local RBOC, and Inter-LATA calls must be handled by an IXC.
Local Area Network (LAN)	Network located in a localized geographical area (office, building, or building complex) providing low-cost shared access and information interchange among network nodes such as terminals, printers, microcomputers, and high-capacity disks.
Logging on	Fixed procedure a user follows when accessing a time-shared computer system from a terminal. When logging on, a user types an account code and a password that uniquely identify the user. The system checks the account and password to make sure they are valid before allowing the user to proceed.
Loop network	Network configured as a closed loop of individual point-to-point communications links interconnected by nodes, each of which retransmits data around the loop until the data arrives at its destination node.
Main Distribution Frame (MDF)	The point in a star topology telephone wiring network that acts as the central hub for all wiring. Usually separates the public network from the premises network.
Mainframe	Literally, the central processing unit of a computer. In common useage, however, a mainframe is a large, powerful computer system capable of high-speed, high-volume data processing. See also host computer.
Menu driven	Mode of user interaction with a computer program that requires the user to pick a command or action using a few simple keystrokes from a menu of commands or actions presented on the computer screen.
Microchip	Specialized, miniature electronic circuit etched on a tiny piece of silicon and enclosed in a plastic or ceramic case. Microchips are the basic underlying components of microcomputers and other high-tech electronic devices.

Microcomputer	The generic term used to refer to computers containing a microprocessor, memory, and mass storage devices. The two basic types on the market are the IBM PC compatible and the Apple Macintosh.
Microprocessor	The centralized processing unit contained in smaller computer devices such as personal computers and many computer peripheral products.
Microwave	Wireless transmission of information using highly directional, high-frequency radio waves. Microwaves are easily concentrated into a narrow beam that is received and transmitted from one line-of-sight station to another until reaching its final destination.
Modem	Contraction for MOdulator/DEModulator. A modem is a communications device that translates digital information into analog information (and vice versa) so that it can be transmitted between digital devices over standard (analog) telephone lines.
Modular telephone jack	Any one of a number of standard telephone connectors for plugging in single-line or multiline telephone instruments.
Modulation	The process of changing digital information into analog information.
Modulator	A device that alters a carrier wave with an information signal in order to communicate the information over a transmission medium.
MOdulator/ DEModulator	See modem.
Morse code	A signalling system used in telegraphy that allows information to be communicated using various combinations of dots and dashes.
Multidrop	A communications link interconnecting several terminals, printers, or other data processing equipment. Also called multipoint.
Multiplexing	Technique used for transmitting a number of different messages concurrently over a single communications channel.
Multipoint	A communications link interconnecting several devices. Also called multidrop.
Multiuser system (MUS)	A microcomputer-based distributed system that serves multiple users simultaneously.
MUS	See multiuser system.

NAK	See negative acknowledge.
Negative acknowledge (NAK)	In a communications protocol, a message indicating a fault in the transmission of data. In XMODEM protocol, for example, a negative acknowledge message tells the originating computer an error was detected in a character read by the receiving computer.
Network	A logical arrangement of computers, terminals, and peripherals interconnected by communication links for the purpose of providing users shared data processing and information exchange capabilities.
Network access	Permission granted a device by the network controller to transmit information on the network. The rules governing network access are called the network access protocol.
Node	Communicating device (computer, terminal, etc.) interconnected by communication links to other devices so as to form a network. See also network.
Off-hook	Telephone company term that describes the active state of a telephone instrument. A telephone is off-hook whenever the receiver is lifted from its cradle. By analogy, a modem is said to go off-hook prior to dialing a telephone number or when answering an incoming call.
Off-line	Condition of a device or piece of equipment not under the control of the central processing unit of a computer.
On-hook	Telephone company term that describes the inactive state of a telephone instrument. A telephone is on-hook whenever the receiver is resting in its cradle; a user puts the instrument on-hook by hanging up the telephone. By analogy, a modem is said to go on-hook whenever it terminates a call and hangs up.
On-line	Condition of a device or piece of equipment under the control of the central processing unit of a computer.
Originate mode	The operating condition of a modem set up to dial a telephone and/or to send data to another system.

Packet	A message containing both control information and data. The control information is used for routing the packet through a network to its final destination. As such, a packet is like an envelope containing a letter: the control information is the address on the envelope; the data is the letter it contains. See also packet switching.
Packet switching	Method for transmitting information in packets within a network. Packets are automatically routed by each encountered network node in a manner that avoids congestion and minimizes the time required for the packet to reach its destination. See also packet.
Parallel data transfer	Technique for transferring data bytes such that all the bits in a byte are transmitted simultaneously. See also serial data transfer.
Parity bit	Check-bit appended to a data byte that serves the purpose of error detection during data transfer. The parity bit is computed to make the number of bits whose value is 1 either always even or always odd. As long as the value of the parity bit is the same in both the transmitted byte and the received byte, the transfer is considered error-free.
PBX	Private Branch Exchange is a business telephone exchange, connected to the telephone network, located on a customer's premises (usually an office or a building) and operated by the customer's employees.
Peripheral	Any equipment distinct from the central computing unit (CPU) that provides additional capability such as printing, data storage, or communications.
Photoelectric diode	An electronic device that generates an electric current when exposed to light. Used in optical applications such as fiber-optic transmission systems.
Point-to-point	Type of communications link that connects a single device to another single device, such as a remote terminal to a host computer.
Polarity	Distinction between the positive and negative poles or electric charges in an electromagnetic circuit. A battery has both a positive and negative pole: the "+" pole has a positive polarity; the "−" pole has a negative polarity.

Polling	Multipoint communications control technique that forces connected devices to transmit information, one after another in a fixed, predetermined order, thus eliminating contention for the communications link.
Protective ground	An EIA RS-232 connection that provides an electrical ground between two electronic devices connected by an RS-232 cable.
Protocol	The rules governing the initiation and termination of communications, interpretation of transmitted data, and detection and correction of errors.
Protocol transfer	Data transfer under protocol control. See also protocol, file transfer.
Pulse dialing	Method of telephone dialing in which digits are transmitted to the central telephone switching office as numbers of alternating makes and breaks of an electric current in the telephone circuit.
Radio	The process of sending and receiving information by electromagnetic waves without a connecting wire.
RD	See receive data.
Receive data (RD)	The EIA RS-232 connection (pin or wire) over which a computer, modem, or other serial device receives data.
Request to send (RTS)	An EIA RS-232 handshaking signal used to ready a modem for transmitting data, and in half-duplex communications, for controlling the direction of data transmission.
Reverse channel	Low-speed communications channel used in half-duplex communications (Bell 202) for controlling line turnaround.
Ribbon cable	Flat, multiconductor cable often used for RS-232 connections between DTE and DCE equipment. The cable is called ribbon cable because it is wide and flat like a piece of ribbon.
Ring network	Communications network, similar to a loop network, in which access is controlled by a permission code. See also token, token passing.
Ringer equivalence	FCC electrical standard for modem equipment connected to the public telephone network.
RJ11C	Standard single-line modular telephone jack for connecting telephones (and direct-connect modems) to the telephone system.

Routing network	Network in which data packets are routed based on addressing information contained in the packet. As a packet travels along from node to node, the path to the next node is dynamically determined based on traffic congestion and routing priorities. See also packet switching.
RS-232	Electronic Industries Association electrical interface standard governing the manufacture of serial data communications equipment.
RTS	See request to send.
Serial data transfer	Technique for transferring data bytes such that the bits in a byte are transmitted single file, one bit after another, down a single conductor. See also parallel data transfer.
Serial interface board	An electronic circuit board that converts data from parallel form to serial form and vice versa. An RS-232 serial interface board conforms to EIA standards for serial data communications equipment. See also serial port.
Serial port	Location on a terminal, computer, or peripheral of the EIA RS-232 serial interface board connector for attaching an RS-232 interface cable.
SIG	See special interest group.
Signal ground	An EIA RS-232 connection that establishes an electrical ground reference for all data and control signals in the interface.
Slotted channel	Network access technique that provides empty data carriers (slots) on a communications link to prevent contention between network nodes. A node can transmit data only when it finds an empty slot on the link.
Smart modem	A modem containing a microprocessor for controlling the configuration and operation of the modem.
Smart telephone	A telephone instrument that contains a microcomputer used for storing and dialing frequently called numbers, redialing, and other time-saving convieniences.
Smart terminal	A terminal containing a microprocessor for controlling the configuration and operation of the terminal and for programming simple applications at the terminal.

Special interest group	Organization of people who share a common interest or goal.
Star network	A network with a single central node to which all other nodes are connected by point-to-point communications links.
Start bit	In asynchronous communications, a bit that signals the start of a data character. See also asynchronous transmission.
Stop bit	In asynchronous communications, a bit (or bits) that signals the end of a data character. See also asynchronous transmission.
Store and forward	Method of routing data through a network such that the data is first stored and then retransmitted by each node along the communications path. See also packet switching.
Strowger rotary switch	The first automatic telephone switching device, named in honor of its inventor, Almon P. Strowger.
Switched network	The network of dial-up telephone lines using circuit switching to provide communications services to network subscribers (users). See also circuit switching.
Synchronous transmission	Mode of data transmission that uses precise clock signals to indentify the beginning and end of each data character.
Sysop	Abbreviation for system operator. Owner and/or operator of a public bulletin board system.
TD	See transmit data.
Telecommunications	The transfer of information over long distances by electronic signalling systems such as telephone, radio, or teletype.
Telecommuting	Using a personal computer and telecommunications for performing a job at home rather than in an office, thereby eliminating the need to commute back and forth.
Telecomputing	Using a terminal or personal computer to access and share the resources of a remote host computer system.
Telephone handset	The transmitter/receiver part of a telehone instrument, usually held in the hand, used for speaking and listening.

Teletext	Telecommunications system that uses television video signalling to broadcast both picture and text information.
TELEX	An automatic teletype exchange (telegram) service, based on 5-digit Baudot code, developed by Western Union.
Terminal emulation	Software technique for making a computer or terminal behave exactly like a different computer or terminal. The emulating device accepts the same data, executes the same programs, and achieves the same results as the emulated device.
Throughput	A measure of the total useful information processed or communicated by a data processing system per unit of time.
Time sharing	A method for operating a data processing system that allows many users to share computing resources at the same time for different purposes. Although the computer services each user, one at a time, in sequence, the high speed of the computer makes it appear that the users are all handled simultaneously.
Token	A special communications code composed of a unique sequence of bits used to control channel access on some types of communications networks. See also token passing.
Token passing	A network access technique for passing the use of a communications channel from node to node in a fixed, predetermined order.
Token Ring	The LAN topology and access scheme recommended by IBM and specified in the 802.5 standard.
Tone dialing	Method of telephone dialing in which digits are transmitted as two-frequency tones to the central telephone switching office.
Topology	The configuration of nodes and links in a communications network.
Transmission medium	The physical links (wire, coaxial cable, fiber optics, microwave) used for transmitting information in a communications network.
Transmit data	The EIA RS-232 connection (pin or wire) over which a computer, modem, or other serial device transmits data.

Twisted pair	A cable formed by twisting together two wires that are insulated from one another. Commonly used for residential telephone service. By twisting the wires together, electrical interference (noise) is minimized.
TWX	Western Union teletype exchange service providing real-time, direct connection between subscribers.
UART	See Universal Asynchronous Receiver Transmitter.
Universal Asynchronous Receiver Transmitter (UART)	Integrated circuit (microchip) that performs all the hardware functions required for serial data transfer, including serial-to-parallel and parallel-to-serial data conversion.
Upload	The process of transferring data files from a local smart terminal or a computer to a remote, time-shared system.
User group	Organization of people who share a common interest in a particular computer or software package and who meet regularly to exchange ideas and information.
Video Conferencing	Similar to a standard telephone conference call except video is also supplied to allow all participants to hear and see each other.
Videotext	Interactive telecommunications system that uses telephone lines for sending and receiving information.
Wide Area Network (WAN)	Type of network that extends LAN connections over a large geographic region and typically uses the public networks to provide the connections.
Word	A unit of data organization or storage (memory, disk, etc.) in a computer system. See also bit, byte.
Word processor	Computer hardware and software system fo preparing, editing, and printing all forms of written communications.
XMODEM protocol	Popular protocol developed by Ward Christensen for personal computer communications.

Exercises

Module One

Discussion Questions:

1. What is the difference between communications and telecommunications?
2. How does improved communications affect business and society?
3. Why are protocols needed for effective communication?

Quiz Questions:

1. The ultimate goal of any communication is to:
    A. Provide a connection between two parties.
    B. Let the other person know you were thinking about them.
    C. Transfer information from one party to another.
    D. Allow for use of enhanced technology.
2. The purpose of a communication protocol is to ensure that nobody is offended. (True) (False)
3. The increasing level of international contact requires improved communication standards because:
    A. Each country may have its own mode of accepted communication.
    B. Different countries may communicate in their own language.
    C. Cultural differences may cause a misunderstanding if standards are not clearly defined.
    D. All of the above
4. Person-to-person communication appears less structured than telecommunication because:
    A. Humans can adapt better to unexpected events.
    B. Computers are able to effectively handle all types of occurrences.
    C. Telecommunications is new and few standards exist.
    D. Telecommunications is more complex than human communications.

5. It is beneficial for all business people to understand a little about telecommunications because:
   A. We all have to use the telephone at some point.
   B. More business is transacted between geographically separate parties and telecommunications bridges that gap.
   C. An understanding of telecommunications provides insight to interpersonal communications.
   D. All of the above

Module Two

Discussion Questions:

1. Was it hard work or luck that allowed Bell to get the first telephone patent?
2. How important were Watson, Hubbard, and Vail to the development of the telephone?
3. Is the telephone network important enough to treat as a national security item?
4. What are the benefits and disadvantages associated with a central telephone company with uniform standards?

Quiz Questions:

1. The original patent given to Alexander Graham Bell is still in effect and all telephones must be bought from the Bell system. (True) (False)
2. Watson was afraid to work for Bell full-time because:
   A. He thought the risk of depending upon the telephone's success was too great.
   B. He did not like working with Bell.
   C. He had another job offer from Western Union.
   D. He lived in different city and did not want to commute.
3. Which company refused to buy the initial telephone patents, then tried to buy them later?
   A. AT&T
   B. Western Union
   C. American Bell
   D. Continental Telephone

4. The first telephone patent was issued in:
   A. 1776
   B. 1894
   C. 1907
   D. 1876
5. Why did Western Union sell its telephone operation to the Bell System?
   A. Because they had too many telephones and needed to unload the inventory.
   B. National Bell was growing too fast and needed the help.
   C. National Bell won a patent infringement suit against Western Union.
   D. Western Union believed that the telephone would never succeed commercially.
6. AT&T became the Bell System's parent company located in New York because:
   A. That is where Bell and Watson lived.
   B. The incorporation laws of New York were more attractive than Massachusetts.
   C. The international access to Europe was easier from New York.
   D. New York was a larger city with more subscribers.
7. Who forced AT&T to sell its interest in Western Union?
   A. AT&T's stockholders
   B. The telephone subscribers
   C. Western Union's stockholders
   D. The federal government
8. In what year was AT&T integrated as part of the post office?
   A. 1918
   B. 1927
   C. 1894
   D. 1984
9. Why does the federal government regulate the telephone network's activities?
   A. Because the telephone network is critical to national security.
   B. If it was not regulated, the Bell System companies might run the little companies out of business.
   C. Because an effectively run telephone network is important to a prospering economy.
   D. All of the above

10. Why is the existing telephone market more confusing to the average consumer than it was in 1979?
    A. More international companies are selling equipment in the U.S.
    B. The weak economy is causing a shrinking of telecommunication budgets.
    C. The consumer must deal with several different companies for the same level of service previously provided by a single company.
    D. There are more telephones in place, making the backbone network more complicated.

Module Three

Discussion Questions

1. Why do you think that the telecommunications industry is moving from analog to digital?
2. What is the relationship between the number of logical states of a signal and the digital information it contains?
3. Give a few more examples of frequency, amplitude, and phase that occur in everyday life.

Quiz Questions

1. Analog signals contain the same amount of information as digital signals and it is independent of the number of samples taken per second. (True) (False)
2. The degree references of a sine wave are derived from:
    A. The amount of difficulty seen in moving the signal.
    B. The relative locations of the wave when compared with a circle.
    C. How far the top of the wave is from the center line.
    D. How often the wave repeats itself in 1 hour.
3. To determine whether the phase of a wave leads or lags another signal, a reference timing point must be chosen. (True) (False)
4. When the frequency of a wave increases, so does:
    A. Its amplitude
    B. The amount of phase difference between it and the reference wave
    C. The number of times it repeats itself in one second
    D. The cost of providing the signal

5. If a waveform has a maximum frequency component of 3000 hertz, then its minimum acceptable Nyquist sampling rate would be:
   A. 1500 samples per second
   B. 6000 samples per second
   C. 3000 samples per second
   D. 4500 samples per second

6. Once a waveform is digitally sampled, it cannot ever be put back into its analog form. (True) (False)

7. When two bits are used for encoding information, it can define a maximum of:
   A. 4 different states
   B. 2 different states
   C. 11 different states
   D. 8 different states

8. What is the American industry standard for digitally encoding a voice signal?
   A. 12 channels per link
   B. 28,000 bits per second
   C. 48,000 bits per second with the x-y companding scheme
   D. 64 kilobits per second using a mu-law companding technique

9. Which of the following best describes a CODEC?
   A. A device used by the CIA for encoding secret information
   B. A device made and marketed by Motorola for their exclusive use
   C. A multiplexing technique used for passing information over short distances
   D. A device that converts analog signals into digital, and digital signals into analog

10. After the analog signal is digitally sampled, it closely resembles its original analog signal. (True) (False)

Module Four

Discussion Questions

1. Discuss the relationship between the various transmission media types and their ability to carry information.

2. Discuss the results of attempting to transmit a signal over a media type that does not have adequate bandwidth for passing all of the information.

3. In what ways are frequency and time division multiplexing similar and different?

Quiz Questions

1. Transmission times over a satellite communication link are delayed by 1/4 second because:
   A. The satellites need to rotate into the proper position to accept the transmission.
   B. The satellites need to communicate with each other before completing the transmission.
   C. It takes the radio waves that long to travel the required distance.
   D. The delay is used on purpose to control network traffic.
2. Which media type is still the most prevalent in American businesses and homes?
   A. Twisted pair
   B. Coaxial cable
   C. Optical fiber
   D. LAN cable
3. Which media type is most immune to electrical interference?
   A. Twisted pair
   B. Coaxial cable
   C. Optical fiber
   D. LAN cable
4. Conventional satellite communications are broadcast back to the earth in a narrow beam that ensures privacy. (True) (False)
5. Optical fiber is rapidly becoming the medium of choice because:
   A. It has much higher bandwidth and can carry more information.
   B. It is immune to external noise.
   C. It has excellent information error characteristics (low bit error rate)
   D. All of the above
6. Why do the RBOCs want to install optical fiber to each house in the country?
   A. It is easier to install and maintain.
   B. The high bandwidth allows for transmission of video, text, and voice.
   C. They manufacture optical fiber cable and are looking for new markets.
   D. The FCC is making them do it.

7. Frequency division multiplexing and time division multiplexing are both digitally based technologies. (True) (False)

8. Which of these media types is the least expensive and has the lowest bandwidth capacity?
   A. Twisted pair
   B. Coaxial cable
   C. Optical fiber
   D. LAN cable

9. Why are satellites placed into geosynchronous orbit?
   A. So that it can be easily found from the earth since it is in the same location.
   B. This orbit is closer to the earth and requires low power transmitters.
   C. This way it can be aimed to control focused transmissions.
   D. Encryption is easier with a stable satellite.

10. What is the difference between a main and intermediate distribution frame?
   A. The telephone company only requires the intermediate distribution frame.
   B. One uses punch down blocks, and the other uses optical fiber.
   C. Fewer wires are on the main than on the intermediate frame.
   D. The intermediate is between the main and the end wiring locations.

Module Five

Discussion Questions

1. Why does the telephone company attempt to transmit as many conversations over the same wiring as is possible?
2. Why is it important to define different types of topologies?
3. When would one topology be advantageous over another?

Quiz Questions

1. Different communication standards may use different types of topologies. (True) (False)

2. Which topology is the most common in telecommunication networks?
   A. Ring
   B. Bus
   C. Hierarchical
   D. Star
3. Which topologies require some type of scheme for controlling user access to the network?
   A. Ring
   B. Bus
   C. Star
   D. All of the above
4. More than one user can access the network at one time in a bus topology. (True) (False)
5. Which of these technologies use the same topology type?
   A. Ethernet
   B. Token Ring
   C. Token Bus
   D. A and C

Module Six

Discussion Questions

1. Discusss the relationship between the accepted telephone numbering scheme and the total number of area codes and numbers available.
2. What are the implications of making cellular sites smaller which increases the total number of people who can be served by a cellular carrier?
3. How has the fax machine explosion affected the way business is conducted?

Quiz Questions

1. Inter-LATA and Intra-LATA calls are treated the same way by the RBOC's. (True) (False)
2. Without the use of hybrid transformer and induction coil, each line between the central office and a residence would require four wires instead of two. (True) (False)

3. What is the frequency range designated for voice telephone conversations?
   A. 2000 hertz
   B. 6000 hertz
   C. 2500 hertz
   D. 4000 hertz

4. Pulse and tone dialing accomplish the same result but with different types of technology. (True) (False)

5. Why is cellular telephone technology more popular today than only a few years ago?
   A. The cost of cellular equipment has decreased substantially.
   B. The RBOCs are selling cellular telephones as primary residential service.
   C. Cellular telephones are being used by businesses to restrict employees' movement.
   D. The Japanese are becoming the dominant cellular carriers in the U.S.

6. What are the minimal additional features recommended for a fax machine?
   A. Type 1 compatibility
   B. A page cutter and document feeder
   C. Color copying
   D. Type 4 compatibility

7. When must an interexchange carrier's (IXC) services be used?
   A. Whenever a call is placed within the same LATA.
   B. It is never used for calls within the same RBOC's region.
   C. Whenever a call is placed between LATAs.
   D. Whenever the IXC has paid for a point-of-presence on the network.

8. Which service would a business use for reduced cost interstate outbound calling traffic?
   A. Local measured traffic service
   B. 800 service
   C. Wide Area Telecommunications service
   D. One plus dialing

9. When using analog telephone technology, how is signalling between the telephone set and the network accomplished?
   A. Using an extra pair of wires
   B. Using tone combinations
   C. Using pre-set timing patterns
   D. Both B and C
10. Either pulse or tone telephones can be used on any type of telephone line. (True) (False)

Module Seven

Discussion Questions

1. What are the impacts on today's telecommunication marketplace that arise from the differences in telephone and data processing industries?
2. Did the need for communication drive the technology development or was it the other way around?
3. How did such a new industry (data processing) make such a dramatic impact on modern life?

Quiz Questions

1. Why did AT&T not use its market presence and enter the data processing industry when it was just developing?
   A. It did not have the money to enter a new business.
   B. Violating the Kingsbury Commitment could have caused another lawsuit.
   C. Divestiture was soon to come and they wanted to save their resources.
   D. AT&T did not have the right technology.
2. Who developed the first transistor?
   A. IBM
   B. NCR
   C. AT&T
   D. Sperry-Rand

3. In what year was the first commercial electronic computer delivered to a paying customer?

   A. 1874

   B. 1964

   C. 1975

   D. 1951

4. Why was the first IBM/PC product so rapidly accepted by the marketplace?

   A. It provided a low-cost alternative to using a mainframe computer and came from IBM.

   B. IBM offered attractive trade-in allowances for PC buyers.

   C. IBM was the only microcomputer manufacturer at the time.

   D. It connected to Local Area Networks (LAN) and allowed sharing of devices.

5. What caused LANs to become an important part of computer networking?

   A. The technology was there, so why not use it.

   B. There were few PC type devices, so networking the existing ones became important.

   C. A large number of PC's can share centralized storage and printing resources on a LAN.

   D. AT&T and IBM jointly marketed the technology.

6. What is the primary difference between centralized and distributed processing?

   A. One allows operator intervention where the other is isolated.

   B. One processes all information on the same computer where the other shares the processing load over many computers.

   C. Centralized processing must have all terminals in the same building.

   D. Distributed processing is only available through computer equipment distributors.

7. What is the percentage ratio of information used inside an organization compared with that used outside the organization?

   A. 80% inside/20% outside

   B. 20% outside/80% inside

   C. 60% outside/30% inside/10% is lost

   D. 50% inside/50% outside

8. IBM sold most of its computers instead of leasing them to their customers. (True) (False)

9. What was the name of the first microcomputer offered for consumer use?

   A. The IBM PC
   B. The Macintosh
   C. The Commodore PET
   D. The Altair

10. The computer industry evolved in a fragmented way with every manufacturer developing its own "best" solution to the customer need. (True) (False)

Module Eight

Discussion Questions

1. Discuss the basic conceptual differences between synchronous and asynchronous communication.
2. Discuss why a modem is necessary for communication over a telephone line.
3. Discuss the differences between serial and parallel communication.

Quiz Questions

1. The primary function of an FSK modem is to:
   A. Change the order of bits as they are transmitted.
   B. Convert 7-bit ASCII characters into 8-bit ASCII characters.
   C. Connect the telephone to the network to allow faster dialing.
   D. Convert digital bits into tones that are transmitted over the telephone line.
2. Which type of communication is generally most efficient?
   A. Synchronous
   B. Asynchronous
   C. Satellite
   D. Terminal emulation
3. Which cable type is most frequently used to connect DTE to DTE?
   A. A standard RS-232-C cable
   B. A null modem cable
   C. A standard 4-wire twisted pair line
   D. Coaxial TV cable

4. The RS-232-C standard is a clearly defined sequence for communication between devices. (True) (False)

5. The primary reason for using error detection is:
   A. To determine who pushed the wrong computer keys.
   B. To allow computers to determine which processor is having problems.
   C. To determine when transmitted information has been corrupted by noise.
   D. To replace the ones with zeroes and vice versa, as needed.

6. Frequency, phase, and RMS level are the most common modem modulation methods. (True) (False)

7. Which communication mode allows for communication in both directions, but only one direction at a time?
   A. Full duplex
   B. Half duplex
   C. Parallel
   D. Simplex

8. There is no difference between the baud rate and the bit per second transmission rate. (True) (False)

9. Which type of device is a modem?
   A. DCE
   B. DTE

10. What are the transmission characteristics that must be accurately defined before asynchronous modem communication can occur?
    A. The transmission speed
    B. The type of parity used
    C. The number of ASCII bits used (7 or 8 bits)
    D. All of the above

Module Nine

Discussion Questions

1. Discuss the steps involved with changing analog signals into digital bitstreams.

2. What is multiplexing, what are the primary types, and why is it beneficial?

3. Discuss the advantages and deficiencies of Centrex, PBX, and key systems.

Quiz Questions

1. Any analog signal is composed of a combination of sine waves of various
   A. Frequencies
   B. Amplitudes
   C. Phases
   D. All of the above

2. A byte of information contains how many bits?
   A. 4
   B. 8
   C. 16
   D. 64

3. Once information is digitized, it is easily understood by any other digital device. (True) (False)

4. Which form of communication is more resistant to noise corruption and typically has a better signal-to-noise ratio?
   A. Digital
   B. Analog

5. What is pair gain?
   A. When an extra pair of wires is installed
   B. When a 4-pair cable is replaced by a 25-pair cable
   C. When the call carrying capacity of the existing wiring is increased by using technology
   D. When equipment is installed that requires additional wiring pairs

6. Which form of telephone system resides in the telephone company's central office?
   A. Key Systems
   B. Centrex
   C. PBX systems
   D. Cellular systems

7. Which type of system is probably best for a 100-person, single building office that primarily communicates internally?
   A. Key Systems
   B. Centrex
   C. PBX systems
   D. Cellular systems

8. Which type of system is probably best for a company with locations in the same general neighborhood, but in physically separate buildings?
    A. Key Systems
    B. Centrex
    C. PBX systems
    D. Cellular systems
9. Which type of system is best for a company that has people continually out of the office but who need to be easily reached?
    A. Key Systems
    B. Centrex
    C. PBX systems
    D. Cellular systems
10. If you were transmitting information over a very long distance and the quality of the received information must be perfect, which technology would probably be best?
    A. Digital
    B. Analog

Module Ten

Discussion Questions

1. Discuss the impact of the microcomputer on society.
2. Would you prefer to use a computer that is completely controlled by you, or have a staff of people you depend upon for information?
3. Which system is better for todays offices: The PC or the Macintosh?

Quiz Questions

1. What part of a microcomputer actually performs the required processing operation?
    A. The hard disk drive
    B. The RAM memory
    C. The microprocessor
    D. The data bus
2. Where is information stored when that particular program is not running on the computer?
    A. The hard disk drive
    B. The RAM memory

C. The microprocessor

D. The data bus

3. Where is program and data information stored while the computer is running?

A. The hard disk drive

B. The RAM memory

C. The microprocessor

D. The data bus

4. Why is a graphical user interface (GUI) like Windows or the Mac important?

A. It takes less time to learn applications.

B. Once one application is learned, the others look about the same.

C. The average user is generally more productive with a GUI.

D. All of the above

5. Which is the most common PC processor being purchased for modern single-user business systems?

A. 8088

B. 80286

C. 6502

D. 80386

6. Which microcomputer system was designed with a total software and hardware approach that it tightly controlled?

A. The Macintosh

B. The Altair

C. The IBM PC

D. Both A and C

7. Which system is produced by many different companies trying to gain sales from the consumer, and creates strong price competition?

A. The Macintosh

B. The Altair

C. The IBM PC

D. Both A and C

8. Which system has the ability to run both DOS and Macintosh-based software?

A. The Macintosh

B. The Altair

C. The IBM PC

D. Both A and C

9. What is it called when the processing power of an entire LAN can be shared by each node on that LAN?
   A. Distributed processing
   B. Centralized processing
   C. Parallel processing
   D. Hierarchical processing
10. When shopping for a microcomputer system, which of the following should you consider first?
   A. The type of hardware
   B. The ultimate benefit of ownership
   C. The cost
   D. The manufacturer

Module Eleven

Discussion Questions

1. Why have local area networks (LAN) become so popular?
2. Discuss the major benefits of using a LAN.
3. Discuss the differences between topologies and media access protocols.
4. What is the difference between a smart terminal connected to a minicomputer and a PC on a LAN?

Quiz Questions

1. Why is a LAN considered by many people to be superior to a centralized processor?
   A. Adding a node to a LAN adds processing power.
   B. LAN's are state-of-the-art and therefore better.
   C. LAN's are easier to manage.
   D. The mainframes break down all the time.
2. What things must be considered when purchasing a network of any kind?
   A. Overall system response time
   B. The overall cost
   C. The reliability of the network
   D. All of the above

3. Which technology allows for multiple information paths over the same medium?
   A. Baseband
   B. Broadband
   C. Token passing
   D. Star topology
4. Which of the following is not a topology type?
   A. CSMA/CD
   B. Star
   C. Ring
   D. Hierarchical
5. Why is a media access protocol required for a LAN to operate properly?
   A. To minimize anxiety while using the LAN
   B. The protocols slow down LAN operation to keep it under control.
   C. Only one path is provided for many user nodes.
   D. It is required for the computers to operate properly.
6. Which of the following was the first LAN protocol adopted for commercial use?
   A. Token ring
   B. Ethernet
   C. Token bus
   D. Arcnet
7. What is the major advantage of using a seamless network?
   A. Since there are no boundaries, the price is lower.
   B. These networks break down less often.
   C. These types of network are less complicated to manage.
   D. The end user does not need to understand the network design to effectively perform his tasks.
8. With the rapid increase in international business, which type of network will probably become more popular in the next decade?
   A. The local area network
   B. The wide area network
   C. The metropolitan area network
   D. The homogeneous router network
9. Which type of device is probably used to connect an Ethernet and Token ring network?
   A. A gateway
   B. A bridge

C. A router

D. A brouter

10. Which type of device would probably be used to connect two Ethernet networks?

    A. A gateway

    B. A bridge

    C. A router

    D. A brouter

Module Twelve

Discussion Questions

1. Discuss the difference between circuit switching and packet switching.

2. Which network is the type most commonly used by the telephone company?

3. Discuss the impact of information type (i.e., voice or data) and timing when evaluating the type of switching to employ.

Quiz Questions

1. Which type of switching allows for easy rerouting of information paths should a link become disabled?

    A. Circuit switching

    B. Datagram switching

    C. Message switching

    D. CSMA/CD

    E. Both B and C

2. Which type of switching is used for electronic and voice mail applications?

    A. Circuit switching

    B. Datagram switching

    C. Message switching

    D. CSMA/CD

    E. Both B and C

3. Which switching type introduces no transmission delay, but requires time for establishing the connection through the network?
   A. Circuit switching
   B. Datagram switching
   C. Message switching
   D. CSMA/CD
   E. Both B and C
4. What is the major benefit associated with a virtual circuit connection over a datagram packet switched connection?
   A. The virtual circuit passes information at a faster rate after the connection is established.
   B. The packet switched path cannot be modified after it is started.
   C. The virtual circuit cannot be broken.
   D. There is no setup time involved with a virtual circuit connection.
5. Which type of technology could have information arriving out of order at the receiving end of the connection?
   A. Circuit switching
   B. Packet switching
   C. Message switching
   D. CSMA/CD
   E. Both B and C

Module Thirteen

Discussion Questions

1. Discuss the benefits and disadvantages of using standards.
2. What is the significance of the OSI model and why does there have to be so many layers?
3. What are some of the problems with using SNA as the industry wide standard?

Quiz Questions

1. How many levels are involved with the OSI model?
   A. 4
   B. 7
   C. 5
   D. 14

2. Which levels of the OSI model are usually irrelevant to the end user?
   A. All layers
   B. No layers
   C. Layers 5 to 7
   D. Layers 1 to 4
3. Who is causing the industry trend toward standardization?
   A. The customers
   B. The technology
   C. The vendors
   D. The ISO and CCITT
4. Ideally, information passed from a higher layer to a lower layer and back again using the same standard should be independent of the type of technology involved? (True) (False)
5. The SNA and OSI models have the same number of layers, so they must be compatible. (True) (False)

Module Fourteen

Discussion Questions

1. What is the difference between a smart modem and a "dumb" modem?
2. Discuss how originate and answer modes are established and how call progress information is provided to the user.
3. Where would you typically use the auto-answer feature?

Quiz Questions

1. Which of the following is *not* a typical modem indicator light?
   A. Auto Answer
   B. FSK
   C. Off Hook
   D. Carrier Detect
2. All modems speak the same language and understand the same command sets. (True) (False)
3. Which type of modem is typically less expensive?
   A. External
   B. Portable computer type
   C. Internal
   D. 9,600 bps

4. Most modems use RS-232-C and require a standard cable when connected to a computer. (True) (False)

5. There are many modem manufacturers that all have their own designs, but most of them are compatible with the Hayes command language. (True) (False)

Module Fifteen

Discussion Questions

1. Why is communication software important to modem operation?
2. What is the difference between electronic mail and a bulletin board service?
3. Is it possible that electronic mail will replace the postal system in the future?

Quiz Questions

1. Which of the following is *not* a communication software package basic feature?
   A. Frequency Shift Keying
   B. Data capture
   C. Terminal emulation
   D. Command/menu driven operation
2. There is only one file transfer protocol used in modem communication. (True) (False)
3. Why is terminal emulation software an important feature?
   A. You may need to connect to different systems that require a special data terminal.
   B. The PC must be told how to look like a data terminal.
   C. Without emulation, communication to other computers would be impossible.
   D. All of the above
4. Which of the following is *not* a common file transfer protocol?
   A. Kermit
   B. D-MODEM
   C. XMODEM
   D. ZMODEM

5. Which of the following would you use to research a specific topic?
   A. MCI Mail
   B. CompuServe
   C. EasyLink
   D. pcAnywhereIV

Module Sixteen

Discussion Questions

1. How would it affect our society if we truly only received one telephone number that we used for our entire life?
2. Is ISDN something that is useful to society, or is it just another scheme devised by the vendors to sell more equipment?
3. How will the unification of Europe affect telephone service in the U.S. and around the world?
4. Why are the number of technologies in test increasing in number, and what would be the benefits of adopting FDDI and BISDN in place of existing technologies?
5. How will TeleMedia affect the way we live our personal and business lives?

Module Seventeen

Discussion Questions

1. Was AT&T a friend to the American public, or a large corporation milking as much profit as possible from subscribers?
2. Did deregulation of the telephone industry and the eventual divestiture of AT&T benefit the American consumer?
3. What would the American telephone network look like if AT&T had not become the dominant carrier?
4. Is there a liability involved with the RBOC's providing regulated telephone service and deregulated information services under the same umbrella organization?
5. Should the RBOCs be allowed to provide optical fiber to each household in America?

Quiz Questions

1. Why is control of the local loop an important issue in **regulatory** issues?
   A. The local loop is under the control of the subscriber who votes for PUC officials.
   B. The carrier could use local loop dominance as a lever against competition.
   C. If inadequate wiring is installed, it will cost more in the long run.
   D. Certain counties do not allow non-union personnel to work on the wiring.
2. Why did the telephone industry become fragmented in the 1890s?
   A. War broke out and control at home was lost.
   B. IBM attempted to buy into the telephone business.
   C. The original patents expired and caused the creation of many new telephone companies.
   D. Federal regulations changed to allows competition.
3. Regulators must walk a tightrope between maintaining a well-run communications infrastructure and not allowing the telephone companies to overcharge the consumer. (True) (False)
4. Why was AT&T initially created?
   A. To sell telephones to residences
   B. To act as the umbrella organization for the other Bell companies
   C. To provide long-distance service to non-Bell companies
   D. As a long-distance carrier to connect New York to the rest of the world
5. Which action made AT&T sell its Western Union stock?
   A. The Sherman Anti-trust Act
   B. The Mann-Elkins Act
   C. Computer Inquiry II
   D. The Kingsbury Commitments
6. What 1949 action stopped AT&T from using public monies to produce telephone equipment for general commercial sale?
   A. The Mann-Elkins Act
   B. Computer Inquiry II
   C. The Consent Decree
   D. Computer Inquiry I

7. What action forced AT&T into giving up its 22 local telephone companies?

   A. The Modified Final Judgement

   B. Computer Inquiry II

   C. The Consent Decree

   D. The Kingsbury Commitments

8. Calls placed between two LATA boundaries must be carried by an inter-exchange carrier (IXC). (True) (False)

9. Which agency controls local regulatory issues?

   A. The public utility commission (PUC)

   B. The federal communication commission (FCC)

10. Which of the above was a direct result of Computer Inquiry III?

   A. Equal Access

   B. Open Network Architecture (ONA)

   C. One-plus dialing plans

   D. The Open Skies Policy

Chapter Quiz Question Answers

Module One

1. C
2. F
3. D
4. A
5. D

Module Two

1. F
2. A
3. B
4. D
5. C
6. B
7. D
8. A
9. D
10. C

Module Three

1. F
2. B
3. T
4. C
5. B
6. F
7. A
8. D
9. D
10. F

Module Four

1. C
2. A
3. C
4. F

5. D
6. B
7. F
8. 8
9. A
10. D

Module Five

1. T
2. D
3. D
4. F
5. D

Module Six

1. F
2. T
3. D
4. T
5. A
6. B
7. C
8. C
9. D
10. F

Module Seven

1. B
2. C
3. D
4. A
5. C
6. B
7. A
8. F
9. D
10. T

Module Eight

1. D
2. A
3. B
4. T
5. C
6. F
7. B
8. F
9. B
10. D

Module Nine

1. D
2. B

3. F
4. A
5. C
6. B
7. C
8. B
9. D
10. A

Module Ten

1. C
2. A
3. B
4. D
5. D
6. A
7. C
8. A
9. C
10. B

Module Eleven

1. A
2. D
3. B
4. A
5. C
6. B
7. D
8. B
9. A
10. B

Module Twelve

1. E
2. C
3. A
4. A
5. E

Module Thirteen

1. B
2. D
3. A
4. T
5. F

Module Fourteen

1. B
2. F
3. C
4. T
5. T

Module Fifteen

1. A
2. F
3. D
4. B
5. B

Module Sixteen

(No Questions)

Module Seventeen

1. B
2. C
3. T
4. D
5. D
6. C
7. A
8. T
9. A
10. B

Bibliography and Recommended
Additional Reading

Freiburger, Paul; Swaine, Paul. *Fire in the Valley: The Making of the Personal Computer*. Berkeley, CA: Osborne, McGraw Hill, 1986.

Sobel, Robert. *IBM vs. Japan: The Struggle for the Future*. Stein and Day, 1986.

Tangney, Brandon; O'Mahony, Donal. *Local Area Networks and Their Applications*. Prentice Hall, 1988.

Madron, Thomas W. *Local Area Networks: The Next Generation*. John Wiley & Sons, Inc., 1990.

Florence, Donne. *Local Area Networks: Developing Your System for Business*. John Wiley & Sons, Inc., 1989.

Stallings, William. *Data and Computer Communications*. Macmillan Publishing Company, 1988.

Sharma, Roshan. *Network Topology Optimization: The Art and Science of Network Design*. Van Nostrand Reinhold, 1990.

Boettinger, H. M. *The Telephone Book*. Riverwood Publishers Limited, 1977.

Rowe, Stanford H. II. *Business Telecommunications*. Macmillan Publishing Company, 1991.

Brigham, E. Oran. *The Fast Fourier Transform*. Prentice-Hall, Inc., 1974.

Brooner, E. G. *The Local Area Network Book*. Howard W. Sams & Co., Inc., 1984.

Emmett, Ariel; Gabel, David. *Direct Connections*. New American Library, 1986.

Lu, Cary. *The Apple Macintosh Book*. Microsoft Press, 1988.

Toffler, Alvin. *Powershift: Knowledge, Wealth and Violence at the Edge of the 21st Century*. Bantam Books, 1990.

Recommended Periodicals

Data Communications (Monthly)
McGraw-Hill, Inc. 212-512-2000
Intensive data communications focus with in-depth technical coverage of related topics.

Teleconnect Magazine (Monthly)
Telecom Library, Inc. 1-800-library
Teleconnect is a products and services magazine that aims at helping users and suppliers choose telecommunication products and services.

Networking Management (Monthly)
Penwell Publishing Company 918-831-9424
This is a publication aimed at the MIS, voice, data, and video communication groups and has a variety of in-depth articles.

Network World (Weekly)
International Data Group 508-875-6400
Provides a manager's overview to the general communications market. Usually has a feature article covering various topics of interest.

Communications Week (Weekly)
A CMP Publication 516-562-5882
Similar publication to Network World but with a heavier data communications focus.

Index